A Book Of

INDUSTRIAL RELATIONS
(HRM SPECIALISATION)

For
MBA Semester - IV
As Per Revised Syllabus
Effective from June 2014

Prof. Sharad D. Geet
M.A. (Eco.), M.Com., LL.B., D.C.L.

Mrs. Asmita A. Deshpande
B.Com., M.B.A.

N2156

Industrial Relations : MBA (S-IV)　　　　　　　　　　**ISBN 978-93-5164-262-6**

Second Edition : December 2015
© : Authors

The text of this publication, or any part thereof, should not be reproduced or transmitted in any form or stored in any computer storage system or device for distribution including photocopy, recording, taping or information retrieval system or reproduced on any disc, tape, perforated media or other information storage device etc., without the written permission of Authors with whom the rights are reserved. Breach of this condition is liable for legal action.

Every effort has been made to avoid errors or omissions in this publication. In spite of this, errors may have crept in. Any mistake, error or discrepancy so noted and shall be brought to our notice shall be taken care of in the next edition. It is notified that neither the publisher nor the authors or seller shall be responsible for any damage or loss of action to any one, of any kind, in any manner, therefrom.

Published By :
NIRALI PRAKASHAN
Abhyudaya Pragati, 1312, Shivaji Nagar,
Off J.M. Road, PUNE – 411005
Tel - (020) 25512336/37/39, Fax - (020) 25511379
Email : niralipune@pragationline.com

Printed By :
Repro Knowledgecast Limited,
Thane

☞ DISTRIBUTION CENTRES

PUNE
Nirali Prakashan : 119, Budhwar Peth, Jogeshwari Mandir Lane, Pune 411002, Maharashtra
Tel : (020) 2445 2044, 66022708, Fax : (020) 2445 1538
Email: bookorder@pragationline.com, niralilocal@pragationline.com

Nirali Prakashan : S. No. 28/27, Dhyari, Near Pari Company, Pune 411041
Tel : (020) 24690204 Fax : (020) 24690316
Email : dhyari@pragationline.com, bookorder@pragationline.com

MUMBAI
Nirali Prakashan : 385, S.V.P. Road, Rasdhara Co-op. Hsg. Society Ltd.,
Girgaum, Mumbai 400004, Maharashtra
Tel : (022) 2385 6339 / 2386 9976, Fax : (022) 2386 9976
Email : niralimumbai@pragationline.com

☞ DISTRIBUTION BRANCHES

JALGAON
Nirali Prakashan : 34, V. V. Golani Market, Navi Peth, Jalgaon 425001,
Maharashtra, Tel : (0257) 222 0395, Mob : 94234 91860

KOLHAPUR
Nirali Prakashan : New Mahadvar Road, Kedar Plaza, 1st Floor Opp. IDBI Bank
Kolhapur 416 012, Maharashtra. Mob : 9850046155

NAGPUR
Pratibha Book Distributors : Above Maratha Mandir, Shop No. 3, First Floor,
Rani Jhanshi Square, Sitabuldi, Nagpur 440012, Maharashtra
Tel : (0712) 254 7129

DELHI
Nirali Prakashan : 4593/21, Basement, Aggarwal Lane 15, Ansari Road, Daryaganj
Near Times of India Building, New Delhi 110002
Mob : 08505972553

BENGALURU
Pragati Book House : House No. 1, Sanjeevappa Lane, Avenue Road Cross,
Opp. Rice Church, Bengaluru – 560002.
Tel : (080) 64513344, 64513355,Mob : 9880582331, 9845021552
Email:bharatsavla@yahoo.com

CHENNAI
Pragati Books : 9/1, Montieth Road, Behind Taas Mahal, Egmore,
Chennai 600008 Tamil Nadu, Tel : (044) 6518 3535,
Mob : 94440 01782 / 98450 21552 / 98805 82331,
Email : bharatsavla@yahoo.com

niralipune@pragationline.com | www.pragationline.com
Also find us on ❋ www.facebook.com/niralibooks

Preface ...

We are earnestly happy to present to the M.B.A. (HRM Specialisation) students, this Text Book on 'Industrial Relations'. This book is written according to the syllabus for M.B.A. - Semester IV.

Our book on 'Business Law' for M.B.A. - Semester III has been well received by the student and teacher community alike. We hope that they will receive this book also with the same enthusiasm.

We are sure that this book will be of immense use to the students of M.B.A. from the viewpoint of their examination and will help them to enhance their knowledge of the Acts prescribed for the examination.

We are very much thankful to Dr. K. R. Shimpi, Principal, Sir. Dr. M. S. Gosavi Institute of Business Studies, Nashik for encouraging us to write this book by giving valuable suggestions.

We express our sincere thanks to Shri. Dineshbhai Furia, Shri. Jignesh Furia, Mr. Malik Shaikh, Mr. Amol Mahabal, Mr. Prasad Chintakindi and the entire staff of Nirali Prakashan, Pune, who have taken pains and keen interest in publishing this book.

Inspite of sincere efforts, some errors might have crept in the book. We hope that we shall be excused for the same.

We shall consider our labour amply rewarded if this book is appreciated by those for whom it is meant.

We extend our good wishes to all students, teachers, and readers with a genuine hope that they will receive this book with great enthusiasm.

PUNE
December 2015

Prof. S. D. Geet
Mrs. Asmita A. Deshpande

Syllabus ...

INDUSTRIAL RELATIONS
HRM (Specialisation) - Core Subject
Course Code : 403

1. Understanding IR: (6 + 2)

Concept, Philosophy of IR, Evolution of IR, Indian Perspective, Parties to IR, Employers' Organizations, Trade Unions, Role of Government, Role of Society.

Approaches to IR: The Dunlop's Approach, The Social Action Approach, The Human Relations Approach, The Gandhian Approach, Theoretical Foundation and Legal Framework of IR in India.

2. The Industrial Disputes Act 1947 (6 + 2)

Sections 2 to 19 Provisions under Chapter V, VA, VC and Chapter VI, VII.

3. Trade Union Act 1926 (8 + 2)

Section 2, Chapter II, III and chapter V, The Maharashtra Recognition of Trade Unions and Prevention of Unfair Labour Practices Act 71, Section 3 and the Provisions under Chapter II, III, IV, V, VI, VII, VIII, X.

4. Industrial Employment (Standing Orders) Act 1946 (6 + 2)

Section 2, 3, 5, 6, 7, 9, 10, 11, 12, 13, 14

The Contract Labour (Regulation and Abolition) Act 1970 Section 2 and all provisions under Chapter III, IV, V, VI and VII.

5. IR Initiative (9 + 2)

Worker's Participation in Management, Concept, Evolution, Implementation, Challenges. Collective Bargaining, Concept, Evolution and Implementation. Study of Best Practices in IR: The students and faculty to identify organizations in the area and study their IR Practices.

***

Contents ...

1. **Understanding IR**   1.1 – 1.30

2. **The Industrial Disputes Act, 1947**   2.1 – 2.62

3. **Trade Union Act, 1926**   3.1 – 3.42

4. **Industrial Employment (Standing Orders) Act, 1946**   4.1 – 4.34

5. **IR Initiative**   5.1 – 5.22

Publisher's Note

Inspite of our best efforts, care and caution, errors might have crept in. The publication is being sold on the condition and understanding that the information given in this book is merely for guidance and reference. It must not be taken as having authority of, or binding in any way on the author, publisher, sellers etc. who do not owe any responsibility for any damage or loss to any person, who may or may not be a purchaser of this publication on account of any action taken on the basis of this publication. However, if any discrepancies, omissions, errors etc. are noticed, kindly bring the same to our notice, so that we can take necessary steps to correct them in the next edition.

***

Chapter 1...

Understanding IR

Contents ...

1.1 Concept
1.2 Philosophy of IR
1.3 Evolution of IR - Indian Perspective
1.4 Parties to IR
    1.4.1 Employer's Organisation
    1.4.2 Trade Unions
    1.4.3 Role of Government
    1.4.4 Role of Society
1.5 Approaches to IR: The Dunlop's Approach, The Social Action Approach, The Human Relations Approach, The Gandhian Approach
1.6 Theoretical Foundation of IR in India
1.7 Legal Framework of IR in India
• Exercise

1.1 Concept

1. Introduction

An industry is a social world in miniature. Industries not only help in producing goods and services but they also provide employment to the people. Different categories of human elements are directly or indirectly involved in industries. Industrial relations play a very vital role in increasing industrial activities. In fact, the economic activity is the central field of industrial relations. The economic system and also labour legislation of a country, besides other factors, affect the industrial relations. A man has to struggle constantly for the purpose of satisfaction of his material wants. No doubt, the industrial revolutions are important for the development of industries. But they create imbalance as they prejudicially affect the rights and interests of the people in different sectors who work in the industries. This results in inequitable distribution of income and wealth. It is so because the means of production are controlled and utilised by the dominant sectors for the maximising the benefit of the people working in the dominant sectors and labour is exploited. This leads to imbalance and disorder in industrial relations. If industrial relations are not smooth, industries cannot develop properly. Economic development is closely related to smooth and good industrial relations and industrial peace. Therefore, industrial relations are not merely a matter between employers and employees. Hence, all the efforts must be done to maintain good and smooth industrial relations.

In an industrial sector of a country, the element of labour goes to constitute one of the most important and basic components; whereas the principal component of a given organisation is invariably its human resource or, people at work. From a country's point of view, human resources are the sum total or aggregate of knowledge, skills, creative abilities, talents, aptitudes as obtaining in its population, in a given point in time. While from the viewpoint of the individual enterprise, its human resources represent the total of the inherent qualities and abilities, acquired knowledge and skills as exemplified in the talents and aptitudes of the employees of that enterprise. Thus, human factor is very crucial for any organisation. In fact, it is the human resource which is of paramount importance in the success of any enterprise, simply because the bulk of problems of any organisational setting are related to human rather than physical, technical or economic nature. The failure to recognise and to utilise this effectively causes immense loss not only to the given enterprise but also to the nation concerned, as a whole.

It goes without saying that maintaining healthy industrial relations is the *minimum prerequisite* for ensuring a proper and smooth working and development of the enterprises concerned. Before we examine the various aspects of 'Industrial Relations,' let us first understand the meaning of the concept of 'Industrial Relations.'

2. Meaning and Definitions of 'Industrial Relations'

Today, industrial activity is continuously expanding and will continue to do so in the future. Based on their individual experiences, the people in the industrial field discuss the various aspects relating to human resources, production and productivity, industrial relations, peace, unrest, etc.

Hence, we find different approaches to the same aspect. The concept of 'industrial relations' is also not an exception to this. We find that there are as many as definitions of it as are the authors, experts on the subject. Each of them has explained the concept of industrial relations based on his/her experiences and ideas. Let us now consider some definitions of 'Industrial Relations' as stated by the experts in order to understand its meaning and nature.

(1) **Prof. Dale Yoder** defines the term 'Industrial Relations' as, *the designation of a whole field of relationships that exist because of the necessary collaboration of men and women in the employment process of the industry.*

(2) **Prof. T. N. Kapoor** made it clear that, *industrial relations refer to a dynamic and developing concept which is not limited to the complex of relations between trade unions and management but also refers to the general web of relationship normally obtaining between employers and employees - a web much more complex than the simple concept of labour-capital conflict.*

(3) **According to Prof. V. B. Singh,** *industrial relations are an integral aspect of social relations arising out of employer-employee interaction in modern industries, which are regulated by the State, the legal system, and the workers' and employers' organisations at the industrial level, and of the pattern of industrial organisation (including management) capital structure (including technology), compensation of labour force and a study of market forces - all at the economic level.*

(4) The International Labour Organisation (ILO) has also pointed out that, *"Industrial relations indicate either the relationship between state and employers' organisation and workers' organisation or the relations between occupational organisations themselves."*

In a broad sense, 'industrial relations' is the topic of study of the personnel or human resource management and, its logical corollary, good industrial relations - one, that is, necessary for the development of a given enterprise and its employees. That apart, it is also important from the viewpoint of not only industrial peace, but also for the industrial and economic development of a given country.

3. Nature and Characteristics or Features of Industrial Relations

Nature of Industrial Relations

Industrial relations do not constitute a simple relationship. They are, in fact, a set of functional, inter-dependent complexities involving various variables, namely, economic, political, social, legal, etc. In other words, they are multi-dimensional in nature.

Industrial relations are the outcome of employment relationship, namely, the relations that exist between the employer and his employees while in the course of conducting work operations in a given industrial enterprise. In this regard, the trade unions, as responsible institutions can also play an important role in shaping industrial relations in many ways.

Further, the appropriate government also influences and shapes the industrial relations by way of rules, agreements, legislation, industrial relation policies, etc. Hence, industrial relations are governed by the system of legislations and regulations relating to the work, workplace and people at work.

Characteristics/Features of Industrial Relations/Features

There are many characteristics or features of the industrial relations which make the nature of industrial relations abundantly clear. Some of them are given below:

(1) The concept of 'Industrial Relations' is a dynamic and evolving concept. It is described as that relationship which exists between employers or management of the enterprise concerned and the employees; or, amongst the employees and their organisations; or, employers, employees and their trade unions and the government. Such relationship necessarily flows out from employment relationship.

(2) Industrial relations do not constitute a simple relationship; they are, in fact, a set of functional, inter-dependent complexities involving various factors or variables, such as, economic, political, social, psychological, legal factors or variables. Further, they can be changed or affected because of the changes in the factors or variables mentioned above.

(3) Industrial relations do not exist in a vacuum. They are created out of employee-employer relationship in a given industrial activity. Without the existence of a minimum of two or more parties, industrial relationship cannot exist. They are - (a) Workers and their organisations; (b) Employers or management of the enterprise; and (c) Government.
The three aforesaid parties thus form the mainstay of industrial relations.

(4) The important objectives of industrial relations are, namely, to develop a healthy labour-management or employee-employer relations; maintenance of industrial peace; avoidance of industrial strife; and, for enabling growth of industrial democracy, etc.

(5) Industrial relations as a part of a branch of personnel management or human resources management is mainly concerns itself, among other things, with the study of the people in relation to their work, the problems arising amongst employees at work. That apart, it also applies equally *vis-à-vis* safeguarding the interests of both the employers and employees.

(6) Industrial relations may be either an individual relation or collective relations. An individual relation implies the relations between an employer and his employees in his/her enterprise; while collective relations are the relations between an employer and his employees or their trade unions at various levels. Thus, the connotation of collective relations is much wider than those of industrial relations. Collective relations also include the relations that one has with the Government, as the regulating authority.

(7) Industrial relations are the product of economic, social, and political system arising out of the employment in the industrial field.

(8) Industrial relations are determined by various factors. These factors can be classified into two groups, namely -
(a) Institutional factors, and (b) Economic factors.

Institutional factors include the labour or industrial legislation, government policy relating to labour and industry, impact and development of the trade unions, etc. In contrast, the economic factors include the ownership of the enterprises, capital structure, technology, composition of labour force, the demand and supply of labour, expectations of workers, economic conditions prevailing in the country concerned, etc.

(9) In a nutshell, the industrial relations are those relations that are affected by the conflicts as well as the co-operative attitude and aptitude of the parties concerned.

4. Scope of Industrial Relations

Industrial relations are an important aspect of social and economic relations arising out of the employer-employee relations and interactions in the industrial field. They are regulated by the Government in different ways. This involves the study of the legal aspects relating to labour and industries, employers' and workers' associations at different levels.

The industrial relations are part and parcel of industrial life and include various aspects, topics for their study. The important aspect or topics which are included in the study of industrial relations are as follows:

(1) It is given that in industrial relations, the relations between the parties relating to the enterprises or industries are studied and they include -
   (a) Employer-employee relations or the relations between the management and the employees working in the given enterprise.
   (b) Employee relations, i.e., relations between the employees working together.
   (c) Relations between the trade unions and the management.
   (d) The relations that exist between the industry, government and the society, at large.

(2) Business enterprises, workers or employees, trade unions do not exist in isolation. They are, in fact, a part of the larger economic, social and political systems. Hence, the study of the industrial relations also includes various environmental issues like, country's labour policy, legal system, attitudes and aptitudes of the employers, employees, trade unions, political and social environments, economic conditions, etc.

(3) The main aspects of the industrial relations are promotion of sound and healthy labour-management relations, maintenance of industrial peace, development of industrial democracy, etc. Hence, various topics relating to these aspects become the part of the study of industrial relations.

(4) The various other aspects relating to the industrial conflicts or industrial disputes too are very important topics from the viewpoint of maintaining good industrial relations. Hence, the causes of industrial disputes are analysed and, accordingly, steps are taken for their resolution. There are statutory and non-statutory measures for conflict resolution. All these aspects are studied in detail in the industrial relations.

(5) Collective bargaining and its types, process of collective bargaining and other related topics are studied in order to find out solutions to the recurrent problems of industrial conflicts or disputes.

(6) The study of certain Acts, such as the Industrial Disputes Act, the Trade Union Act, Payment of Bonus Act, the Factories Act, etc., are necessary for improving the industrial relations. Hence, the study of the related labour laws is included in the scope of the industrial relations.

(7) Welfare measures, whether statutory or non-statutory provided by the employers, trade unions, government, etc., creates, maintains and improves the labour-management relations which substantially contribute to industrial peace. Hence, their study becomes inevitable in industrial relations.

5. Objectives of Industrial Relations

The following are the objectives and importance of Industrial Relations which may be outlined as below:

(1) To protect and safeguard the interests of both employer(s) and employees by creating proper understanding and goodwill amongst the concerned parties, i.e., employers, employees and their unions in the industrial field which participate in the process of production and distribution of the goods and services.

(2) To bring about industrial peace and develop harmonious relations. Such harmonious industrial relations are essential for not only increasing the overall productivity of the employees but also the production of goods and services.

(3) To enhance the economic status of the employees by increasing their wage rates and by giving other benefits. This, in turn, helps to increase the productivity by lessening the tendencies of high turnover and absenteeism.

(4) To eliminate, or remove the causes of strikes, lock-outs, *gheraos* by considering the difficulties of the employees. For this purpose, reasonable wages, improved working conditions and standard of living and fringe benefits can be provided wherever and whenever possible.

(5) To regulate the production and industrial activities by minimising industrial conflicts through state control or by any other possible means.

(6) To establish and develop the industrial democracy based on labour partnership in sharing of profits and also of managerial decisions, i.e., workers' participation in management.

(7) To avoid industrial conflicts/disputes and thereby its consequences.

(8) To encourage and develop the trade unions' working so as to improve the strength of the employees.

(9) To establish proper rapport between the management/employer and employees.

(10) To solve the problems of the employees through mutual negotiations and consultation with the employer/management.

(11) To lay down such considerations as may promote proper understanding and thereby facilitate co-operation in order to ensure better participation of the employees and thus enhance the overall industrial productivity.

6. Importance of Industrial Relations

Good Industrial Relations would mean industrial peace which is necessary for better and higher production. Hence, healthy industrial relations are the key to the progress of individuals, management, industry and nation. Their significance may be discussed as below:

(1) Uninterrupted Production: The most important benefit of industrial relations is that it ensures continuity of production. This means, continuous employment for all, from the managerial level to the workforce. All available resources are utilised to their fullest, resulting in maximum possible production, which, in turn, translates into an uninterrupted flow of income for all concerned. Therefore, smooth running of an industry is of vital importance for several other industries, especially, if the products are intermediaries or inputs to exporters if these are export goods; to consumers and workers if these are goods of mass consumption.

(2) **Reduction in Industrial Disputes:** Good industrial relations help in minimising industrial disputes. Disputes are reflections of the failure of fulfilling basic human urges or motivations to secure adequate satisfaction or expression. Strikes, lockouts, go-slow tactics, *gheraos* and grievances are some of the reflections of industrial unrest. Good industrial relations help promote an atmosphere of industrial peace in which disputes are settled through cooperation and do not spring up as industrial unrest. In short, good industrial relations help promote cooperation and thereby enable increased production.

(3) **High Morale:** Good industrial relations improve the morale of the employees. This is achieved when every worker feels that he is a co-owner of the gains of industry. This induces employees to work with zest as they feel that the interest of the employer and employees is one and the same, i.e., to increase production. To maintain good industrial relations, an employer needs to realise that the gains of industry are not for him alone, but are one that need to be shared equally and generously with his workers. In other words, the achievement of unity of thought and action between the workers and management is the main by-product of industrial peace. This, in turn, boosts the morale of workers and has a positive effect on production.

(4) **Mental Revolution:** The main object of industrial relations is to create a complete overhaul in the outlook of workers and employees, termed as 'mental revolution'. The leadership in the ranks of workers, employees and the Government need to work out a new relationship in consonance with the spirit of true democracy, wherein they both think of themselves as partners in the industry. This can be achieved when the role of workers in such a partnership is recognised. However, the workers also need to recognise an employer's authority and respect it. Industrial peace ultimately lies in a transformed outlook on the part of both – one that would eventually lead to increased production, and thereby benefiting both the parties.

(5) **New Programmes:** Good industrial relations would involve setting up of new programmes for workers and of development, such as training facilities, labour welfare facilities etc. This serves to increase the efficiency of workers resulting in higher worker morale, which, in turn, translates into higher and better production at lower costs.

(6) **Reduced Wastage:** Good industrial relations are maintained on the basis of cooperation and acceptance of each others' views and ideas. This helps to increase production by bringing about a reduction in wastage of resources, be they-human, material or machines.

7. Factors Determining Good Industrial Relations

Good industrial relations depend on a lot of different factors. Some of the obvious ones are listed as follows.

(1) History of Industrial Relations: Every enterprise has its own good and bad history of industrial relations. A good history is marked by a harmonious relationship between the management and workers. A bad history, in contrast, is characterised by militant strikes, lockouts and gheraos. Both types of history have a tendency to perpetuate themselves. A militant relationship propagates itself and there is a tendency for militancy to continue. The same holds true for a harmonious relationship.

(2) Economic Satisfaction of Workers: It has been recognised by psychologists that human needs have a certain priority and the basic need for survival can be classified as the most important one. Most humans are dominated by this need for survival and work to satisfy this need. It is more so in underdeveloped countries where workers live under extremely harsh conditions and have to fight for basic sustenance. Thus, an important prerequisite for good industrial relations is economic satisfaction of the workers.

(3) Social and Psychological Satisfaction: Once the basic need for survival is met, other social and psychological urges of workers need to be fulfilled for maintaining good industrial relations. An organisation is a joint venture wherein an environment of close human and social relationships is created, within which each participant feels that he is not only fulfilling his needs but also is contributing towards the well-being of others. To maintain this supportive climate, not only economic rewards but also social and psychological rewards, such as, workers' participation in management, job enrichment, suggestion schemes, redressal of grievances etc., is required.

(4) Off-the-job Conditions: Humans are complex beings and an employer employs the whole individual rather than certain separate characteristics of that individual to work for him. All of the person's traits go into making him a whole man. His home life though separate from his work life, affects his work life and his emotional well-being affects his physical well-being. Hence, to improve industrial relations, it is not enough for an employer to look after the worker's factory life alone, but his off-the-job conditions should also be looked into and improved.

(5) Enlightened Trade Unions: A strong and enlightened labour movement which helps to promote the status of labour, without harming the interests of management is a crucial imperative for maintaining good industrial relations. A responsible union should encourage employees to shoulder their responsibilities in such a way as to beneficially contribute towards the industry. Also, they should exhort workers to produce more, persuade the management to pay more, mobilise public opinion on vital labour issues and help the Government to enact progressive labour laws.

(6) Negotiating Skills and Attitudes of Management and Workers: In industrial relations, representation for both, management and workers comes from a variety of backgrounds in terms of training, education, experience and attitudes. These varying backgrounds play a major role in shaping the character of industrial relations. Well-trained and experienced negotiators who are motivated by a desire for industrial peace create a bargaining atmosphere which is conducive to the writing of a just and equitable collective agreement; while ignorant, inexperienced and ill-trained negotiators are unsuccessful as they fail to recognise that collective bargaining deals not just with the economic interests of the two parties but also *vis-a-vis* their emotions. Collective bargaining requires careful preparation and top-notch competence and, therefore, they cannot be accomplished by some easy trick or gimmick. Both parties need to have trust and confidence in each other and empathise with each other, i.e., they should be able to perceive a problem from the opposite angle with an open mind. The factors which help create mutual trust are namely, respect for the law and vision.

(7) Public Policy and Legislation: There are three major forces which determine industrial relations: They are - the employer, the union, and the Government. It also applies equally insofar as regulating employee relations go. The Governments in all countries, at times, intervenes in the management-union relationships by enforcing labour laws and by seeing to it that the goals of a society as a whole take precedence over those of both parties. Governmental intervention helps in three different ways:

- It helps in identifying and solving the given problem(s) before they become serious.
- It provides a formalised channel for both the workers and employers to vent their emotions and dissatisfaction.
- It acts as a check and balance on the arbitrary and capricious management practices.

(8) Better Education: Industrial workers, especially, in India are uneducated if not illiterate and are therefore easily swayed by unscrupulous trade union leaders who have their own agendas to implement. The solution for this is to simply educate them. Education empowers the workers, by way of upgrading their skills, which, in turn, not only yields better financial returns for them but also helps them in achieving a standing in the society. All these go to instil a sense of loyalty and responsibility to their organisation, in the immediate sense, and, to the society at large, in the ultimate sense.

(9) Nature of Industry: Every organisation goes through its highs and lows. During the lows, cost-cutting is the norm. Very often, labour costs need to be cut, leading to salary cuts and unemployment. This naturally triggers discontent amongst the workforce and, as a result, destroys good industrial relations.

1.2 Philosophy of IR

The term 'industrial relations,' consists of two terms, namely - 'industry' and 'relations'. While 'industry' refers to "any productive activity in which an individual (or a group of individuals) is (are) engaged". By 'relations,' is meant "the relationships that exist within the industry, on the one hand, and between the employer and his workmen, on the other." Taken collectively, the term 'industrial relations,' serves to explain the relationship between employees and management which stem directly or indirectly from union-employer relationship.

In a nutshell, industrial relations are basically the interactions between employers, employees and the government and the institutions and associations through which such interactions are mediated.

That apart, industrial relations have both broad as well as a narrow outlook. Originally, industrial relations were broadly defined to include the relationships and interactions between employers and employees. From this perspective, industrial relations cover all aspects of the employment relationship, including human resource management, employee relations and union-management (or labour) relations. Now, its meaning has become more specific and restricted. Accordingly, industrial relations pertains to the study and practice of collective bargaining, trade unionism and labour-management relations, while human resource management is a separate, largely distinct field that deals with non-union employment relationships and the personnel practices and policies of employers.

The relationships which arise at and out of the workplace generally include the relationships between individual workers, the relationships between workers and their employer, the relationships between employers, the relationships employers and workers have with the organisations formed to promote their respective interests, and the relations between those organisations, at all levels. Industrial relations, also includes the processes through which these relationships are expressed (such as, collective bargaining, workers' participation in decision-making and grievance and dispute settlement) and the management of conflict between employers, workers and trade unions, when it arises.

Today, industry is a broad term for any kind of economic production and is classified into four sectors. These four key industrial economic sectors are:

1. The *primary sector*, which is largely involved in raw material extraction and includes industries like mining and farming;
2. The *secondary sector*, where refining, construction and manufacturing are involved;
3. The *tertiary sector*, which deals with providing services like law and medicine, distribution of manufactured goods; and
4. The *quaternary sector*, which focuses on technological research, design and development, such as computer programming and biochemistry.

The early industries were involved in the manufacture of goods for trade, which included weapons, clothing, pottery etc. Industrial relations can be traced back to medieval Europe, where industry came to be dominated by the guilds in cities and towns. They supported and looked out for their member's interests, and maintained standards of workmanship and ethical conduct.

The industrial revolution paved the way for the development of factories for large-scale production, with consequent changes in the society. Originally, the factories were steam-powered, but later, they transitioned to electricity. Then, came the assembly line and today, automation is being used to replace human operators.

1.3 Evolution of IR - Indian Perspective

During the first decade of this 21st century and the last two decades of 20th century, it was discovered that industrial tensions are one of the most tangible manifestations of disagreements and conflicts of interests in India. Generally, the employers and their employees have to face various issues or problems, such as, the fair rates of wages and salaries, working conditions, the interpretation of contracts of employment, privileges, responsibilities of trade unions, etc.

Without a doubt, the aforesaid clashes are nothing new, but they, in their present day form, do reflect a major development in the society. The problems of industrial relations, as we understand it today, were not in existence in the past when the system of industrial production was very simple. With the advent of modern industries, post industrial revolution, things *vis-à-vis* production has changed dramatically.

Today, on the other hand, labour is not merely an unorganised mass of ignorant and unconscious workers as it was in the past. As a result, the employers have to deal with their employees through the medium/agency of trade unions. The trade unions have substantially increased the strength and consciousness of their members.

The trade unions now play a very important role in the field of industrial relations. In a sense, to a great extent, industrial peace depends much on the actions, reactions and interactions of the trade unions. Besides, the employers and their organisations, employees and their organisations, the other party affecting industrial relations is the Government.

It is found that the Government regulates the labour/ industrial relations in all countries of the world. In some countries, the Governments of the respective countries have laid down certain bare minimum rules for observance by the employers and their employees.

While in some other countries, the legislation covers a wide area of relationships between the employers and the employees. In India, the Government of India has enacted procedural and substantive laws to regulate the industrial relations. In order to know the development of the industrial relations in India, we have to consider basically three important factors or aspects, namely:

(1) Labour policy and labour legislation,
(2) Growth of the trade unions, and
(3) Industrial disputes and their settlement.

Labour Policy and Labour Legislation

During the pre-independence days and especially, during the early period of the colonial rule, the British rulers in India were mainly concerned with getting an ample supply of cheap labour for the production of goods for the industries mostly owned by their fellow brethren.

Naturally, the regulation of labour and their employment mainly aimed at keeping the labour costs of the industries owned by the British in India as low as possible. It is, therefore, not surprising that the British rulers did not take any pains *vis-a-vis* improving the working conditions of the Indian workers. Their conditions only started changing after 1918, i.e., after the end of the First World War.

The International Labour Organisation [ILO] was established in 1919 with a view to solve the workers' problems. The important objects of ILO are to remove injustice and hardship faced by the workers all over the world over besides improving their living conditions with a view to establish universal and lasting peace based upon social justice. The influence of the functioning of the ILO on the labour policy and labour legislation in India cannot be underestimated.

After 1920, the Government started taking certain steps to improve the working conditions of the workers employed in the factories and to provide a certain amount of security. The influence of the ILO and the pressure of public opinion in India due to the extremely unsatisfactory conditions of factory workers compelled the Government to pass certain Acts for introducing the measures to improve the same.

To name a few - The Workmen's Compensation Act, 1923, the Trade Unions Act, 1926, the Trade Disputes Act, 1929, the Payment of Gratuity Act, 1936, the Employers' Liability Act, 1938 were amongst the most significant legislative measures passed by the Government of India to protect the interests of the employees.

The Royal Commission on Labour was appointed in 1929 by Government of India. The report of the Commission brought the labour problems in India in sharp focus and also provided the comprehensive data regarding the conditions of the Indian workers. The important consequence of the report of the Royal Commission was passing of the Factories Act, 1934, and the Payment of Wages Act, 1936. Though the limited statutory provisions were made by the Government of India during the period of the British rule, there did not emerge a very comprehensive labour policy covering various aspects of industrial relations during the pre-independence period.

In the post-independence period, the Government of free India took steps necessary to develop economy in all directions. The Industrial Truce Resolution, 1947, set the tone and direction of new labour policy. The major emphasis in this was on the mutuality of interests of management and labour and the method to be adopted laid stress on mutual discussion and settlement of disputes in a proper manner. That resolution gave a proper push to the industrial relations in the expected direction.

In 1950, the Constitution of India was adopted. The Constitution has emphasised that:
(1) There should be no exploitation of the workers, weaker sections of the society,
(2) There should be fair distribution of the national income among the people,
(3) There should be provision for social security for the needy and distressed workers/employees and
(4) There should be promotion of industrial harmony for the continuous development of the industrial sector.

Thus, the Directive Principles of the State Policy as embodied in the Constitution of India lay special stress on the goal of 'Welfare State,' by directing the Government to follow certain principles which are essential to secure a social order for the promotion of welfare of the people.

In this regard, it has been clearly stated in the Constitution of India that, "The State shall endeavour to secure by suitable legislation or economic organisation, or in any other way, to all workers, agricultural, industrial or otherwise, work a living wage, conditions of work ensuring a decent standard of life and full enjoyment of leisure and social and cultural opportunities." This reflects the attitude of the constitution as regards workers and their working and living conditions.

The Indian Government decided to adopt economic planning for the development of her economy. The Five-Year Plan provides a broad framework and approach to the Government of India in so far as framing suitable labour policy - one, that is, in alignment with its overall economic development strategy.

The Second Five Year Plan (1956-1961) aimed at the goal of establishing a socialistic pattern of society and also emphasised the need of creating an industrial democracy as a prerequisite for establishing it.

The wage issue was at the heart of the problem of industrial relations and, even today, it continues to occupy an important place in the context of healthy industrial relations. Recognising the importance of the problem, the First Five Year Plan recommended the increase in wages of the workers to remove the anomalies or where the existing wage rates were abnormally low. It was decided to set up the permanent wage boards with a tripartite composition in each State and at the Centre to deal comprehensively with all aspects relating to wages of the workers employed.

It was realised that, the creation of the industrial democracy and industrial peace were necessary for the healthy development of industrial relations. Labour legislation and the enforcement machinery set up for its implementation, at best, could only provide a suitable framework wherein the employers and their employees could function.

From this point of view, under the Industrial Disputes Act, amended in 1950, a three-tier system of Labour Court, Industrial Tribunals and the National Tribunal were set up. A Code of Discipline was also evolved in 1958 in order to reduce the industrial disputes. Thus, efforts were made to strengthen the industrial relations during 1950-1960, i.e., during the first two five year plans.

In the next decade, the attention was focussed on the fixation of minimum wage rates, reduction in disparities, wage differential, etc. Special attention was given to three aspects during the Forth Five-Year Plan Period, namely:

(1) Improvement in the field of labour legislation for the protection, safety and welfare of workers,

(2) Orientation of workers and employers in order to solve the labour problems, and

(3) Execution of programmes, which had a large bearing on the welfare of workers for workers' education, provision of facilities for imparting higher skills and training to workers, social securities, etc.

The Fifth Five Year Plan envisaged better food, nutrition and health standards, higher standard of education and training, improvement in discipline and morale, more productive technology and management practices.

The Sixth Five Year Plan (1980-85) laid more stress on effective implementation of the measures in the different legislative enactments and also in extending the coverage of the Employees State Insurance Scheme, the Employees' Provident Fund and Family Pension Scheme.

Special programmes were planned by the State Governments too for the agricultural workers, artisans, handloom weavers, leather workers, fishermen and other unorganised workers in the urban as well as in the rural areas. During the Sixth Plan period, bonus payments and some social security benefits were brought under the statutory arrangements.

It was in mid-1991, that the Government of India announced the new economic policy for the seven major areas of our economy, namely, trade policy, industrial policy, fiscal policy, agricultural policy, financial policy, poverty alleviation and employment policy, human resource policy.

The New Economic Policy of 1991 has consolidated and reinforced the process of industrial restructuring. The era of privatisation, globalisation and liberalisation has begun because of the New Economic Policy. The process of industrial restructuring began in the decade of 1990 introduced the radical measures to release the Indian industries from an artificial environment of high protection and regulations. The process is still continued.

Modern industrialisation and economic growth which have taken place in the first six-seven years of the 21st century call for the increased use of legislation not merely for tackling the existing labour, social and economic problems but also for creating such industrial conditions as would seem to be very conductive for establishing a just and healthy conditions.

It is expected that the employers and their employees shall realise the importance of industrial democracy and good industrial relations for productivity and efficiency of industry.

They must make all efforts to resolve their disputes through the route of joint consultation so as to fulfil the purpose of sound industrial relations. In this regard, the Government would like to help them by amending the existing acts, if necessary, and, passing suitable new acts whenever and wherever necessary.

From the brief view taken so far as regards the labour policy and the efforts of the Government to protect the interests of the workers, we come to know that the Government has tried to give proper shape to the employee-employer relations or industrial relations by passing various Acts.

A large number of labour legislations have been enacted to promote the conditions of the workers working in different sectors of the economy. The important Acts passed to protect the interests of the employees and to improve the industrial relations are mentioned as below.

1. The Factories Act, 1948.
2. The Workmen's Compensation Act, 1923.
3. The Employees' State Insurance Act, 1948.
4. The Employees' Provident Fund (and Miscellaneous Provisions) Act, 1952.
5. The Payment of Gratuity Act, 1972.
6. The Maternity Benefit Act, 1961.
7. The Payment of Wages Act, 1936.
8. The Minimum Wages Act, 1948.
9. The Industrial Disputes Act, 1947.
10. The Industrial Employment (Standing Orders) Act, 1946.
11. The Trade Unions Act, 1926.
12. The Payment of Bonus Act, 1965.
13. The Indian Mines (Amendment) Act, 1959.
14. The Coal Mines (Conservation and Safety) Act, 1952.
15. The Plantation Labour Act, 1951.
16. The Indian Railway Act, 1930.
17. The Indian Merchant Shipping Act, 1923.
18. The Indian Dock Labourers' Act, 1923.
19. The Dock Workers' (Regulation of Employment) Act, 1948.
20. The Contract Labour (Regulation and Abolition) Act, 1970.
21. The Bombay Industrial Relations Act, 1946.
22. The Maharashtra Recognition of Trade Unions and Prevention of Unfair Labour Practices Act, 1971.

23. The Bombay Shops and Establishment Act, 1948.
24. The Employment of Children Act, 1938 which was replaced by The Child Labour (Prohibition and Regulation) Act, 1986.
25. Equal Remuneration Act, 1976.
26. The Bonded Labour System (Abolition) Act, 1976.
27. The Employers' Liability Act, 1938.
28. The Employment Exchanges (Compulsory notification of Vacancies) Act, 1959.

1.4 Parties to IR

The parties involved in industrial relations are:

1. **Employers:** The employers have certain rights with respect to the work force. The right to hire or fire rests with them. They have the right to relocate, close or merge the factory or introduce technological changes. These rights affect the workers' interest and, if not carried out sensitively, can lead to conflict situations.

2. **Employees:** Workers always try to improve the terms and conditions of their employment. They like to be involved in the decision-making process of the management. They like to have a platform where they can exchange views and air their grievances. If the management is open and shares a good relationship with their workers, it will earn their trust and loyalty; if not, it could lead to situations where labour unions lock horns with management by resorting to lock-outs and strikes.

3. **Government:** Industrial relations are influenced and regulated by the state and central governments through laws, rules, agreements etc. Labour and tribunal courts also come under this category.

The parties involved in industrial relations as given above are important components of the industrial relations system. These should, therefore, be studied in detail.

An industrial relations system consists of the whole gamut of relationships between employees and employees and between employees and employers which are managed by the means of conflict and co-operation.

A sound industrial relations system is one in which relationships between management and employees (and their representatives) on the one hand and, between them and the State, on the other, are more harmonious and co-operative than one of conflict. This serves to create an environment conducive to economic efficiency and the motivation, productivity and development of the employee morale and, which, in turn, generate employee loyalty and mutual trust.

(1) Industry: The Industrial Disputes Act, 1947, defines an industry as, any systematic activity carried on by cooperation between an employer and his workmen for the production, supply or distribution of goods or services with a view to satisfy human wants or wishes, whether or not any capital has been invested for the purpose of carrying on such activity; or such activity is carried on with a motive to make any gain or profit. Thus, an industry is a whole gamut of activities that are carried on by an employer with the help of his employees and labourers for production and distribution of goods to earn profits.

(2) Employer: An employer can be defined from different perspectives as -
- a person or business that pays a wage or fixed payment to other person(s) in exchange for the services of such persons.
- a person who directly engages a worker/employee in employment.
- any person who employs, whether directly or through another person or agency, one or more employees in any scheduled employment in respect of which minimum rates of wages have been fixed.

As per Industrial Disputes Act, 1947, an employer means:
- in relation to an industry carried on by or under the authority of any department of [the Central Government or a State Government], the authority prescribed in this behalf, or where no authority is prescribed, the head of the department;
- in relation to an industry carried on by or on behalf of a local authority, the chief executive officer of that authority

(3) Employee: Employee is person who is hired by another person or business for a wage or fixed payment in exchange for personal services and who does not provide the services as part of an independent business.
- An employee is any individual employed by an employer.
- A person who works for a public or private employer and receives remuneration in wages or salary by his employer while working on a commission basis, piece rate or time rate.
- An employee, as per Employees' State Insurance Act, 1948, is any person employed for wages in or in connection with work of a factory or establishment to which the Act applies.

In order to qualify to be an employee, under ESI Act, a person should belong to any of the following categories:
- those who are directly employed for wages by the principal employer within the premises or outside in connection with work of the factory or establishment.

- those employed for wages by or through an immediate employer in the premises of the factory or establishment in connection with the work thereof.
- those employed for wages or through an immediate employer in connection with the factory or establishment outside the premises of such factory or establishment under the supervision and control of the principal employer or his agent.
- employees whose services are temporarily lent or let on hire to the principal employer by an immediate employer under a contract of service (employees of security contractors, labour contractors, house keeping contractors etc., come under this category).

(4) Employment: The state of being employed or having a job.

(5) Labour market: The market in which workers compete for jobs and employers compete for workers. It acts as the external source from which organisations attract employees. These markets obtain because different conditions characterise different geographical areas, industries, occupations, and professions at any given time.

(6) Trade Union or **Labour Union:** It is an organisation of workers who have banded together to achieve common goals in key areas, such as, wages, working hours and working conditions. The trade union, through its leadership, bargains with the employer on behalf of union members (rank and file members) and negotiates labour contracts (collective bargaining) with employers. This may include the negotiation of wages, work rules, complaint procedures, rules governing hiring, firing and promotion of workers, benefits, workplace safety and policies. The agreements negotiated by the union leaders are binding on the rank and file members and the employer and, in some cases, on other non-member workers as well.

To conclude, industrial relations can be explained as the relationships which arise at and out of the workplace and, generally, include the relationships between individual workers, the relationships between workers and their employer, the relationship the employers and workers have with the organisations formed to promote their respective interests and the relations between those organisations, at all levels.

Industrial relations also includes the processes through which these relationships are expressed (such as, collective bargaining, workers' participation in decision-making, and grievance and dispute settlement), and the management of conflict between employers, workers and trade unions, when it arises. The field of industrial relations (also, called labour relations) looks at the relationship between management and workers, particularly groups of workers who are represented by a union.

A sound industrial relations system is one where a harmonious and cooperative environment is created between the management and employees on the one hand and, the company and the State, on the other, so as to help attain economic efficiency. Alternately, if there is a situation wherein there is conflict rather than cooperation in the relationship, then, it would lead to lack of motivation, loss of productivity and loyalty, which, in turn, would have an adverse impact on economic efficiency.

1.4.1 Employer's Organisation

The employers and employers' organisations play an important role in the setting up and formulating of industrial relations policies of the government. According to **Mr. Naval Tata**, employers' organisations are essential because of the following reasons -

1. For the development of healthy and stable industrial relations,
2. To promote collective bargaining at different levels,
3. To bring about a unified employer's viewpoint on the issues of industrial relations to the government in a concerned manner, and
4. To represent in the meetings of ILC and SLC boards in conformity with tripartite approach to labour matters.

On these basis, an employer's strategy in the area of employment relations must focus on achieving -

- appropriate attitudinal and behavioural changes, not only at enterprise, but at other levels;
- a modern policy, legislative and institutional framework which ensures an effective industrial relations system;
- compensation systems linked to enterprise performance;
- a more literate, skilled and adaptable workforce, which is capable of experimentation and innovation;
- more flexible forms of work organisation and management; and
- culture-sensitive management strategies, as firms invest both within and beyond the region.

Today's employers should be seeking modern labour policies, legislation and institutions which encourage industrial harmony (by emphasising prevention not resolution of conflict). In particular, legislation should be proactive and facilitative in relation to the parties' needs and avoid unnecessary complexity, while maintaining fair and reasonable minimum employment standards. The legislative framework should also give greater emphasis to the need of labour-management cooperation (as mentioned above) and settlement of grievances and disputes in the workplace (assisted by conciliation, if necessary).

The employers' organisations like trade unions, face a difficult situation in assisting their constituents in the face of the new demands being placed on them by globalisation. Not only do they face the need to become more representative and better able to provide services to their members (by recruiting new members from a broader cross-section of the business and industrial community), like unions they confront very different situations from country to country, and differ in their capacities as regards fulfilling their functions effectively.

A key function of employers' organisations has always been to act as the mouthpiece for employers in seeking to influence the broad policy environment in a manner conducive to their constituents' interests (in this respect, it might be noted that the IR function was originally and, in many cases, has remained the cornerstone of the operations of many employers' organisations). This representational role will remain significant. But "the ultimate credibility of the employers' organisations will depend on the provision of quality services to enterprises and their capacity and skill in negotiating on behalf of employers" (de Silva 1996:3). In this regard, considerable emphasis is now being given within the region concerned insofar as developing employers' organisations as strong professional organisations. Priority is being given to strategic planning; developing direct services to members across a range of issues (for e.g., labour law, IR/HRM, labour market information, human resource development etc.) and providing the necessary internal capacities to deliver these services (which require knowledgeable, well-trained technical staff, supported by sophisticated research and information bases).

More specifically, in the area of IR/HRM, employers' organisations need to have a role which is proactive and preventive, i.e., primarily concerned with promoting among their members (and with government and trade unions), the need for sound workplace relations which emphasise the importance of improved cooperation and consultation and effective negotiation to address workplace issues, thereby avoiding (or, at least, limiting) industrial disputes and providing a basis for achieving sustainable improvements in enterprise performance.

To achieve this objective, it is suggested that employers' organisations should organise their operations around two functional poles, supported by a range of subsidiary services. The 'twin poles' would consist of developing and/or maintaining an effective representational role and developing a sound information database.

An active representational role to governments and trade unions, in relation to national labour policies and legislation (as noted above), but also for securing public understanding and/or support on certain issues, remains a critical priority for employers' organisations. Many of the issues where influence is sought to be brought to bear are sensitive, have potential labour cost implications and/or are important to employers' day-to-day operations and, therefore, need careful handling. The employers' organisations need to be prepared to have a view on an increasingly broader range of issues (for e.g., skills development, including in the context of training and re-training and covering both delivery and compensation aspects; industry (including investment and taxation) policy; the implications for business of privatisation strategies; and the like.

1.4.2 Trade Unions

The workers' individual capacity to bargain with their employers is weak, and therefore, they find themselves short-changed in the sense that, their demands are not given due need, leave alone its proper satisfaction by their respective employers. This leads to worsening of industrial relations between the employers and employees, respectively, which, in turn, leads to industrial disputes. In fact, the genesis of trade unionism can be traced to the growth of modern industrial establishments involving the employment of a large workforce often in conditions wherein the worker is rendered helpless *vis-a-vis* negotiating his terms of contract at an individual level.

Conversely, if the trade unions are strong, many problems of the workers can be solved and thereby better industrial relations can be promoted and maintained. There should be some machinery or mechanism for settling the issue of relations between the employers and their employees. Besides others, a trade union is the best and socially most desirable organisation, to conduct bargaining on behalf of workers' organisations and is an essential basis for the establishment of industrial peace. Trade unionism developed along proper lines can definitely lessen violent class conflicts, and thus, prove to be very beneficial not only to both employers' and employees' interests but also insofar as ensuring smooth industrial development. Hence, it is considered that no other agency formed or promoted to look after the interests of the workers can be a real substitute for trade unions. The organisation of workers, i.e., a trade union is, therefore, not only necessary but inevitable.

Of late, it is found that the role of trade unions in making policies at the plant, industry and even at the national level is growing. The powerful amongst them have been known to exert pressure as regards formulating policies which affect the wages, bonus, outside recruitments, promotions, safety measures, working conditions etc., not only at the local levels but also at the national level. Trade unions, as a body, not only help to protect the interests of their members but also play a key role in maintaining good industrial relations by settling the industrial disputes to a great extent.

1.4.3 Role of Government

The Government and the factory owner must completely understand the labour psychology and therefore a change in their outlook and attitude is necessary to secure industrial peace. Nothing should be done under threat or coercion but on a clear understanding that whatever is good and is due to the labourer, must be given.

Industry owners should treat the workers as co-partners. Workers in the country too must understand fully that if they desire to secure their due place in the industrial world, they must think more in terms of responsibilities and duties. Sabotage and violence of all kinds, bitterness in thought, word and deed must be eschewed. An improvement in labour regulations will provide an opportunity to accelerate manufacturing growth and development of the nation.

1.4.4 Role of Society

Whether we have good jobs and how we work has a fundamental effect on the quality of our lives. Unemployment causes social isolation and economic deprivation. When there is high level of unemployment, there is social tension and upheaval. Too much employment has its own set of woes. People who work for long hours often suffer from health issues and family problems. There is a need to strike a work life balance to ensure a healthy, happy and productive populations.

1.5 Approaches to IR: The Dunlop's Approach, The Social Action Approach, The Human Relations Approach, The Gandhian Approach

1. The Dunlop's Approach

John Dunlop put forth his theory on Industrial Labour Relations in 1950. According to Dunlop, the modern industrial relations system consists of three players:

(1) Management organisations, i.e., employers,
(2) Workers and formal/informal ways they are organised, i.e., labour unions and
(3) Government agencies.

These players and their organisations are located within three environmental constraints: the market, distribution of power in society and technology. Within this environment, the players interact with each other, negotiate and use economic/political power in the process of determining rules that constitute the output of the industrial relations system. Dunlop's model identifies three key factors to be kept in mind while conducting an analysis of the management-labour relationship:

(4) Environmental or external factors: economic, technological, political, legal and social forces that impact employment relationships.
(5) Characteristics and interactions of the key players in the employment relationship: labour, management and the Government.
(6) Rules that are derived from these interactions and which govern the employment relationship.

Effectively, industrial relations, is a system which guides the rules of the workplace. Such rules are the result of interactions between the three players, i.e., the workers/ unions, employers and associated organisations and the government. It believes that, management, labour and the government possess a shared ideology which helps to define their roles within the relationship and provide stability to the system.

2. The Social Action Approach

(1) G. Margerison, an industrial sociologists, holds the view that the core of industrial relations is the nature and development of the conflict itself.

(2) Margerison argued that conflict is the basic concept that should form the basis of the study of industrial relations.

(3) According to this approach, there are two major conceptual levels of industrial relations. One is the intra-plant level where situational factors like job content, work task, and technology, and interaction factors produce three types of conflict i.e. distributive, structural, and human relations. These conflicts are being resolved through collective bargaining, structural analysis of the socio-technical systems and man-management analysis respectively.

(4) The second level is outside the firm and mainly concerns with the conflict resolved at the intra-organisation level. However, this approach rejects the special emphasis given to rule determination by the "System and Oxford Model". In its place, it suggests a method of inquiry, which attempts to develop sociological models of conflicts.

3. The Human Relations Approach

(1) In the words of Keith Davies, human relations are "the integration of people into a work situation that motivates them to work together productively, co-operatively and with economic, psychological and social satisfactions."

(2) According to him, the goals of human relations are: (a) to get people to produce, (b) to co-operate through mutuality of interest, and (c) to gain satisfaction from their relationships.

(3) The human relations school founded by Elton Mayo and later propagated by Roethlisberger, Whitehead, W. F. Whyte, and Romans offers a coherent view of the nature of industrial conflict and harmony.

(4) The human relations approach highlights certain policies and techniques to improve employee morale, efficiency and job satisfaction. It encourages the small work group to exercise considerable control over its environment and in the process helps to remove a major irritant in labour-management relations.

(5) But there was reaction against the excessive claims of this school of thought in the sixties. Some of its views were criticised by Marxists, pluralists, and others on the ground that it encouraged dependency and discouraged individual development, and ignored the importance of technology and culture in industry.

(6) Taking a balanced view, however, it must be admitted that the human relations school has thrown a lot of light on certain aspects such as communication, management development, acceptance of workplace as a social system, group dynamics, and participation in management.

4. The Gandhain Approach

(1) Gandhiji can be called one of the greatest labour leaders of modern India. His approach to labour problems was completely new and refreshingly human. He held definite views regarding fixation and regulation of wages, organisation and functions of trade unions, necessity and desirability of collective bargaining, use and abuse of strikes, labour indiscipline, workers participation in management, conditions of work and living, and duties of workers.

(2) The Ahmedabad Textile Labour Association, a unique and successful experiment in Gandhian trade unionism, implemented many of his ideas.

(3) Gandhiji had immense faith in the goodness of man and he believed that many of the evils of the modern world have been brought about by wrong systems and not by wrong individuals. He insisted on recognising each individual worker as a human being. He believed in non-violent communism.

(4) Gandhiji laid down certain conditions for a successful strike. These are: (a) the cause of the strike must be just and there should be no strike without a grievance; (b) there should be no violence, and (c) non-stikers or-blacklegs- should never be molested.

(5) He was not against strikes but pleaded that they should be the last weapon in the armoury of industrial workers and hence should not be resorted to, unless all peaceful and constitutional methods of negotiations, conciliation and arbitration are exhausted.

(6) His concept of trusteeship is a significant contribution in the sphere of industrial relations. According to him, employers should not regard themselves as sole owners of mills and factories of which they may be the legal owners. They should regard themselves only as trustees, or co-owners. He also appealed to the workers to behave as trustees, not to regard the mill and machinery as belonging to the exploiting agents but to regard them as their own, protect them and put to the best use they can.

(7) In short, the theory of trusteeship is based on the view that all forms of property and human accomplishments are gifts of nature and as such, they belong not to any one individual but to society as a whole. Thus, the trusteeship system is totally different from other contemporary labour relations systems. It aimed at achieving economic equality and the material advancement of the "have-nots" in a capitalist society by non-violent means.

(8) Gandhiji realised that relations between labour and management can either be a powerful stimulus to economic and social progress or an important factor in economic and social stagnation. According to him, industrial peace was an essential condition not only for the growth and development of the industry itself, but also in a great measure, for the improvement in the conditions of work and wages.

(9) At the same time, he not only endorsed the workers' right to adopt the method of collective bargaining but also actively supported it.

- He also pleaded for perfect understanding between capital and labour, mutual respect, recognition of equality, and strong labour organisation as the essential factors for happy and constructive industrial relations. For him, means and ends are equally important.

1.6 Theoretical Foundation of IR in India

There are many theories regarding industrial relations. The most important ones are:

1. Unitary Perspective,
2. Pluralistic Perspective,
3. Marxist/Radical Perspective,
4. Dunlop's Theory.

1. Unitary Perspective: The unitary perspective visualises the given organisation to be an integrated and harmonious whole, wherein the management and the workforce have a common goal. Its ideal is that of one big happy family, where mutual cooperation is the key. The concept of unitarism is predominantly believed to be managerial in its emphasis and application, as it demands unstinting loyalty from all its employees. Here, the existence of trade unions is believed to be quite unnecessary and conflict is seen to be disruptive.

Unitary approach from the employees' perspective:

- Working practices should be flexible. Individuals should be oriented towards business process improvement. For this, they should possess multiple skills and be ready to tackle any task with efficiency.
- If a union is recognised, its role is to further improve communication between groups of staff and the company.
- The emphasis is on good relationships and sound terms and conditions of employment.
- Employee participation in workplace decisions is encouraged. This helps in empowering individuals in their roles and emphasises teamwork, innovation, creativity, discretion in problem-solving, quality and improvement groups etc.
- The skills and expertise of managers should support the endeavours of the employees.

Unitary approach from an employer's viewpoint:

- Staffing policies should try to unify, validate effort, inspire and motivate employees.
- The organisation's wider objectives should be properly communicated and discussed with the staff.

- Reward systems should be designed in such a way as to foster and secure loyalty and commitment.
- Line managers should take responsibility for their team/staffing.
- Staff-management conflicts arise due to lack of information and inadequate presentation of the management's policies.
- The personal objectives of every individual employed in the business should be discussed with them and integrated with the organisation's needs.

2. Pluralistic Perspective: Pluralism, as a theory, believes that an organisation is made up of powerful and divergent sub-groups, each with its own set of objectives and leaders and their legitimate loyalties. In particular, the two predominant sub-groups in the pluralistic perspective are the management and trade unions. Thus, the role of management leans heavily towards persuasion and coordination and backs away from enforcing and controlling. Trade unions are considered legitimate representatives of employees; conflict is dealt with by collective bargaining. If managed well, collective bargaining is viewed as a tool for positive change and evolution. This system has a greater propensity towards conflict and realistic managers would expect conflict to occur. Thus, they should be able to anticipate and resolve conflicts by securing beforehand agreed procedures for settling disputes.

The requirements for following this approach are:

- The firm concerned should have industrial relations and personnel specialists who could give valuable input to managers and provide specialist services in respect of staffing and matters relating to union consultation and negotiation.
- Independent external arbitrators should be used to assist in the resolution of disputes.
- Union recognition should be encouraged and union representatives given the scope to carry out their representative duties.
- Comprehensive collective agreements should be negotiated with the union.

3. Marxist/Radical Perspective: According to the Marxist perspective, in a capitalist society, there is a huge chasm between the interests of the management and labour. This view regards the capitalist economic system as the root of all evil and the basis of all inequality of power and economic wealth. Here, the unions' conflict with the given management as a natural response to the workers' exploitation at the hands of the capitalists is seen as inevitable. This view of industrial relations is a by-product of a theory of capitalist society and social change.

Marx argued that:
- Weakness and contradiction intrinsic to the capitalist system would result in revolution and the rise of socialism over capitalism.
- Capitalism would promote monopolies.
- Wages (costs to the capitalist) would be minimised to a subsistence level.
- Capitalists and workers would compete to win ground and establish their supremacy, constant win-lose struggles would be evident.

4. **Dunlop's Theory:** Refer to Article 1.5 (Point 1) of this chapter.

1.7 Legal Framework of IR in India

Labour legislation has great impact on industrial relations. Labour laws and legislation are responsible for the formulation of industrial relations in India. Arun Monappa, in his book 'Industrial Relations', states the objectives of labour legislations, thus -

(1) protecting workers from exploitation,
(2) strengthening industrial relations,
(3) providing machinery for settling industrial disputes and welfare of workers.

Industrial Law has played a crucial role in shaping industrial relations of our country. The relevant labour laws seek to protect the interests of weaker section in industrial relations. In India, labour legislation began over 125 years ago, beginning with the Apprentice Act. The era of protective labour laws began with the enactment of Factories Act, which is still continuing and literally has been taken over by our judiciary.

Arun Monappa says that labour laws regulate not only conditions of work of industrial establishments, but also industrial relations, payment of wages, registration of trade unions, provision of security measures for workers, defining of legal rights and obligations of employees and employers and also making available provision of guidelines for their relationship.

Law is essential for maintaining peaceful environment for the growth of the industry. Labour legislation in India has developed with the growth of the industry. In the eighteenth century, India was not only a agricultural country but a great manufacturing country too. Asian and European markets were mainly fed by the looms supplied by India, but the British Government in India as a matter of policy discouraged the Indian manufacturers in order to encourage the rising manufacturers of England. Their policy was to make India subservient to the industries of Great Britain and to make Indian people grow only raw materials. The British oppression in India continued for a considerable time which led to the growth of Indian nationalism and to a vigorous renaissance. Nationalism has an obvious economic aspect to it, which was reflected in our country through manifest urge for economic reforms and for industrialisation. In the twentieth century, the national movement took a new turn and there was a common demand for Indian goods.

In India, the plantation industry in Assam was the first to attract legislative control. The method of recruitment of workers in this industry was full of hardships. Workers were employed through professional recruiters. Workers were not allowed by the planters to leave the tea gardens. A number of Acts were passed from 1863 onwards to regulate such recruitments. These legislations protected the interests of the employers more than safeguarding the interests of the workers. The Factories Act was passed in 1934 and the Mines Act in 1923. The Workmen's Compensation Act, 1923, was passed to protect the interest of the workers.

The following Acts have been enacted to promote the conditions of labour and regulate the relation between employer and employee keeping in view the development of industry and national economy:

- The Apprentices Act
- The Bonded Labour System (Abolition) Act
- The Child Labour (Prohibition & Regulation) Act
- The Children (Pledging of Labour) Act
- The Contract Labour (Regulation & Abolition) Act
- The Employees' Provident Funds and Misc. Provisions Act
- The Employees' State Insurance Act
- The Employers' Liability Act
- The Employment Exchange (Compulsory Notification of Vacancies) Act
- The Equal Remuneration Act
- The Factories Act
- The Industrial Disputes Act
- The Industrial Employment (Standing Orders) Act
- The Inter-state Migrant Workmen (Regulation of Employment and Conditions of Service) Act
- The Labour Laws (Exemption from Furnishing Returns & Maintaining Registers by Certain Establishments) Act
- The Maternity Benefit Act
- The Minimum Wages Act

- The Payment of Bonus Act
- The Mines Act
- The Payment of Gratuity Act
- The Payment of Wages Act
- The Sales Promotion Employees (Conditions of Service) Act
- The Shops and Establishments Act
- The Trade Union Act
- The Workmen's Compensation Act
- The Weekly Holidays Act

Mahatma Gandhi had once said, 'A nation may do without its millionaires and without its capitalists, but a nation can never do without its labour.' In India, a number of labour legislations have been enacted to promote the condition of the labour keeping in view the development of industry and national economy. But, for industrial regeneration, it is necessary that the partners of the industry must remedy their respective defects.

Since independence, both legislation and public opinion have done a lot to better the condition of the workers. At the same time, it is the duty of the workers and their organisations to improve the work efficiency and thereby help in securing higher profits through better production. The prosperity of the industry should be shared by the management with both the workers and, the community, at large.

Workers are the dominant partners in the industrial undertakings and without their active cooperation, good work, discipline, integrity and character, the industry will not be able to produce effective results and thereby profits. If the human element refuses to cooperate, the industry will fail to run. Therefore, the profit of the industry must be shared between employers, workers and community.

The Government and the factory owner must completely understand the labour psychology and therefore a change in their outlook and attitude is necessary to secure e industrial peace. Nothing should be done under threat or coercion but on a clear understanding that whatever is good and is due to the labourer, must be given.

Industry owners should treat the workers as co-partners. Workers in the country too must understand fully that if they desire to secure their due place in the industrial world, they must think more in terms of responsibilities and duties. Sabotage and violence of all kinds, bitterness in thought, word and deed must be eschewed. An improvement in labour regulations will provide an opportunity to accelerate manufacturing growth and development of the nation.

Exercise

1. What is Industrial Relations? State its characteristics.
2. State the scope of Industrial Relations.
3. Explain the importance of Industrial Relations.
4. State the philosophy of Industrial Relations.
5. Explain the evolution of Industrial Relations.
6. Explain the various parties to Industrial Relations.
7. Discuss the various approaches to Industrial Relations.
8. Write short notes on:
   (a) Nature of industrial relations.
   (b) Indian perspective to industrial relations.
   (c) Theoretical foundation of industrial relations in India.
   (d) Legal framework of industrial relations in India.

Chapter 2...

The Industrial Disputes Act, 1947

Contents ...

2.1 Sections 2 to 19
2.2 Provisions under Chapter V - Strikes and Lockouts
2.3 Provisions under Chapter V A - Lay-off and Retrenchment
2.4 Provisions under Chapter VC - Unfair Labour Practices
2.5 Provisions under Chapter VI - Penalties
2.6 Provisions under Chapter VII - Miscellaneous
• Exercise

2.1 Sections 2 to 19

1. Introduction

The First World War which broke out in 1914, lasted for about four years. At the close of the war, there was a great outbreak of industrial unrest which led to the passing of the first Industrial Trade Disputes Act. This Act was known as the Trade Disputes Act, 1929. Chapter III and Chapter IV of this Act were related to the establishment of tribunals for investigation and settlement of trade disputes.

During the Second World War, several emergency measures were introduced by the Central Government. In 1942, Rule 81-A was added with a view to restrain strikes and lock-outs. This Rule 81-A gave powers to the Central Government to make orders prohibiting strikes, lock-outs etc., with regard to any trade disputes unless reasonable notice was given. At the close of the year 1942, the Government promulgated an order under Rule 81-A, whereby the party proposing to go on strike or lock-outs was required to issue an advance fourteen days' notice for doing so.

Shortly, thereafter, the Industrial Disputes Act, 1947, was passed which embodies the important provisions of the Trade Disputes Act, 1929, as well as the important principles of Rule 81-A. The Industrial Disputes Act, 1947, too was amended several times. The Industrial Disputes (Amendment) Act, 1982, provided for extensive changes. It had recast many terms used in the main Act, such as, Workman, Industry, Industrial Establishments, etc. The rules regarding closure, lay-off, reinstatement, retrenchment, etc., too were altered. Moreover, certain new concepts as well as rules had been introduced, namely, a time limit for adjudication of disputes, a model grievances redressal procedure etc. The latest amendment was carried out in August, 1996. This Act, i.e., The Industrial Disputes (Amendment) Act, 1996, received the assent of the President of India on 16th August, 1996.

2. Objects of the Act

The Industrial Disputes Act, 1947, can be described as a milestone in the history of Industrial Laws in India. It is one of the self-contained Acts. It provides one with the necessary machinery and procedure for the investigation and settlement of industrial disputes. The Act is mainly passed:

(1) To secure and maintain industrial peace by preventing and settling industrial disputes between the employers and workmen, or employers and employees.

(2) To promote those measures that is necessary for securing amity and good relations between employers and workmen through the mechanism of internal works committees.

(3) To promote good relations through an external machinery of conciliation, Courts of Inquiry, Labour Courts, Industrial Tribunals and National Tribunals.

(4) To ameliorate the condition of workmen by redressal of grievances of workmen through a statutory machinery.

(5) To provide for job security to the workmen employed in industries.

(6) To prevent illegal strikes and lock-outs.

(7) To encourage collective bargaining.

3. Definitions

(1) Appropriate Government [Section 2(a)]

'Appropriate Government' means –

(a) In relation to any industrial dispute concerning any industry carried on by or under the authority of the Central Government or by a railway company or concerning any such industry as may be specified in this behalf by the Central Government or in relation to an industrial dispute concerning a Dock Labour Board established under Section 5-A of the Dock Workers (Regulation of Employment) Act, 1948 (9 of 1948), or the Industrial Finance Corporation of India established under Section 3 of the Industrial Finance Corporation Act, 1948, or the Employees State Insurance Corporation established under Section 3 of the Employee's State Insurance Act, 1948, or the Board of Trustees constituted under Section 3-A of the Coal Mines Provident Fund and Miscellaneous Provisions Act, 1948, or the Central Board of Trustees and the State Boards of Trustees constituted under Section 5-A and Section 5-B, respectively, of the Employees Provident Fund and Miscellaneous Provisions Act, 1952, or the Indian Airlines and Air India Corporations established under Section 3 of the Air India Corporations Act, 1953, or the Life Insurance Corporation of India established under Section 3 of the Life Insurance Corporation Act, 1956, or the Oil and

Natural Gas Commission established under Section 3 of the Oil and Natural Gas Commission Act, 1959, or the Deposit Insurance and Credit Guarantee Corporation established under Section 3 of the Deposit Insurance and Credit Guarantee Corporation Act, 1961 (47 of 1961), or the Central Warehousing Corporations Act, 1962 (58 of 1962), or the Unit Trust of India established under Section 3 of the Unit Trust of India Act, 1963 (52 or 1963), or the Food Corporation of India established under Section 3, or a Board of Management established for two or more contiguous States under Section 16, of the Food Corporations Act 1964 (37 of 1964), or the International Airports Authority of India constituted under Section 3 of the International Airports Authority of India Act, 1971 (43 of 1971), or a Regional Rural Bank established under Section 8 of the Regional Rural Banks Act, 1976 (21 of 1976), or the Export Credit and Guarantee Corporation Limited or the Industrial Reconstruction Corporation of India Limited; Rural Bank established under Section 3 of the Regional Rural Banks Act, 1976 (21 of 1976), or [the Banking Service Commission established under Section 3 of the Banking Service Commission Act, 1975 (42 of 1975), a banking or an Insurance Company, a mine, an oilfield, a Cantonment Board or a major port, the Central Government; and

(b) In relation to any other industrial dispute, the State Government.

(2) Arbitrator [Section 2(aa)]

In the Industrial Disputes Act, 1947, the definition of 'Arbitrator' is given in Section 2 wherein it is only stated that **'Arbitrator'** includes an umpire.

(3) Average Pay [Section 2(aaa)]

'Average pay' means the average of the wages payable to a workman;

(a) in the case of monthly paid workman, in the three complete calendar months;

(b) in the case of weekly paid workman, in the four complete weeks;

(c) in the case of daily paid workman, the twelve full working days, preceding the date on which the average pay becomes payable if the workman had worked for three complete calendar months or four complete weeks or twelve full working days, as the case may be, and where such calculation cannot be made, the average pay shall be calculated at the average of the wages payable to a workman during the period he actually worked.

From the above definition, it becomes clear that Section 2(aaa) lays down the basis as to how the average pay of a workman is to be calculated.

When the average pay cannot be calculated on the above mentioned basis, the average is to be calculated as the average of wages payable to a workman during the period he actually worked. While calculating the average wages to a daily paid workman, weekly or other holidays should be excluded.

(4) Muster Roll

Muster roll simply means official list. Section 25-D of the Industrial Disputes Act, 1947, provides that notwithstanding that workmen in any industrial establishment have been laid off, it is the duty of every employer to maintain for the purposes of Sections 25-A to 25-J, a muster roll and also to provide for the making of entries properly therein by workmen who may present themselves for work at the establishment at the appointed time during normal working hours. Thus, muster roll proves to be very useful for calculating an average pay.

(5) Award [Section 2(b)]

'Award' means an interim or a final determination of any industrial dispute or of any question relating thereto by any Labour Court, Industrial Tribunal or National Industrial Tribunal and includes an arbitration award made under Section 10-A.

From the above mentioned definition of 'award,' it becomes clear that award is of the following two kinds or types.

(a) Interim or a final determination of industrial dispute or of any other question relating thereto by any Labour Court, Industrial Tribunal or National Tribunal, and

(b) An arbitration award made under Section 10-A. The important provisions relating to award have been made in Sections 16, 17, 17-A.

(6) Board [Section 2(c)]

'Board' means a Board of conciliation constituted under this Act.

Section 5 of the Industrial Disputes Act, 1947, provides for the constitution of a Board of Conciliation.

The appropriate Government may as occasion arises, by notification in the Official Gazette, constitute a Board of Conciliation for promoting the settlement of any industrial dispute. Thus, the settlement of an industrial dispute is the main purpose behind the constitution of a Board of Conciliation. A Board of Conciliation consists of a chairman and two or four members as the appropriate Government thinks it fit. The chairman of a Board of Conciliation shall be an independent person. The other members of a Board of Conciliation are appointed in equal numbers to represent the two parties to the dispute. Each party is to recommend the names of their representatives. But, if they do not recommend the names of their representatives, the appropriate Government selects such members.

Provisions relating to the constitution, duties of Board of Conciliation have been made in Sections 5 and 13 of this Act, which we shall consider at an appropriate place.

(7) Closure [Section 2(c)]

'Closure' means the permanent closing down of the place of employment or part thereof.

The definition of the term 'closure' is given in the State Acts of Maharashtra and Madhya Pradesh, which is as follows:

"'Closure' means the closing of any place or a part of a place of employment or the total or partial suspension of work by an employer or the total partial refusal by an employer to continue to employ persons employed by him whether such closing, suspension or refusal is or is not in consequence of an industrial dispute."

By closure of an undertaking is meant the closing of industrial activity and, as a result, workmen employed in such undertaking are rendered jobless. When an undertaking is closed, compensation is required to be paid to the workmen working in such undertaking. Provisions have been made in Section 25-FFF of the Industrial Disputes Act, 1947, regarding the compensation to be paid to workmen in case of closing down of undertaking.

(8) Conciliation Officer [Section 2(d)]

'Conciliation Officer' means Conciliation Officer appointed under this Act.

The Appropriate Government appoints such number of persons as it thinks fit to be conciliation officers by notification in the Official Gazette. A conciliation officer can be appointed for a specified area or specified industries in a specified area or for one or more specified industries and either permanently or for a limited period. Such conciliation officers are charged with the duty of mediating in and promoting the settlement of industrial disputes.

The conciliation officers thus appointed are the public servants within the meaning of Section 21 of the Indian Penal Code, 1960. The provisions relating to the appointment and duties of the conciliation officers have been made in Sections 4 and 12, respectively.

(9) Conciliation Proceeding [Section 2(e)]

'Conciliation proceeding' means any proceeding held by a conciliation officer of Board under this Act.

(10) Controlled Industry [Section 2(ee)]

'Controlled Industry' means any industry the control of which by the Union has been declared by the Central Act to be expedient in the public interest.

Here, it must be remembered that only when the declaration is made by the Central Act that the control of industry by the Union is necessary or suitable in the public interest. then and only then, an industry is called a controlled industry.

(11) Court [Section 2(f)]

'Court' means a court of enquiry constituted under this Act.

Section 6 of this Act empowers the Appropriate Government to appoint a Court of Inquiry for enquiring into any matter appearing to be connected with or is relevant to an industrial dispute. A court may consist of one independent person or of such number of independent persons, as the Appropriate Government may think it fit and where a court of inquiry consists of two or more members, one of them is appointed as the chairman. All members of the Court of Inquiry are deemed to be public servants within the meaning of Section 21 of the Indian Penal Code.

(12) Employer [Section 2 (g)]

'Employer' means
(a) In relation to an industry carried on by or under the authority of any department of the Central Government or a State Government, the authority prescribed in this behalf, or where no authority is prescribed, the head of the department;

(b) In relation to an industry carried on by or on behalf of a local authority, the chief executive officer of that authority.

This definition of an 'employer' is not exhaustive. But, it must also be noted that, it does not limit its sphere merely to businesses run by the Government or local authority. This Act applies to all industries carried on either by an individual or an association.

(13) Executive [Section 2(gg)]

'Executive' in relation to a trade union, means the body by whatever name called, to which the management of the affairs of the trade union is entrusted.

(14) Industry [Section 2(J)]

'Industry' means any systematic activity carried on by co-operation between an employer and his workmen (whether such workmen are employed by such employer directly or by or through any agency, including a contractor) for the production, supply or distribution of goods or services with a view to satisfy human wants to wishes (not being wants or wishes which are merely spiritual or religious in nature), whether or not –

(i) Any capital has been invested for the purpose of carrying on such activity; or

(ii) Such activity is carried on with a motive to make any gain or profit and includes –

   (a) Any activity of the Dock Labour Board established under Section 5-A of the Dock Workers (Regulation of Employment) Act, 1948.

   (b) Any activity relating to the promotion of sales or business or both carried on by an establishment.

(15) Industrial Dispute [Section 2(k)]

'Industrial dispute' means any dispute or difference between employers and employers or between employers and workmen, or between workmen and workmen, which is connected with the employment or non-employment or the terms of employment or with the conditions of labour, of any person.

For any dispute to be considered an industrial dispute, it should satisfy the following essentials:

(a) There must be a difference or dispute (i) between employers and employers (ii) between workmen and workmen or (iii) between workmen and employers.

(b) A workman concerned with the dispute should not be employed in any administrative or managerial capacity.

(c) Industrial dispute must pertain to an industrial matter or

(d) It may be connected with the employment or non-employment or the terms of employment.

(e) Industrial dispute may be concerned with the condition of labour of any person.

Industrial dispute implies a real and substantial difference having some element of persistency and continuity till resolved and, if not adjusted timely, it is likely to endanger the industrial peace of the given undertaking.

(16) Industrial Establishment or Undertaking [Section 2(ka)]

'Industrial establishment or undertaking' means an establishment or undertaking in which any industry is carried on;

Provided that where several activities are carried on in an establishment or undertaking or undertakings and only one or some of such activities is or are an industry or industries, then –

(a) if any unit of such establishment or undertaking carrying on any activity, being an industry, is severable from the other unit or units of such establishment or undertaking such unit shall be deemed to be a separate industrial establishment or undertaking;

(b) If the predominant activity or each of the predominant activities carried on in such establishment or undertaking or any unit thereof is an industry and the other activity or each of the other activities carried on in such establishment or undertaking or unit thereof is not severable from and is, for the purpose of carrying on, or aiding the carrying on of, such predominant activity or activities, the entire establishment or undertaking or, as the case may be, unit thereof shall be deemed to be an industrial establishment or undertaking.

(17) Insurance Company [Section 2(kk)]

'Insurance Company' means an insurance company as defined in Section 2 of the Insurance Act, 1938, having branches or other establishments in more than one state.

(18) Labour Court [Section 2(kkb)]:

'Labour Court' means a Labour Court constituted under Section 7.

According to Section 7 of this Act, the Appropriate Government may constitute one or more Labour Courts for the adjudication of industrial disputes relating to any matter specified in the Second Schedule. The Appropriate Government may also entrust certain other functions to Labour Courts. A Labour Court consists of one person only who is appointed by the Appropriate Government [Section 7(2)].

The provisions relating to jurisdiction, duties, qualifications, disqualifications etc., have been made in Section 7 of the Industrial Disputes Act, 1947.

(19) Major Port [Section 2(1a)]

'Major port' means a major-port as defined in clause (8) of Section 3 of the Indian Ports Act, 1908.

(20) Mine [Section 2(1b)]

'Mine' means a mine as defined in clause J of Section 2(1) of the Mines Act, 1952.

(21) National Tribunal [Section 2(11)]

'National Tribunal' means a National Industrial Tribunal Constituted under Section 7-B.

The Central Government is authorised under this Act to constitute one or more National Industrial Tribunals for the adjudication of industrial disputes, which involve questions of national importance or such disputes in which the industrial establishments situated in more than one state are interested or affected by such disputes. A National Tribunal consists of one person only and such person is appointed by the Central Government. Certain functions or duties are entrusted to National Tribunal, as the Central Government deems fit.

(22) Office-bearer [Section 2(111)]

'Office-bearer' in relation to a trade union includes any member of the executive thereof, but does not include an auditor.

(23) Prescribed [Section 2(m)]

'Prescribed' means prescribed by rules made under this Act.

(24) Public Utility Service [Section 2(n)]

'Public utility service' means:
(a) Any railway service or any transport service for the carriage of passengers or goods by air;
　(i) Any service in, or in connection with the working of, any major port of dock;
(b) Any section of an industrial establishment on the working of which the safety of the establishment or the workmen employed therein depends;
(c) Any postal, telegraph or telephone service;
(d) Any industry which supplies power, light or water to the public;
(e) Any system of public conservancy or sanitation;
(f) Any industry specified in the First Schedule which the Appropriate Government may, if satisfied that public emergency or public interest so requires, by notification in the Official Gazette, declare to be public utility service for the purposes of this Act, for such period as may be specified in the notification.

Provided that the period so specified shall not, in the first instance, exceed six months but may by a like notification, be extended from time to time, by any period not exceeding six months, at any one time, if in the opinion of the Appropriate Government, public emergency or public interest requires such extension;

(25) Railway Company [Section 2(o)]

'Railway Company' means any railway company as defined in Section 3 of the Indian Railways Act, 1890.

(26) Settlement [Section 2(p)]

'Settlement' means a settlement arrived at in the course of conciliation proceeding and includes a written agreement between the employer and workmen arrived at otherwise than in the course of conciliation proceeding where such agreement has been signed by the parties thereto in such manner as may be prescribed and a copy thereof has been sent to an officer authorised in this behalf by the Appropriate Government and Conciliation Officer.

(27) Trade Union [Section 2(gg)]

'Trade Union' means a trade union registered under the Trade Union Act, 1926,

According to Section 2(h) of the Trade Union Act, 1926, a trade union means any combination formed primarily for the purpose of regulating the relations between workmen and employers or between workmen and workmen or between employers and employers for imposing restrictive conditions on the conduct of any trade or business and includes any federation of two or more trade unions.

(28) Tribunal [Section 2(r)]

'Tribunal' means an Industrial Tribunal constituted under Section 7-A and includes an Industrial Tribunal constituted before the 10th March 1975, under this Act.

Industrial Disputes Act, 1947, provides for the constitution of one or more Industrial Tribunals. The Appropriate Government may constitute one or more Industrial Tribunals for the adjudication of industrial disputes relating to any matter specified in the Second Schedule or the Third Schedule appended to this Act.

(29) Village Industries [Section 2(rb)]

'Village Industries' has the same meaning assigned to it in clause (h) of Section 2 of the Khadi and Village Industries Commission Act, 1956.

(30) Wages [Section 2(rr)]

'Wages' means all remuneration capable of being expressed in terms of money, which would, if the terms of employment, express or implied, were fulfilled, be payable to a workman, in respect of his employment or of work done in such employment, and includes –

(a) Such allowances (including dearness allowance) as the workman is for the time being entitled to;

(b) Such value of any house accommodation, or of supply of light, water, medical attendance or other amenity of any service or of any concessional supply of food grains of other articles;

(c) Any travelling concession; but does not include –
   (i) Any bonus;
   (ii) Any contribution paid or payable by the employer to any pension fund or provident fund or for the benefit of the workman under any law for the time being in force;
   (iii) Any gratuity payable on the termination of his service;

(d) Any commission payable on the promotion sales or business or, both.

In the above mentioned definition of 'wages', the two terms, namely, bonus and gratuity are used. Let us make clear the meaning of these two terms.

(31) Bonus

Bonus is an extra payment made to workmen by their employer in addition to their wages, allowances and usual fringe benefits. The Payment of Bonus Act, 1965, has made various provisions so far as payment of bonus is concerned. The payment of bonus to the workmen to whom the Payment of Bonus Act is applicable does not depend on the profit of their employers or their will. According to its provisions, the bonus is required to be paid to the employers.

(32) Workman [Section 2(s)]

'Workman' means any person (including an apprentice) employed in any industry to do any manual, unskilled, skilled, technical, operations, clerical or supervisory work for hire or reward, whether the terms of employment, be express or implied, and for the purposes of any proceeding under this Act in relation to an industrial dispute, includes any such person who has been dismissed, discharged or retrenched in connection with, or as a consequence of, that dispute, or whose dismissal, discharge, or retrenchment has led to that dispute, but does not include any such person –

(a) Who is subject to the Air Force Act, 1950 or the Army Act, 1950 or the Navy Act, 1957; or

(b) Who is employed in the Police Service or as an officer or other employee of a prison; or

(c) Who is employed mainly in a managerial or administrative capacity; or

(d) Who, being employed in a supervisory capacity, draws wages exceeding one thousand and six hundred rupees per month or exercises, either by the nature of the duties attached to the office or by reason of the powers vested in him, functions mainly of a managerial nature.

4. Machinery for Settlement of Industrial Disputes

In the preamble of the Industrial Disputes Act, 1947, it is stated that, "An Act to make provisions for the investigation and settlement of industrial disputes and for certain other purposes." Thus, this Act intends the prevention and settlement of industrial disputes by making necessary provisions and, for that purpose, various authorities with sufficient powers are constituted under it to bring about settlement between the parties concerned. These authorities are both internal as well as external.

The three modes, namely, voluntary settlement and conciliation, adjudication and arbitration have been provided for settlement of disputes under the Industrial Disputes Act, 1947. Works Committees, Conciliation Officers, Boards of Conciliation and Courts of Inquiry are the authorities under this Act which make use of conciliation as a method of settlement of industrial disputes. These authorities are meant to facilitate settlement of industrial disputes or, if needed, inquire into them, but in no case, can they make any awards, i.e., one, that would be binding on the parties concerned.

The adjudication authorities, in this regard, are - labour courts, Industrial Tribunals and National Tribunal.

The provisions relating to voluntary reference of dispute to arbitration have been made in Section 10-A, have already been studied by us while considering the definition of arbitrator.

Conciliation Machinery

(1) Works Committees [Section 3]

A 'works committee' is a forum provided for under this Act for expressing the difficulties of the parties concerned as regards their disputes. It endeavours to maintain cordial relationship even though there are disputes or differences between the parties to the disputes. The success of work committees mainly depends on the efforts and co-operation of both the parties to the disputes.

Section 3(1) of this Act provides for a Works Committee. According to this section, in the case of any industrial establishment in which one hundred or more workmen are employed or have been employed on any day in the preceding twelve months, the Appropriate Government may, by general or special order, require the employer to constitute in the prescribed manner, a Works Committee consisting of representatives of both employers and workmen engaged in the establishment.

However the number of representatives of workmen on the committee shall not be less than the number of representatives of the employer. The representatives of the workmen shall be chosen in the prescribed manner from among the workmen engaged in the establishment and in consultation with their trade union, if any, registered under the Indian Trade Unions Act, 1926. Section 3(2) further provides that it shall be the duty of the Works Committee to promote measures for securing and preserving amity and good relations between the employer and workmen and, to that end, to comment upon matters of their common interest or concern and endeavour to compose any material difference of opinion in respect of such matters.

The Industrial Disputes Act, 1947, prescribes the use of voluntary negotiations as the first option for settling industrial disputes. In this regard, Works Committees play a prominent role. 'Works Committee' comprise joint committees having an equal number of representatives from both the employers and workmen. The constitution of Works Committee is a must in an industrial establishment wherein one hundred or more workmen are employed on any day in preceding twelve months. In a nutshell, a Works Committee is an internal or in-house media meant for facilitating the settlement of industrial disputes within a given industry.

Functions of a Works Committee

Sub-section 2 of Section 3 of this Act enumerates the duties or functions of a Works Committee as follows:

(a) To remove the disparities between employers and workmen;

(b) To promote measures for securing and preserving amity and friendly and good relations between the employers and workmen;

(c) To that end, to comment upon all matters of their common interest or concern;

(d) To make efforts to compose any material difference of opinion in respect of various matters. These matters include so many aspects, such as, welfare of workers, provision and supervision of various recreational facilities, training of workmen and their wages, bonus, gratuity, working conditions including discipline, promotions, transfers, etc. Thus, it seems that there is no subject concerning the relation between the employers and workmen which the Works Committee is precluded from considering. However, the following points must be remembered in this connection.

(i) The findings of the Works Committee are advisory or recommendatory and not mandatory, in nature. It cannot decide and pass final judgement. Its duty is only to comment since it is mainly a negotiating organ. It is the function of the Works Committee to promote measures for harmonious and friendly and good relations between the employers and workmen.

(ii) Works Committees are not intended to supersede or supplement the trade unions for the purpose of collective bargaining. They are not authorised to consider real changes or substantial changes in the service conditions. They are not a substitute for trade unions.

(2) Conciliation Officers [Section 4]

Section 4 of the Industrial Disputes Act, 1947, provides for conciliation officer. According to Section 4(1), the Appropriate Government, by notification in the Official Gazette, may appoint such number of persons as it thinks fit, to be conciliation officers, charged with the duty of mediating in and promoting the settlement of industrial disputes. Section 4(2) further states that a Conciliation Officer may be appointed for a specified area or for specified industries in a specified area or for one or more specified industries either permanently or for a limited period. Thus, Section 4 makes it clear that a conciliation officer may be appointed by the Appropriate Government:

(a) Either permanently or for a limited period;

(b) For a specified area or for a specified industry in a specified area; or

(c) For one or more specified industries.

The Appropriate Government appoints such number of Conciliation Officers as it thinks fit.

The Conciliation Officers thus appointed are the public servants within the meaning of Section 21 of Indian Penal Code, 1960 [Section 11(6) of Industrial Disputes Act, 1947].

Duties of the Conciliation Officers [Section 12]:

The main duties of the conciliation officers consist of mediating in and promoting the settlement of industrial disputes.

According to Section 12 of this Act, the duties of the Conciliation Officers are as follows –

(a) To Hold Conciliation Proceedings

Where any industrial dispute exists or is apprehended, the Conciliation Officer may, or where the dispute relates to a public utility service and a notice of strike or lock-out under Section 22 of this Act has been given, shall hold conciliation proceedings in the prescribed manner [Section 12(1)].

Thus, it is obligatory on the part of Conciliation Officers to hold conciliation proceedings in public utility services where:

(i) An industrial dispute exists, or

(ii) An industrial dispute is apprehended; or

(iii) Where notice of a strike or a lock-out is given under Section 22 of this Act.

(b) Investigation of an Industrial Dispute

For the purpose of bringing about a settlement of the dispute without delay, the Conciliation Officer shall investigate the dispute and all matters affecting the merits and the right settlement of the dispute, and may do all such things as he thinks fit for the purpose of inducing the parties to come to a fair and amicable settlement of the dispute [Section12(2) Thus, it is expected that the Conciliation Officers should take necessary steps to conduct conciliation proceedings expeditiously and, for doing so, certain discretionary powers are vested with the Conciliation Officers for conducting the proceedings in such a manner as they think proper.

(c) Memorandum of Settlement

If the settlement of the dispute or of any matter in dispute arrived at in the course of the conciliation proceedings, the Conciliation Officer shall send a report thereof to the Appropriate Government or an officer authorised in this behalf by it together with a memorandum of the settlement signed by the parties to the dispute [Section 12(3)].

(d) Submission of Report with Facts to the Appropriate Government

If no settlement is arrived at, the conciliation officer, as soon as practicable after the close of the investigation, shall send to the Appropriate Government a full report setting forth the steps taken by him for ascertaining the facts and circumstances relating to the dispute and, for bringing about a settlement thereof, together with a full statement of such facts and circumstances, and the reason on account of which in his opinion a settlement could not be arrived at [Section 12(4)].

(e) Reference to a Board, Labour Court, Tribunal or National Tribunal

On a consideration of the report referred to in sub-section 4 of Section 12, if the Appropriate Government is satisfied that there is a case for reference to a Board, Labour Court; Tribunal or National Tribunal, it may make such reference. Where the appropriate Government does not make such reference, it shall record and communicate to the parties' concerned its reasons therefor [Section 12(5)].

(f) Submission of Report within Fourteen Days

A report under this section shall be submitted within fourteen days of the commencement of the conciliation proceedings or within such shorter period as may be fixed by the Appropriate Government [Section 12(6)]. Provided that subject to the approval of the Conciliation Officer the time for the submission of the report may be extended by such period as may be agreed upon in writing by all the parties to the dispute [Proviso to Section 12(6)].

Commencement and Conclusion of Conciliation Proceedings

According to Section 20(1), a conciliation proceeding shall be deemed to have commenced on the date on which a notice of strike or lock-out under Section 22 is received by the Conciliation Officer. It is deemed to have concluded –

(a) Where a settlement is arrived at, when a memorandum of settlement is signed by the parties to the dispute, or

(b) Where no settlement is arrived at, when the report of the conciliation office by the Appropriate Government [Section 20(2)].

(3) Board of Conciliation [Section 5]

Section 5 of the Industrial Disputes Act, 1947, provides for the constitution of a Board of Conciliation, Section 5 is reproduced as below –

The Appropriate Government may as occasion arises, by notification in the Official Gazette, constitute a Board of Conciliation for promoting the settlement of any industrial dispute [Section 5(1)].

A Board shall consist of a chairman and two or four other members as the Appropriate Government thinks fit [Section 5(2)].

The chairman shall be an independent person and the other members shall be persons appointed in equal numbers to represent the parties to the dispute and any person appointed to represent a party shall be appointed on the recommendation of the party [Section 5(3)]. Provided that if any party fails to make a recommendations as aforesaid within the prescribed time, the Appropriate Government shall appoint such person as it thinks fit to represent that party [Proviso to Section 5(3)].

Validity of Sitting of a Board of Conciliation

A Board having the prescribed quorum may act, notwithstanding the absence of the Chairman or any of its members or any vacancy in its number [Section 5(4)]. Provided that if the Appropriate Government notifies the Board that the services of the Chairman or of any other member have ceased to be available, the Board shall not act until a new chairman or member, as the case may be, has been appointed [Proviso to Section 5(4)].

Quorum of the Board of Conciliation

The quorum necessary to constitute a sitting of a Board of Conciliation is as follows –

(a) Where the number of members is three Quarum - two members; and

(b) Where the number of members is five Quarum - three members.

Reference of Disputes to a Board of Conciliation

Where the Appropriate Government is of the opinion that any industrial dispute exists or is apprehended, it may at any time, by order in writing, refer the dispute to a Board of Conciliation for promoting a settlement thereof [Section 10(1)].

Where the parties to an Industrial Disputes Act apply in the prescribed manner, whether jointly or separately, for a reference of the dispute to a Board of Conciliation, the Appropriate Government, if satisfied that the persons applying represents the majority of such party, shall make reference, accordingly [Section 10(2)].

Duties of a Board of Conciliation

Thus, a Board of Conciliation is a body of persons appointed by the Appropriate Government by notification in the Official Gazette for the purpose of promoting the settlement of an industrial dispute. Section 13 of this Act provides for the following duties of the Board of Conciliation. They are, namely –

(a) **Efforts to Bring About a Settlement :** Where a dispute has been referred to a Board of conciliation under this Act, it shall be the duty of the Board to bring about a settlement of the same and, for this purpose, the Board shall in such manner as it thinks fit and without delay, investigate the dispute and all matters affecting the merits and the right settlement thereof and may do all such things as it thinks fit for the purpose of inducing the parties to come to a fair and amicable settlement of the dispute [Section 13(1)].

(b) **Submission of the Memorandum of Settlement:** If a settlement of the dispute or any of the matters in dispute is arrived at in the course of conciliation proceedings, the Board shall send a report thereof to the Appropriate Government together with a memorandum of the settlement signed by the parties to the dispute [Section 13(2)].

(c) **Submission of Report with Facts, Circumstances etc.:** If no settlement is arrived at, the Board shall, as soon as practicable after the close of the investigation, send to the Appropriate Government, a full report setting forth proceedings and steps taken by the Board for ascertaining the facts and circumstances relating to the disputes and for bringing about a settlement thereof, together with full statement of such facts and circumstances, its findings thereon, the reasons on account of which, in its opinion, a settlement could not be arrived at and its recommendations for determination of the dispute [Section 13(3)].

(d) **Communication to the Parties:** If on the receipt of a report under sub-section 13(3) in respect of a dispute relating to public utility service, the Appropriate Government does not make a reference to a Labour Court, Tribunal or National Tribunal under Section 10, it shall record and communicate to the parties concerned its reasons therefor [Section 13(4)].

(e) **Submission of Reports within Two Months:** The Board of conciliation shall submit its report under this section within two months from the date on which the dispute was referred to it or within such shorter period as may be fixed by the Appropriate Government [Section 13(5)].

Provided that the Appropriate Government may, from time to time extend the time for the submission of the report by such further periods not exceeding two months in the aggregate. It is further provided that the time for submission of the report may be extended by such period as may be agreed to in writing by all parties to dispute.

Form of Report and Publication of Report

The report of a Board of Conciliation must be in writing and is required to be signed by all members of the Board. However, any member can submit a dissenting report. Every report together with the minute of dissent is required to be published by the Appropriate Government within thirty days from its receipt [Sections 16(1) and 17(1)].

All Members of a Board of Conciliation are Public Servants

It is made amply clear in the provisions of Section 11(6) that all members of a Board of Conciliation are deemed to be public servants within the meaning of Section 21 of the Indian Penal Code, 1860.

Procedure to be Followed by a Board of Conciliation

Subject to any rules that may be made in this behalf, a Board of Conciliation shall follow such procedure as it may think fit [Section 11(1)].

Commencement and Conclusion of Proceeding

A conciliation proceeding is deemed to commence from the date of order referring the dispute to the Board of Conciliation [Section 20(1)] and it is deemed to have concluded – (a) when a memorandum of the settlement is signed by the parties to the dispute or (b) when the report of the Board of Conciliation is published [Section 20(2)].

Finality of the Governments Order

It is made clear in Section 9(1) that no order of the Appropriate Government or of the Central Government appointing any person as the Chairman or any other member of a

Board of Conciliation shall be called into question in any manner, and no act or proceeding before any Board of Conciliation shall be called into question in any manner on the ground merely of the existence of any vacancy in, or defect in the constitution of such Board of condition.

(4) Courts of Inquiry [Section 6]

Where conciliation officers do not become successful, a Board of Conciliation takes over. The functions of such Board of Conciliation are the same as those of conciliation officers. The purpose of constituting the Boards of Conciliation is to bring about the settlement of industrial disputes. The next step in the process of settlement of industrial disputes under this Act is adjudication, for which various provisions are made in it in Sections 6, 7, 7-A and 7-B. Now, let us study one important aspect of adjudication first, i.e., Courts of Inquiry.

Composition and Appointment of Members of a Court of Inquiry

The provisions relating to composition and appointment of members of a Court of Inquiry have been made in Section 6 of this Act, which are as follows –

The Appropriate Government may as occasion arises, by notification in the Official Gazette, constitute a Court of Inquiry for enquiring into any matter appearing to be concerned with or relevant to an industrial dispute [Section 6(1)].

A court may consist of one independent person or of such number of independent persons as the Appropriate Government may think fit and where a Court consists of two or more members, one of them shall be appointed as the Chairman [Section 6(2)].

Quorum of a Court of Inquiry

According to the Rule 14 of the Industrial Disputes (Central) Rules, 1957, the quorum necessary to constitute a sitting of a Court of Inquiry shall be as follows –

(a) Where the number of members is not more than two, the quorum required is one.
(b) Where the number of members is more than two but less than five, the required quorum is two.
(c) Where the number of members is five or more, the same would be three.

Validity of sitting of a Court of Inquiry

A Court having the prescribed quorum, may act, notwithstanding the absence of the Chairman or any of its members of any vacancy in its number [Section 6(3)].

Provided that, if the Appropriate Government notifies the Court that the services of the Chairman have ceased to be available, the court shall not act until a new chairman has been appointed [Proviso to Section 6(3)].

Duties of a Court of Inquiry

The powers, duties etc. of various authorities concerned with investigation and settlement of industrial disputes are narrated in Sections 11, 14 and also in Sections 16 to 21 of Chapter IV of the Industrial Disputes Act, 1947.

The relevant portion of these sections is reproduced as below:

(a) **Appointment of Assessor or Assessors:** A Court of Inquiry may, if it so thinks fit, appoint one or more persons having special knowledge of the matter under consideration as assessor or assessors, to advise it in the proceedings before it [Section 11(5)].

(b) **Holding of an Enquiry and Submission of Report:** A court shall inquire into the matters referred to it and report thereon to the Appropriate Government ordinarily within a period of six months from the commencement of its inquiry [Section 14].

(c) **Report in Writing:** The report of a Court of Inquiry shall be in writing and shall be signed by all the members of the Board or Court as the case may be [Section 16(1)]. Provided that nothing in this section shall be deemed to prevent any member of the Court from recording any minute of dissent from a report or from any recommendation made therein [Proviso to Section 16(1)].

Publication of a report of a Court of Inquiry

Every report of a Court of Inquiry together with any minute of dissent recorded therewith shall, within a period of thirty days from the date of its receipt by the Appropriate Government, be published in such a manner as the Appropriate Government thinks fit [Section 17(1)].

Procedure to be followed by a Court of Inquiry

Subject to any rules that may be made in this behalf, a Court of Inquiry shall follow such procedure as it may think fit [Section 11(1)].

Reference of an Industrial Dispute to a Court of Inquiry

Where the Appropriate Government is of the opinion that any industrial dispute exists or is apprehended, it may at any time, by order in writing, refer any matter appearing to be connected with or relevant to the dispute to a Court of Inquiry for Inquiry [Section 10(1)]. In Section 10(2), it is further stated that where the parties to an industrial dispute apply in the prescribed manner, whether jointly or separately, for a reference of the dispute to a Court of Inquiry, the Appropriate Government if satisfied that the persons applying represent the majority of each party, shall make the reference, accordingly.

All Members of a Court of Inquiry are Public Servants

All members of a Court of Inquiry are deemed to be public servants within the meaning of Section 21 of the Indian Penal Code, 1860 [Section 11(6)].

Finality of orders constituting a Court of Inquiry

No order for the Appropriate Government or of the Central Governmont, as the case may be, appointing any person as the Chairman or any other member of a Court of Inquiry shall be called into question in any manner, and no act or proceeding before any Court of Inquiry shall be called into question in any manner on the ground merely of the existence of any vacancy in, or defect in the constitution of such Court of Inquiry [Section 9(1)].

Adjudication Machinery

Labour courts, Industrial Tribunals and National Tribunals are adjudication authorities constituted under the Industrial Disputes Act, 1947, for the settlement of industrial disputes and bring about industrial peace. Let us now consider the provisions of this Act relating to appointments, constitution, qualifications, duties and powers etc., of these authorities.

(1) Labour Courts [Section 7]

The ultimate legal remedy for settling an unresolved industrial dispute is its reference to adjudication by the Appropriate Government. The Industrial Disputes Act, 1947, empowers the Appropriate Government to Constitute a Labour Court, Industrial Tribunals or National Tribunal to adjudicate Industrial Disputes [Sections 7, 7-A, 7-B].

According to Section 7 of the Industrial Disputes Act, 1947, the Appropriate Government may, by notification in the Official Gazette, constitute one or more Labour Courts for the adjudication of industrial disputes relating to any matter specified in the Second Schedule (which is given below) and for performing such other functions as may be assigned to them under this Act [Section 7(l)]. A Labour Court shall consist of one person only to be appointed by the Appropriate Government [Section 7(2)].

Jurisdication of Labour Courts

The Second Schedule to the Industrial Disputes Act, 1947, specifies various matters within the jurisdiction of Labour Court.

Second Schedule

The matters within the Jurisdication of the Labour Courts are as follows:

(a) The propriety or legality of an order passed by an employer under the standing orders;

(b) The application and interpretation of standing orders;

(c) Discharge or dismissal of workmen including reinstatement of, or grant of relief to, workmen wrongfully dismissed;

(d) Withdrawal of any customary concession or privilege;

(e) Illegality or otherwise of strike or lock-out, and

(f) All matters other than those specified in the Third Schedule.

Qualifications and Disqualifications of a Person to be Appointed as a Presiding Officer of a Labour Court

Section 7(3) of this Act prescribes the qualifications of persons to be appointed as the presiding officers. According to Section 7(3), a person shall not be qualified for appointment as the Presiding Officer of a Labour Court, unless –

(a) he is or has been a Judge of a High Court; or

(b) he has been a District Judge or an Additional District Judge for a period of not less than three years; or

(c) he has held any judicial office in India for not less than seven years; or

(d) he has been the Presiding Officer of a Labour Court constituted under any Provincial Act or State Act for not less than five years.

Disqualifications to become Presiding Officer of a Labour Court

Section 7-C provides that no person shall be appointed to, or constitute in, the office of the presiding officer of a Labour Court; Tribunal or National Tribunal, if –

(a) He is not an independent person; or

(b) He has attained the age of sixty-five years.

Duties of a Labour Court

The duties of a Labour Court are as follows:

(a) **To Adjudicate:** It is the duty of a Labour Court to adjudicate upon the industrial disputes relating to any matter specified in the Second Schedule which is already given above and to perform all such other functions as may be assigned to it under this Act [Section 7(1)].

(b) **To hold Proceedings and Submission of Awards:** Where an industrial dispute has been referred to a Labour Court for adjudication, it shall hold its proceedings expeditiously and shall, within the period specified in the order referring such industrial dispute or the further period extended under the second proviso to sub-section 2-A of Section 10, submit its award to the Appropriate Government [Section 15].

Powers of a Labour Court

The important powers of a Labour Court are as follows:

(a) **Power to Enter the Premises:** The Presiding Officer of a Labour Court may for the purpose of inquiry into any existing or apprehended industrial dispute enter the premises occupied by any establishment to which the dispute relate, after giving a reasonable notice [Section 11(2)]

(b) **Powers of the Civil Court:** According to Section 11(3), every Labour Court shall have the same powers as are vested in a Civil Court under the Code of Civil Procedure, 1908, when trying a suit, in respect of the following matters, namely –

(i) Enforcing the attendance of any person and examining him on oath.

(ii) Compelling the production of documents and material objects.

(iii) Issuing commissions for the examination of witness(es).

(iv) In respect of such matters as may be prescribed.

(c) **Powers in respect of Judicial Proceedings:** Every inquiry or investigation by a Labour Court shall be deemed to be a judicial proceeding within the meaning of Sections 193 and 228 of the Indian Penal Code, 1860 [Section (3)(d)]

(d) **Power of Appointing an Assessor or Assessors:** A Labour Court, if it so thinks fit, may appoint one or more persons having special knowledge of the matter under consideration as an assessor or assessors to advice it in the proceeding before it [Section 11(5)].

(e) **Some Powers of a Civil Court and Status of Civil Court :** Every Labour Court is deemed to be a Civil Court for the purposes of Sections 345, 346, and 348 of the Code of Criminal Procedure, 1973 (2 of 1974) [Section 11(8)].

(f) **Power to Set Aside the Order of Discharge, Dismissal of Workman and to Direct Reinstatement :** Where an industrial dispute relating to the discharge or dismissal of a workman has been referred to a Labour Court for adjudication and, in the course of adjudication proceedings, the Labour Court is satisfied that the order of discharge or dismissal, as the case may be, was not justified, it may by its award, set aside such order of discharge or dismissal and direct the re-instatement of the workman on such terms and conditions, if any, as it thinks fit, or give such other relief to the workman including the award of any lesser punishment in lieu of discharge or dismissal as the circumstances of the case may require [Section 11-A]. It is also provided that in any proceeding under Section 11-A, the Labour Court shall rely only on the materials on record and shall not take any fresh evidence in relation to the matter [Proviso to Section 11-A].

(g) **Powers of a Labour Court to allow Costs:** It is stated in Section 11(7) that, "Subject to any rules made under this Act, the costs of, and incidental to, any proceeding before a Labour Court, the Labour Court shall have full powers to determine by and to whom and to what extent and subject to what conditions, if any, such costs are to be paid, and to give all necessary directions for the purposes aforesaid and such costs may, on an application made to the Appropriate Government by the person entitled, to be recovered by that Government in the same manner as an arrear of land revenue."

Thus, Section 11(7) empowers a Labour court to determine the costs of any proceedings before it and also to determine by whom and to what extent and subject to what conditions, if any, such costs are to be paid. A Labour Court is also empowered to give all necessary directions for the purposes aforesaid.

The Presiding of a Labour Court is a Public Servant:

It is made clear in the provisions of Section 11(6), that the Presiding Officer of a Labour Court is deemed to be a public servant within the meaning of Section 21 of the Indian Penal Code, 1860.

Procedure to be followed by a Labour Court:

Subject to any rules that may be made in this behalf, a labour court shall follow such procedure as it may think fit [Section 11(1)].

Finality of the Orders of the Government Constituting a Labour Court

No order of the Appropriate Government appointing any person as the presiding officer of a Labour Court shall be called into question in any manner, and no act or proceeding before any Labour Court shall be called into question in any manner on the ground merely of the existence of any vacancy in, or defect in the constitution of such Labour Court [Section 9(1)].

Filling of a Vacancy in the Office of Presiding Officer of a Labour Court

If, for any reason, a vacancy (other than a temporary vacancy) occurs in the office of the Presiding Officer of a Labour Court, the Appropriate Government shall appoint another person in accordance with the provisions of this Act to fill the vacancy, and the proceeding may be continued before the Labour Court from the stage at which the vacancy is filled [Section 8].

Reference of Disputes to a Labour Court

(a) Where the Appropriate Government is of the opinion that any industrial dispute exists or is apprehended, it may at any time, by order in writing, refer the dispute or any matter to be connected with, or relevant to the dispute, if it relates to the matter specified in the Second Schedule, to a Labour Court for adjudication [Section 10(1)(c)].

(b) Where the dispute relates to any matter specified in the Third Schedule and is not likely to affect more than one hundred workmen, the Appropriate Government may, if it so thinks fit, make the reference to a Labour Court under Section 10(1)(c) which is reproduced above [Proviso to Section 10(1)].

(c) Where the dispute in relation to which the Central Government is the Appropriate Government, it shall be competent for that Government to refer the dispute to a Labour Court constituted by the State Government [Proviso to Section 10(1)].

(d) Where the parties to an industrial dispute apply in the prescribed manner, whether jointly or separately, for a reference of the dispute to a Labour Court, the Appropriate Government, if satisfied that the persons applying represent the majority of each party, shall make the reference, accordingly [Section 10(2)].

Points of Reference and Jurisdiction

Where in an order referring an industrial dispute to a Labour Court or in a subsequent order, the Appropriate Government has specified the points of dispute for adjudication, the Labour Court shall continue its adjudication (jurisdiction) to those points and matters incidental thereto [Section 10(4)].

Prohibition of any Strike or Lock-out

Section 10(3) states that, "Where an industrial dispute has been referred to a Labour Court under this section, the Appropriate Government may, by order, prohibit the continuance of any strike or lock-out in connection with such dispute which may be in existence on the date of reference.

Forms of Award

The award of a Labour Court must be in writing and it must be signed by its Presiding Officer [Section 16(2)].

Publication of Award

According to the provisions of Section 17(1), every award of a Labour Court must be published within a period of thirty days from the date of its receipt by the Appropriate Government and it must be published in such a manner as it thinks fit.

It is stated in Section 17(2) that, "Subject to the Provisions of Section 17-A, the award published under Section 17(1) shall be final and shall not be called into question by any Court in any manner whatsoever."

Period for Submitting of an Award

An order referring an industrial dispute to a Labour Court under Section 10 shall specify the period within which such Labour Court shall submit its award on such dispute to the Appropriate Government [Section 10(2-A)].

Where such industrial dispute is connected with an individual workman, no such period shall exceed three months [Proviso to Section 10(2-A)]. But where the parties to an industrial dispute apply in the prescribed manner, whether jointly or separately, to the Labour Court for extension of such period or for any other reason, and the Presiding Officer of such Labour court considers it necessary or expedient to extend such period, he may for reasons to be recorded in writing, extend such period by such further period, as he may think fit [Proviso to Section 10(2-A)].

In computing any period specified in this section, the period, if any, for which the proceedings before the Labour Court had been stayed by any injunction or order of a Civil Court shall be excluded [Proviso to Section 10(2-A)].

It is also further provided in the Section 10(2-A) that no proceedings before the Labour Court shall lapse merely on the ground that any period specified under this sub-section had expired without such proceeding being completed.

On the Death of Parties, Proceedings do not Lapse

The provisions made in Section 10(8) of this Act relates to the proceedings pending on the death of the parties to the dispute. Section 10(8) lays down that, "No proceedings pending before a Labour Court in relation to an industrial dispute shall lapse merely by reason on the death of any of the parties to the dispute being a workman, and such labour court shall complete such proceedings and submit its award to the Appropriate Government."

(2) Industrial Tribunals [Section 7-A]

Constitution and Jurisdiction: Section 7-A of the Industrial Disputes Act, 1947, provides for the constitution of one or more Industrial Tribunals. According to Section 7-A(1), the Appropriate Government, by notification in the Official Gazette, may constitute one or more Industrial Tribunals for the adjudication of industrial disputes relating to any matter whether specified in the Second Schedule (which is already given elsewhere) or the Third Schedule and for performing such other functions as may be assigned to them under this Act. The Third Schedule appended to this Act is reproduced as below:

The Third Schedule

The matters within the jurisdiction of Industrial Tribunals are as follows:

(a) Wages including the period and mode of payment;

(b) Compensatory and other allowances;

(c) Hours of work and rest intervals;

(d) Leave with wages and holidays;
(e) Bonus, profit-sharing, provident fund and gratuity;
(f) Shift working otherwise than in accordance with standing orders;
(g) Classification of discipline;
(h) Rules of discipline;
(i) Rationalisation;
(j) Retrenchment of workmen and closure of establishment; and
(k) Any other matter that may be prescribed.

A Tribunal shall consist of one person only to be appointed by the Appropriate Government [Section 7-A(2)].

Qualifications and Disqualifications of Presiding Officer of a Tribunal

A person shall not be qualified for appointment as the Presiding Officer of a Tribunal unless –

(a) He is or has been, a Judge of a High Court; or
(b) He has been a District Judge or an Additional District Judge for a period of not less than three years [Section 7-A(3)].

Disqualification of Presiding Officer of a Tribunal

No person shall be appointed to, or continue in the office of the presiding officer of a Tribunal, if –

(a) He is not an independent person; or
(b) He has attained the age of sixty-five years [Section 7-C].

Appointment of Assessors

The Appropriate Government may, if it thinks fit, appoint two persons as assessors, to advise the Tribunal in the proceedings before it [Section 7-A(4)].

Duties of Industrial Tribunals

Section 15 of this Act describes the duties of Tribunals and, accordingly, "Where an industrial dispute has been referred to a Tribunal for adjudication, it shall hold its proceedings expeditiously and shall within the period specified in the order referring such industrial dispute or the further period extended under the second proviso to sub-section 2(A) of Section 10, submit its award to the Appropriate Government.

Powers of an Industrial Tribunal

The powers of an Industrial Tribunal are given in Section 11 (Chapter IV) of the Industrial Disputes Act, 1947. These powers are enumerated as below:

(a) The Presiding Officer of a Tribunal may for the purpose of inquiry into any existing or apprehended industrial dispute, after giving a reasonable notice, enter the premises occupied by any establishment to which the dispute relates [Section 11(2)].

(b) Every Tribunal shall have the same powers as are vested in a Civil Court under the Code of Civil Procedure, 1908, when trying a suit, in respect of the following matters, namely -

(i) Enforcing the attendance of any person and examining him on oath;

(ii) Compelling the production of documents and material objects;

(iii) Issuing commissions for the examination of witness(es);

(iv) In respect of such other matters, as may be prescribed.

Every inquiry or investigation by a Tribunal is deemed to be a judical proceeding within the meaning of Sections 193 and 228 of the Indian Penal Code, 1860. Every court of inquiry is deemed to be Civil Court for the purposes of Sections 345, 346 and 348 of the Code of criminal Procedure, 1973.

(c) Power of Appointing an Assessor or Assessors: A Tribunal, if it so thinks fit, may appoint one or more persons having special knowledge of the matter under consideration as an assessor or assessors to advice it in the proceeding before it [Section 11(5)].

(d) Some Powers of a Civil Court and Status of Civil Court: Every Tribunal is deemed to be Civil Court for the purposes of Sections 345, 346 and 348 of the Code of Criminal Procedure, 1973 (2 of 1974) [Section 11(8)].

(e) Power to give Relief in case Discharge, Dismissal of Workman and to Direct Reinstatement: Where an industrial dispute relating to the discharge or dismissal of a workman has been referred to a Tribunal for adjudication and, in the course of adjudication proceedings, the Tribunal is satisfied that the order of discharge or dismissal, as the case may be, was not justified, it may by its award set aside such order of discharge or dismissal and direct re-instatement of the workman on such terms and conditions, if any, as it thinks fit, or give such other relief to the workman including the award of any lesser punishment in lieu of discharge or dismissal as the circumstances of the case may require [Section 11-A]. It is also provided that in any proceeding under Section 11-A, the Tribunal shall rely only on the materials on record and shall not take any fresh evidences in relation to the matter [Proviso to Section 11-A].

(f) Power of an Industrial Tribunal to Allow Costs: It is stated in Section 11(7) that, "Subject to any rules made under this act, the costs of, and incidental to, any proceeding before an Industrial Tribunal shall have full powers to determine by and to whom and to what extent and, subject to what conditions, if any, such costs are to be paid, and to give all necessary directions for the purposes aforesaid and such costs may, on an application made to the Appropriate Government by the person entitled, to be recovered by that Government in the same manner as an arrear of land revenue.

Thus, Section 11(7) empowers an Industrial Tribunal to determine the costs of any proceedings before it and also to determine by whom and to what extent and the subject to what conditions if any, such costs are to be paid. An Industrial Tribunal is also empowered to give all necessary directions for the purposes aforesaid.

The Presiding Officer of Tribunals is a Public Servant

It is made clear in the provisions of Section 11(6) that the presiding officer of a Tribunal is deemed to be a public servant within the meaning of Section 21 of the Indian Penal Code, 1860.

Procedure to be followed by a Tribunal

Subject to any rules that may be made in this behalf, a Tribunal shall follow such procedure as it may think fit [Section 11(1)].

Finality of the Orders of the Government

No order of the Appropriate Government appointing any person as the Presiding Officer of a Tribunal shall be called into question in any manner and no act or proceeding before any Tribunal shall be called into question in any manner on the ground merely of the existence of any vacancy in or defect in the constitution of such Tribunal [Section 9(1)].

Filling of a Vacancy in the Office of Presiding Officer of a Tribunal

If, for any reason, a vacancy (other than a temporary vacancy) occurs in the office of the Presiding Officer of a Tribunal, the Appropriate Government shall appoint another person in accordance with the provisions of this Act to fill the vacancy; and the proceeding may be continued before the Tribunal from the stage at which the vacancy is filled [Section 8].

Reference of disputes to a Tribunal

(a) Where the Appropriate Government is of the opinion that any industrial dispute exists or is apprehended, it may at any time, by order in writing, refer the dispute or any matter to be connected with, or relevant to the dispute, if it relates to the matter specified in the Second Schedule or the Third Schedule to a Tribunal for adjudication [Section 10(1)(c)].

(b) Where the dispute in relation to which the Central Government is the Appropriate Government, it shall be competent for that Government to refer the dispute to an Industrial Tribunal constituted by the State Government [Proviso to Section 10(1)].

(c) Where the parties to an industrial dispute apply in the prescribed manner, whether jointly or separately for a reference of the dispute to a Tribunal, the Appropriate Government, if satisfied that the persons applying represent the majority of each party, shall make the reference, accordingly [Section 10(2)].

Points of Reference and Jurisdiction

Where in an order referring an industrial dispute to a Tribunal or in a subsequent order, the Appropriate Government has specified the points of dispute for adjudication the Tribunal shall continue its adjudication (jurisdiction) to those points and matters incidental thereto [Section 10(4)].

Prohibition of any Strike or Lock-out

Section 10(3) states that, "where an industrial dispute has been referred to a Tribunal under this section, the Appropriate Government may by order, prohibit the continuance of any strike or lock-out in connection with such dispute which may be in existence on the date of reference."

Order of Inclusion of either an Industrial Establishment or a Group or Class of Establishments

Where a dispute concerning any establishment or establishments has been or is to be referred to an Industrial Tribunal under Section 10 and the Appropriate Government is of the opinion, whether on an application made to it in this behalf or otherwise, that the dispute is of such nature that any other establishment, group or class of establishments of a similar nature is likely to be interested in, or affected by, such dispute, the Appropriate Government may, at any time of making the reference or at any time thereafter but before the submission of award, include in that reference such establishment, group or class of establishments, whether or not at the time of such inclusion any dispute exists or is apprehended in that establishment group or class of establishments [Section 10(5)].

Form of Award

The award of a Tribunal must be in writing and it must be signed by its Presiding Officer [Section 16(2)].

Publication of Award

According to the provisions of Section 17(1), every award of a Tribunal must be published within a period of thirty days from the date of its receipt by the Appropriate Government and it must be published in such manner as it thinks fit.

It is stated in Section 17(2) that, "Subject to the provisions of Section 17-A, the award published under Section 17(1) shall be final and shall not be called into question by any court in any manner whatsoever."

Period for Submitting of an Award

An order referring an industrial dispute to an Industrial Tribunal under Section 10 shall specify the period within which such Tribunal shall submit its award on such dispute to the Appropriate Government [Section 10(2-A)].

Where such industrial dispute is connected with an individual workman, no such period shall exceed three months [Proviso to Section 10(2-A)]. But where the parties to an industrial dispute apply in the prescribed manner, whether jointly or separately, to the Industrial Tribunal for extension of such period or for any other reason, and the Presiding Officer of such Tribunal considers it necessary or expedient to extend such period, he may for reasons to be recorded in writing, extend such period by such further period as he may think fit [Proviso to Section 10(2-A)].

(3) National Industrial Tribunal [Section 7-B]

Constitution of National Tribunal, its composition and appointment of presiding officer

The Central Government, by notification in the Official Gazette, may constitute one or more National Industrial Tribunals for the adjudication of industrial disputes which, in the opinion of the Central Government, involve questions of national importance or are of such a nature that industrial establishments situated in more than one state are likely to be interested in, or affected by, such disputes [Section 7-B(1)].

A National Tribunal shall consist of one person only to be appointed by the Central Government [Section 7-B(2)].

Qualifications and disqualifications of a presiding officer of National Industrial Tribunal [Section 7-B (3) and 7-C]:

Qualifications and disqualifications: A person shall not be qualified for the appointment as the presiding officer of National Tribunal unless he is or has been a Judge of a High Court [Section 7-B(3)].

No person shall be appointed to, or continue in, the office of the presiding officer of a National Tribunal if –

(a) He is not an independent person; or
(b) He has attained the age of sixty-five years [Section 7-C].

Appointment of Assessors [Section 7-B(4)]

Assessors: The Central Government may, if it thinks fit, appoint two persons as assessors to advise the National Industrial Tribunal in the proceedings before it [Section 7-B(4)].

Duties of a National Tribunal

(a) **Proceedings and Award:** Where an industrial dispute has been referred to a National Tribunal for adjudication, it shall hold its proceedings expeditiously and shall within the period specified in the order referring such industrial dispute or the further period extended under the second proviso to sub-section 2(A) of Section 10, submit its award to the Appropriate Government [Section 15].

(b) **Disputes of National Importance:** The National Tribunals are to adjudicate industrial disputes which, in the opinion of the Central Government –
   (i) involve various questions of national importance; or/and
   (ii) are of such a nature that industrial establishments situated in more than one state is likely to be interested in, or affected by, such industrial disputes.

Powers of a National Tribunal

The powers of a National Tribunal are given in Section 11 (Chapter IV) of the Industrial Disputes Act, 1947. These powers are enumerated as below:

(a) The presiding officer of a National Tribunal may for the purpose of inquiry into any existing or a apprehended industrial dispute, after giving a reasonable notice, enter the premises occupied by any establishment to which the dispute relates [Section 11(2)].

(b) According to Section 11(3), every National Tribunal shall have the same powers as are vested in a civil court under the Ccode of Civil Procedure, 1908, when trying a suit, in respect of the following matters, namely –

(i) Enforcing the attendance of any person and examining him on oath;

(ii) Completing the production of documents and material objects;

(iii) Issuing commissions for the examination of witness(es);

(iv) In respect of such other matters as may be prescribed.

Every inquiry or investigation by a National Tribunal is deemed to be a judicial proceeding within the meaning of Sections 193 and 228 of the Indian Penal Code, 1860. Every National Tribunal is deemed to be Civil Court for the purposes of Sections 345(1), 346 and 348 of the Code of Criminal Procedure, 1973.

(c) Power of Appointing an Assessor or Assessors: A National Tribunal, if it so thinks fit, may appoint one or more persons having special knowledge of the matter under consideration as an assessor or assessors to advise it in the proceeding before it [Section 11(5)].

(d) Some Powers of a Civil Court and Status of Civil Court: Every National Tribunal is deemed to be a Civil Court for the purposes of Sections 345(1), 346 and 348 of the Code of Criminal Procedure, 1973 (2 of 1974) [Section 11(8)]

(e) Power to Set Aside the Order of Discharge, Dismissal of Workman and to Direct Reinstatement: Where an industrial dispute relating to the discharge or dismissal of a workman has been referred a National Tribunal for adjudication and in the course of adjudication proceeding, the National Tribunal is satisfied that the order of discharge or dismissal, as the case may be, was not justified, it may by its award set aside the order of such discharge or dismissal and direct the re-instatement of the workman on such terms and conditions, if any, as it thinks fit, or give such other relief to the workman including the award of any lesser punishment in lieu of discharge or dismissal as the circumstances of the case may require [Section 11-A]. It is also provided that in any proceeding under Section 11-A, the National Tribunal shall rely only on the materials on record and shall not take any fresh evidence in relation to the matter [Proviso to Section 11-A].

(f) Powers of a National Tribunal to allow costs: It is stated in Section 11(7) that, "Subject to any rules made under this Act, the costs of, and incidental to, any proceeding before a National Tribunal, the National Tribunal shall have full powers to determine by and to when and to what extent and subject to what conditions, if any, such costs are to be paid, and to give all necessary directions for the purposes aforesaid and such costs may, on an application made to the Appropriate Government by the person entitled, to be recovered by that Government in the same manner as an arrear of land revenue."

Thus, Section 11(7) empowers a National Tribunal to determine the costs of any proceedings before it and also to determine by whom and to what extent and subject to what conditions, if any, such costs are to be paid. A National Tribunal is also empowered to give all necessary directions for the purposes aforesaid.

The Presiding Officer of a National Tribunal is a Public Servant

It is made clear in the provisions of Section 11(6) that the presiding officer of a National Tribunal is deemed to be a public servant within the meaning of Section 21 of the Indian Penal Code, 1860.

Procedure to be followed by a National Tribunal

Subject to any rules that may be made in this behalf, a National Tribunal shall follow such procedure as it may think fit [Section 11(1)].

Finality of the Order of the Government

No order of the Appropriate Government appointing any person as the Presiding Officer of a National Tribunal shall be called into question in any manner and no act or proceeding before any National Tribunal shall be called into question in any manner on the ground merely of the existence of any vacancy in, or defect in the constitution of such Labour Court [Section 9(1)].

Fitting of a Vacancy in the Office of Presiding Officer of a National Tribunal

If, for any reason, a vacancy (other than a temporary vacancy) occurs in the office of the presiding officer of a National Tribunal, the Appropriate Government shall appoint another person in accordance with the provisions of this Act to fill up the vacancy and the proceeding may be continued before the National Tribunal from the stage at which the vacancy is filled [Section 8].

Reference of Disputes to National Tribunal

(a) Where the Central Government is of the opinion that any industrial dispute exists or is apprehended, and -

    (i) the dispute involves any question of national importance or;

    (ii) that is of such a nature that industrial establishments situated in more than one state are likely to be interested in, or affected by such dispute, and

    (iii) that the dispute should be adjudicated by a National Tribunal, then –

The Central Government may, whether or not it is the Appropriate Government in relation to that dispute, at any time, by order in writing, refer the dispute or any matter appearing to be connected with, or relevant to the dispute whether it relates to any matter specified in the Second Schedule or the Third Schedule [these schedules are already reproduced elsewhere], to a National Tribunal for adjudication [Section 10(1-A)].

(b) Where the parties to an industrial dispute apply in the prescribed manner, whether jointly or separately, for a reference of the dispute to a National Tribunal, the Appropriate Government, if satisfied that the persons applying represent the majority of each party, shall make the reference, accordingly [Section 10(2)]

Points of Reference and Jurisdiction

Where in an order referring an industrial dispute to a National Tribunal or in a subsequent order, the Appropriate Government has specified the points of dispute for adjudication, the National Tribunal shall continue its adjudication (jurisdiction) to those points and matters incidental thereto [Section 10(4)].

Prohibition of any Strike or Lock-out

Section 10(3) states that, "Where an industrial dispute has been referred to a National Tribunal under this section, the Appropriate Government may by order, prohibit the continuance of any strike or lock-out in connection with such dispute which may be in existence on the date of reference.

Order of Inclusion of either an Industrial Establishment or a Group or Class of Establishments

Where a dispute concerning any establishment or establishments has been, or is to be referred to a National Tribunal under Section 10 and, the Appropriate Government, is of the opinion, whether on an application made to it in this behalf or otherwise, that the dispute is of such nature that any other establishment group or class of establishments of a similar nature is likely to be interested in or affected by such dispute, the Appropriate Government may, at any time of making the reference or at any time thereafter but before the submission of award, include in that reference such establishment group or class of establishments, whether or not at the time of such inclusion any dispute exists or is apprehended in that establishment group or class of establishments [Section 10(5)].

Form of Award

The award of a National Tribunal must be in writing and it must be signed by its Presiding Officer [Section 16(2)].

Publication of Award

According to the provisions of Section 17(1), every award of a National Tribunal must be published within a period of thirty days from the date of its receipt by the Appropriate Government and it must be published in such manner as it thinks fit.

It is stated in Section 17(2) that, "'Subject to the provisions of Section 17-A, the award published under Section 17(1) shall be final and shall not be called into question by any court in any manner whatsoever."

Period for Submitting of an Award

An order referring an industrial dispute to the National Tribunal under Section 10 shall specify the period within which such National Tribunal shall submit its award on such dispute to the Appropriate Government [Section 10(2-A)].

Where such industrial dispute is connected with an individual workman, no such period shall exceed three months [Proviso to Section 10(2-A)]. But where the parties to an industrial dispute apply in the prescribed manner, whether jointly or separately, to the National Tribunal for extension of such period or for any other reason, and the Presiding Officer of such National Tribunal considers it necessary or expedient to extend such period, he may for reasons to be recorded in writing, extend such period by such further period as he may think fit [Proviso to Section 10(2-A)].

In computing any period specified in this section, the period, if any, for which the proceedings before the National Tribunal had been stayed by any injunction or order of a Civil Court shall be excluded [Proviso to Section 10(2-A)].

It is also further provided in the Section 10(2-A) that no proceedings before the National Tribunal shall lapse merely on the ground that any period specified under this sub-section had expired without such proceeding being completed.

On the Death of Parties, Proceedings do not Lapse

The provisions made in Section 10(8) of this Act relates to the proceedings pending on the death of the parties to the dispute. Section 10(8) lays down that -

"No proceedings pending before National Tribunal in relation to an industrial dispute shall lapse merely by reason on the death of any of the parties to the dispute being a workman, and such National Tribunal shall complete such proceedings and submit its award to the Appropriate Government."

Barring the Other Authorities under this Act for Adjudication of an Industrial Dispute Pending before the National Tribunal

Where any reference has been made under Section 10(1-A) to a National Tribunal [Please see the provisions of Section 10(1-A)] given under the heading, 'Reference of disputes to National Tribunal'], then notwithstanding anything contained in this Act, no Labour Court or Tribunal shall have jurisdiction to adjudicate upon any matter which is under adjudication before the National Tribunal, and accordingly,

(a) if the matter under adjudication before the National Tribunal is pending in a proceeding before a Labour Court or the Tribunal, the proceeding before the Labour Court or the Tribunal, as the case may be, insofar as it relates to such matter shall be deemed to have been quashed on such reference to the National Tribunal; and

(b) it shall not be lawful for the Appropriate Government to refer the matter under adjudication before the National Tribunal to any Labour Court or Tribunal for adjudication during the pendency of the proceeding in relation to such matter before the National Tribunal.

In this sub-section, which is mentioned above, the expressions, 'Labour Court' or 'Tribunal' includes any Court or Tribunal or any other authority constituted under any law relating to investigation and settlement of industrial disputes in force in any state [Explanation to Section 10(6)].

(4) Voluntary Reference to Arbitration

Section 10-A of the Industrial Disputes Act, 1947, provides for the voluntary reference of disputes to arbitration. Where any industrial dispute exists or is apprehended and the employer and the workmen agree to refer the dispute to arbitration, they may do so by an agreement in writing in the form prescribed by the rules and signed in the manner laid down in the rules. However, the reference to the arbitration must be made before the dispute has been referred to any authority under Section 10. The definition of 'Arbitrator' and the provisions relating to voluntary reference of a dispute to arbitration are discussed as follows.

Definition of 'Arbitrator' and Provisions relating to Voluntary Reference of a Dispute to Arbitration

Arbitrator [Section 2(aa)]

In the Industrial Disputes Act, 1947, the definition of 'Arbitrator' is given in Section (aa) and it is only stated that **'Arbitrator' includes an umpire**. However, the provisions relating appointment of an umpire and to voluntary reference of dispute to arbitration have been made in Section 10-A, which is as follows:

(a) Time to making Voluntary Reference of Dispute to Arbitration and who can make such reference: Where any industrial dispute exists or is apprehended and the employer and the workmen agree to refer the dispute to arbitration, they may, at any time before the dispute has been referred under Section 10 to a Labour Court or Tribunal or National Tribunal, by a written agreement, but save as aforesaid refer the dispute to arbitration [Section 10-A(1)].

Thus, the reference to arbitration must be made before the dispute has been referred to any authority under Section 10. Such reference to arbitration can be made by the employer and the workmen on the agreement amongst themselves where any industrial dispute exists or is apprehended.

(b) To whom Arbitration Reference can be made: Section 10-A(1) makes it amply clear that voluntary reference of dispute to arbitration shall be made to such person or persons including the Presiding Officer of a Labour Court, Industrial Tribunal or National Tribunal as an arbitrator or arbitrators as may be specified in the arbitration agreement.

(c) Appointment of an Umpire: The parties to the dispute can select any person as an arbitrator or persons as arbitrators. But, where an arbitration agreement provides for a reference of the dispute to an even number of arbitrators, then, that agreement shall provide for the appointment of another person as an umpire. The umpire thus appointed shall enter upon the reference if the arbitrators are equally divided in their opinion, and the award of the umpire shall prevail and shall be deemed to be the arbitration award for the purposes of this Act [Section 10-A(1-A)].

(d) Form of Arbitration Agreement: An arbitration agreement referred to in Section 10-A(1) shall be in such form and shall be signed by the parties thereto in such manner as may be prescribed [Section 10-A(2)].

(e) Provisions relating to Forwarding a Copy of the Arbitration Agreement to the Appropriate Government and the Conciliation Officer: Section 10-A(3) states that, "A copy of the arbitration agreement shall be forwarded to the Appropriate Government and the conciliation officer and the Appropriate Government shall, within one month from the date of the receipt of such copy, publish the same in the Official Gazette."

(f) Opportunity to Employers and Workmen who are not Parties to the Arbitration Agreement but are involved in the Dispute to represent their Case : Where an industrial dispute has been referred to arbitration and the Appropriate Government is satisfied that the persons making the reference represent the majority of each party, the Appropriate Government may, within one month, issue a notification in such manner as may be prescribed, and when any such notification is issued, the employers and workmen who are not parties to the arbitration agreement but are involved in the dispute, shall be given an opportunity of representing their case before the arbitrator or arbitrators, as the case may be [Section 10-A(3-A)]

(g) Duty of the Arbitrators: It is the duty of the arbitrator or arbitrators to investigate the dispute and then to submit the arbitration award duly signed to the Appropriate Government. Section 10-A(4) lays down that, **"The arbitrator or arbitrators shall investigate the dispute and submit to the Appropriate Government, the arbitration award signed by the arbitrator or arbitrators, as the case may be."**

(h) Prohibition of Continuance of Strike or Lock-out: When a dispute is referred to arbitration, the Appropriate Government may prohibit the continuance of any strike or lock-out by issuing an order. Section 10-A[4-A] states that, "where an industrial dispute has been referred to arbitration and notification has been issued under Section 10-A(3-A), the Appropriate Government may, by order, prohibit the continuance of any strike or lock-out in connection with such dispute which may be in existence on the date of the reference."

(i) Arbitration Act, 1940, not to apply: According to Section 10-A(5), "Nothing in the Arbitration Act, 1940 (10 of 1940), shall apply to arbitration under this section." Thus, when a dispute is referred to arbitration under Section 10-A, the provisions of the Arbitration Act, 1940, do not apply to arbitration under Section 10-A of the Industrial Disputes Act, 1947.

Filling of Vacancies and Finality of Orders [Section 8]

According to Section 8 of this Act, if, for any reason a vacancy (other than temporary absence) occurs in the office of the Presiding Officer of a Labour Court, Tribunal or National Tribunal or in the office of the Chairman or any other members of a Board or Court, then in the case of a National Tribunal, the Central Government, and in any other case, the Appropriate Government, shall appoint another person in accordance with the provisions of this act to fill the vacancy, and the proceeding may be continued before the Labour Court Tribunal, National Tribunal, Board or Court, as the case may be, from the stage at which vacancy is filled.

Finality of Orders Constituting Boards etc. [Section 9]

No order of the appropriate Government or of the Central Government appointing any person as the Chairman or any other member of a Board or of a Court or as the Presiding Officer of a Labour Court, Tribunal or National Tribunal shall be called in question in any manner; and no act or proceeding before any Board or Court shall be called in question in any manner on the ground merely of the existence of any vacancy in, or defect in the constitution of, such Board or Court [Section 9 (1).

No settlement arrived at in the course of a conciliation proceeding shall be invalid by reason only of the fact that such settlement was arrived at after expiry of the period referred to in sub-section (6) of Section 12 or sub-section (5) of Section 13, as the case may be [Section 9 (2)]. (Sections 12 and 13 are already explained in this chapter).

Where the report of any settlement arrived at in the course of conciliation before a Board is signed by the Chairman and all the other members of the Board, no such settlement shall be invalid by reason only of the casual or unforeseen absence of any of the members including Chairman of the Board, during any state of the proceeding [Section 9 (3)].

Notice of Change [Section 9-A and 9-B]

In Chapter II-A [Section 9-A and 9-B) of this Act, provisions have been made relating to the notice of change.

According to Section 9-A, no employer, who proposes to affect any change in the conditions of service applicable to any workmen *in respect of any matter specified in the Fourth Schedule*, shall affect such change –

(1) Without giving to the workmen likely to be affected by such change a notice in the prescribed manner of the nature of the change proposed to be effected; or

(2) Within twenty-one days of giving such notice.

Provided that no notice shall be required for affecting such change (a) where the change is affected in pursuance of settlement of award and (b) where the workmen likely to be affected by the change are persons to whom the Fundamental and Supplementary Rules, Civil Services Rules, Revised Leave Rules etc. are applicable.

The conditions of service for change of which notice is required to be given are mentioned in the Fourth Schedule given below:

The Fourth Schedule

Conditions of service for change of which notice is to be given –

(1) Wages including the period and mode of payment.
(2) Contribution paid or payable, by the employer to any provident fund or pension fund or for the benefit of the workmen under any law for the time being in force;
(3) Compensatory and other allowances;
(4) Hours of work and intervals;
(5) Leave with wages and holidays;
(6) Starting, alteration or discontinuance of shift working otherwise than, in accordance with standing orders;
(7) Classification by grades;
(8) Withdrawal of any customary concession or privilege or change in usages;
(9) Introduction of new rules of discipline, or alteration of existing rules; except in so far as they are provided in standing orders;

(10) Rationalisation, standardisation or improvement of plant or technique which is likely to lead to retrenchment of workmen;

(11) Any increase or reduction (other than casual) in the number of persons employed or to be employed in any occupation or process of department or shift not occasioned by circumstances over which the employer has no control.

No notice is required for certain changes

No notice is required to be given to an employer, who proposes to effect any change in the conditions of service applicable to any workmen in respect to any matter specified in the Fourth Schedule where the change is affected in pursuance of any settlement of award and where the workmen likely to be affected by the change are persons to whom the Fundamental and Supplementary Rules, Civil Services Rules, Revised Leave Rules etc. are applicable.

Power of Government to Exempt [Section 9-B]

Where the appropriate Government is of the opinion that the application of the provisions of Section 9-A to any class of industrial establishments or to any class of workmen in any industrial establishment affects the employees in relation thereto so prejudically, that such application may cause serious repercussion on the industry concerned and that public interest so requires, the appropriate Government may, by notification in the Official Gazette, direct the provisions of the said section *shall not apply, or shall subject to such conditions as may be specified in the notification*, to that class of industrial establishment or to that class of workmen employed in any industrial establishment.

Reference to Certain Individual Disputes to Grievance Settlement Authorities [Section 9-C]

Section 9-C of this Act provides for setting up of Grievance Settlement Authorities and reference of certain individual disputes to such authorities. The employer in relation to every industrial establishment in which fifty or more workmen are employed or have been employed on any day in the preceding twelve months, shall provide for, in accordance with rules made in that behalf under this Act, a Grievance Settlement Authority for the settlement of industrial disputes connected with an individual workman employed in the establishment [Section 9-C (1)].

Where an industrial dispute connected with an individual workman arises in an establishment referred to in sub-section (1) above, a workman or any trade union of workmen of which such workman is a member, refer, in such manner as may be prescribed, such dispute to the Grievance settlement Authority provided for by the employer under that sub-section for settlement of disputes [Section 9-C (2)].

The Grievance Settlement Authority referred to in Section 9-C (1) shall follow such procedure and complete its proceedings within such period as may be prescribed [Section 9-C (3)].

No reference shall be made under Chapter III with respect to any dispute referred to in this section unless such dispute has been referred to the Grievance Settlement Authority concerned and the decision of that authority is not acceptable to any of the parties to the disputes. [Section 9-C (4)].

Reference of Disputes to Board, Courts, etc. [Section 10]

In Chapter III of this Act, provisions have been made for reference of disputes to various authorities. These provisions are as under.

Where the appropriate Government is of the opinion that any industrial dispute exists or is apprehended, it may at any time, by order in writing –
(1) Refer the dispute to a Board for promoting a settlement thereof, or
(2) Refer any matter appearing to be connected with or relevant to the dispute, to a Court of inquiry; or
(3) Refer any dispute or any matter appearing to be connected with or relevant to, the dispute, if it relates to any matter specified in the Second Schedule (which is already reproduced elsewhere in this chapter), to a Labour Court for adjudication; or
(4) Refer the dispute or any matter appearing to be connected with, or relevant to, the dispute, whether it relates to any matter specified in the Second Schedule or the Third Schedule to a Tribunal for adjudication [Section 10 (1)].

Provided that where the dispute relates to any matter specified in the Third Schedule and is not likely to affect more than one hundred workmen, the appropriate Government may, if it thinks fit, make the reference to a Labour Court under clause C of Section 10 (1). [Proviso to Section 10 (1)].

Provided further that where the dispute relates to a public utility service and a notice under Section 22 has been given, the appropriate Government shall, unless it considers that the notice has been frivolously or vexatiously given or that it would be inexpedient so to do; make reference under this subsection notwithstanding that any other proceeding under this Act in respect of the dispute may have commenced [Proviso to Section 10 (1)].

Provided also that where the dispute in relation to which the Central Government is the appropriate Government, it shall be competent for that Government to refer the dispute to a Labour Court or an Industrial Tribunal, as the case may be, constituted by the State Government [Proviso to Section 10 (1)].

Where the Central Government is of the opinion that any industrial dispute exists or is apprehended and the dispute involves any question of national importance or is of such a nature that industrial establishments situated in more than one state are likely to be interested in or affected by such dispute and that dispute should be adjudicated by a National Tribunal, then the Central Government may, whether or not it is the appropriate Government in relation to that dispute at any time, by order in writing, refer the dispute or any matter appearing to be connected with, or relevant to the dispute, whether it relates to any matter specified in the Second Schedule, to a National Tribunal for adjudication [Section 10 (1-A)].

Where the parties to any industrial dispute apply in the prescribed manner whether jointly or separately, for a reference of the dispute to a board, Court, Labour Court, Tribunal or National Tribunal, the appropriate Government, if satisfied that the persons applying represent the majority of each party, shall make the reference accordingly [Section 10 (2)].

An order referring an industrial dispute to a Labour Court, National Tribunal or Tribunal under this section shall specify the period within which such Labour Court, Tribunal or National Tribunal shall submit its award on such dispute to the appropriate Government [Section 10 (2-A)].

Provided that where such industrial dispute is connected with an industrial workman, no such period shall exceed three months.

Provided further that where the parties to an industrial dispute apply in the prescribed manner, whether jointly or separately, to the Labour Court, Tribunal or National Tribunal for extension of such period or for any other reason, and the Presiding Officer of such Labour Court, Tribunal or National Tribunal considers it necessary or expedient to extend such period, he may for reasons to be recorded in writing, extend such period by such further period as he may think fit.

Provided also that in computing any period specified in this sub-section, the period, if any, for which the proceedings before the Labour Court, Tribunal or National Tribunal had been stayed by any injuction or order of a Civil Court shall be excluded.

Provided also that no proceedings before a Labour Court, Tribunal or National Tribunal shall lapse merely on the ground that any period specified under this sub-section had expired without such proceedings before completed.

Where an industrial dispute has been referred to a Board, Labour Court, Tribunal or National Tribunal under this section the appropriate Government may by order prohibit the continuance of any strike or lock-out in connection with such dispute which may be existence on the date of reference [Section 10 (3)].

Wherein an order referring an industrial dispute to a Labour Court, Tribunal or National Tribunal under this section or in a subsequent order, the appropriate Government has specified the points of disputes for adjudication, the Labour Court, or the Tribunal or the National Tribunal, as the case may be, shall confine its adjudication to those points and matters incidental thereto [Section 10 (4)].

Where a dispute concerning any establishment or establishments has been, or is to be, referred to a Labour Court, Tribunal, or National Tribunal under this Section and the appropriate Government is of opinion, whether on an application made to it in this behalf or otherwise, that the dispute is of such a nature that any other establishment, group or class of establishments of a similar nature is likely to be interested in, or affected by such dispute, the appropriate Government may, at the time of making the reference or at any time thereafter but before the submission of the award, include in that reference such establishment, group or class of establishments, whether or not at the time of such inclusion any dispute exists or is apprehended in that establishment, group or class of establishments. [Section 10 (5)].

Where any reference has been made to a National Tribunal under Section 10 (1-A), then, notwithsanding anything contained in this Act, no Labour Court or Tribunal shall have jurisdiction upon any matter which is under adjudication before the National Tribunal. [Section 10 (6)].

Where any industrial dispute, in relation to which the Central Government is not the appropriate Government, is referred to a National Tribunal, then notwithstanding anything contained in this Act, any reference in Sections 15, 17, 19, 33-A, 33-B and 36-A to the appropriate Government in relation to such dispute shall be construed as a reference to the Central Government, but, save as aforesaid and as otherwise expressly provided in this Act, any reference in any other provision of this Act to the appropriate Government in relation to that dispute shall mean a reference to the State Government [Section 10 (7)].

No proceedings pending before a Labour Court, Tribunal or National Tribunal in relation to an industrial dispute shall lapse merely because of the death of day of the parties to the dispute being a workman and such Labour Court, Tribunal or National Tribunal shall complete such proceedings and submit its award to the appropriate Government [Section 10 (8)].

Procedure and Powers of the Authorities [Section 11]

We have already considered the duties of various authorities appointed by the Appropriate Government or the Central Government, as the case may be, under this Act. The procedure to be followed and powers given to the authorities are also explained in Chapter IV of this Act. Let us consider them briefly. Section 11 of this Act provides for the procedure and powers of Conciliation Officers, Boards, Courts and Tribunals.

Section 11: Procedure and Powers of Conciliation Officers, Boards, Courts and Tribunals

(1) Subject to any rules that may be made in this behalf, an arbitrator, a Board, Court, Tribunal or National Tribunal shall follow such procedure as the arbitrator or other authority concerned may think fit.

(2) A Conciliation Officer or a member of a Board or Court or the Presiding Officer of a Labour Court, Tribunal or National Tribunal may, for the purpose of inquiry into any existing or apprehended industrial dispute, after giving reasonable notice, enter the premises occupied by the establishment to which the disputes relate.

(3) Every Board, Court, Labour Tribunal and National Tribunal shall have the same powers as are vested in a Civil Court under the Code of Civil Procedure, 1908, when trying a suit in respect of the following matters, namely:

   (a) Enforcing the attendance of any person and examining him on oath;

   (b) Compelling the production of documents and material objects;

   (c) Issuing summons for the examination of witness(es);

(d) In respect of such other matters as may be prescribed, and every inquiry or investigation by a Board, Court, Labour Court, Tribunal and National Tribunal shall be deemed to be a judicial proceeding, within the meaning of Sections 193 and 228 of the Indian Penal Code.

(4) A Conciliation Officer may enforce the attendance of any person for the purpose of examination of such person or call for and inspect any document which he has ground for considering to be relevant to the industrial dispute or to be necessary for the purpose of verifying the implementation of any award or carrying out any other duty imposed on him under this Act, and for the aforesaid purposes, a Conciliation Officer shall have the same powers as are vested in a Civil Court under the Code of Civil Procedure, 1908, in respect of enforcing the attendance of any person and examining him or of compelling the production of documents.

(5) A Court, Labour Court, Tribunal or National Tribunal may, if it thinks fit, appoint one or more persons having special knowledge of the matter under consideration as assessor or assessors to advise it in the proceeding before it.

(6) All Conciliation Officers, members of a Board or Court and the Presiding Officers of a Labour Court, Tribunal or National Tribunal shall be deemed to be public servants within the meaning of Section 21 of the Indian Penal Code.

(7) Subject to any rules made under this Act, the costs of, and incidental to any proceeding before a Labour Court, Tribunal or National Tribunal shall be in the discretion of that Labour Court, Tribunal or National Tribunal and the Labour Court, Tribunal or National Tribunal, as the case may be, shall have full powers to determine by and to when and to what extent and subject to what conditions, if any, such costs are to be paid, and to give all necessary directions for the purposes aforesaid and, such costs may, on an application made to the Appropriate Government by the person entitled, be recovered by the Government in the same manner as an arrear of land revenue.

(8) Every Labour Court, Tribunal or National Tribunal shall be deemed to be a Civil Court for the purposes of Ssections 345, 346 and 348 of the Code of Criminal Procedure, 1973.

Section 11-A makes amply clear the powers of Labour Courts, Tribunals and National Tribunals to give appropriate relief in case of discharge or dismissal of workmen. Section 11-A reads as follows:

Section 11-A: Power of Labour Courts, Tribunal and National Tribunals to give appropriate relief in case of discharge or dismissal of workman

Where in industrial dispute relating to the discharge or dismissal of a workman has been referred to a Labour Court, Tribunal or National Tribunal for adjudication and, in the course of the adjudication proceedings, the Labour Court, Tribunal or National Tribunal, as the case may be, is satisfied that the order of discharge or dismissal was not justified, it may, by its award, set aside the order of discharge or dismissal and direct reinstatement of the workman on such terms and condition, if any, as it thinks fit, or give such other relief to the workman including the award of any lesser punishment in lieu of discharge or dismissal as the circumstances of the case may require.

Provided that in any proceeding under this section, the Labour Court, Tribunal or National Tribunal, as the case may be, shall rely only on the materials on record and shall not take any fresh evidence in relation to the matter.

Form of Report or Award [Section 16 (1)]

According to Section 16 (1), the report or award of a Board or Court must be in writing and shall be signed by all the members, as the case may be. It is further provided that nothing in this Section 16 (1) shall be deemed to prevent any member of the Board or Court from recording any minute of dissent from a report or from any recommendation made therein [Proviso to Section 16 (1)].

The Award of a Labour Court or Tribunal or National Tribunal shall be in writing and shall be signed by its Presiding Office [Section 16 (2)].

Publication of Reports and Awards

According to Section 17 (1) every report of a Board or Court together with any minute of dissent recorded therewith, every arbitration award and every award of a Labour Court, Tribunal or National Tribunal must be published within a period of thirty days from the date of its receipts by the appropriate Government in such manner as, the appropriate Government thinks fit and proper. Further it is provided that subject to the provisions of Section 17 - A (which is reproduced below), the award published under Section 17 (1) shall be final and shall not be called in question by any Court in any manner whatsoever [Section 17 (2)]. This implies that the awards thus published cannot be challenged.

Commencement of the Award [Section 17-A]

Section 17-A (1) states that an award, including an arbitration award, shall become enforceable on the expiry of thirty days from the date of its publication as provided in Section 17 (1). However, if the appropriate Government is of the opinion, in any case of award where the award has been given by a Labour Court or Tribunal in relation to an industrial dispute to which it is a party or if the Central Government is of the opinion, in any case where the award has been given by a National Tribunal, that it will be in expedient to give effect to the whole or any part of the award, the appropriate Government or the Central Government, as the case may be, may be notification in the Official Gazette, declare that the award shall not become enforceable on the expiry of the said period of thirty days.

Thus, this Section 17-A empowers the Government not to make the award given by a Labour Court a Tribunal or a National Tribunal, as the case may be, enforceable in whole or in part, if the appropriate Government thinks that it will be in expedient to do so. The concerned Government however, has to do so by giving proper notification in the Official Gazette. Then obviously such award or an arbitration cannot become enforceable on the expiry of the period of thirty days from the date of its receipt by the appropriate Government.

Section 17 A (2) makes it clear that "where any declaration has been made in relation to an award under the proviso to sub-section (1), the appropriate Government or the Central Government may, within ninety days from the date of publication of the award under Section 17, make an order rejecting or modifying the award, and shall, on the first available opportunity, lay the award together with a copy of the order before the Legislature of the State, if the order has been made by a State Government or before Parliament, if the order has been made by the Central Government.

Where any award as rejected to modified by an order made under sub-section (2) is laid before the Legislature of a State or before Parliament, such award shall become enforceable on the expiry of fifteen days from the date on which it is so laid; and where no order under sub-section (2) is made in pursuance of a declaration under the proviso to sub-section (1), the award shall become enforceable on the expiry of the period of ninety days referred to in sub-section (2) [Section 17 A (3)].

Section 17 A (4) provides that subject to the provisions of sub-section (1) and sub-section (3) regarding the enforceability of an award, the award shall come into operation with effect from such date as may be specified therein, but where no date is so specified, it shall come into operation on the date when the award becomes enforceable under Section 17 (1) or Section 17 A (3) as the case may be.

Provisions Relating to Full Wages to Workman Pending Proceedings in Higher Courts [Section 17-B]

Section 17-B makes provisions relating to full wages to a workman during the period of pendency of such proceedings because of the cause mentioned in this section in the High Court or in the Supreme Court. These provisions are stated below.

"Where in any case, a Labour Court, Tribunal or National Tribunal by its award directs reinstatement of any workman and the employer prefers any proceedings against such award in a High Court or the Supreme Court, the employer shall be liable to pay such workman, during the period of pendency of such proceedings in the High Court or the Supreme Court, full wages last drawn by him, inclusive of any maintenance allowance admissible to him under any rule if the workman had not been employed in any establishment during such period and an affidavit by such workman had been filed to that effect in such Court".

It is also provided that where it is proved to the satisfaction of the High Court or the Supreme Court that such workman had been employed and had been receiving adequate remuneration during any such period or part thereof, the Court shall order that no wages shall be payable under this section for such period or part, as the case may be [Proviso to Section 17-B].

Persons on whom Settlements and Awards are Binding

According to Section 18, settlements and awards are binding on the following persons.

(1) A settlement arrived at by agreement between the employer and workman otherwise than in the course of conciliation proceeding shall be binding on the parties to the agreement [Section 18 (1)].

(2) Subject to the provisions of sub-section (3) an arbitration award which has become enforceable shall be binding on the parties to the agreement who referred the dispute to arbitration [Section 18 (2)].

(3) A settlement arrived at in the course of conciliation proceedings under this Act or an arbitration award in a case where a notification has been issued under sub-section (3-A) of Section 10-A or an award of a Labour Court, Tribunal or National Tribunal which has become enforceable shall be binding on –
  (a) All parties to the industrial dispute;
  (b) All other parties summoned to appear in the proceedings as parties to the Dispute, unless the Board, [arbitrator] [Labour Court, Tribunal or National Tribunal], as the case may be, records the opinion that they were so summoned without proper cause;
  (c) Where a party referred to in clause (a) or clause (b) is an employer, his heirs, successors or assigns in respect of the establishment to which the dispute relates;
  (d) Where a party referred to in clause (a) or clause (b) is composed of workmen, all persons who were employed in the establishment or part of the establishment, as the case may be, to which the dispute relates on the date of the dispute and all persons who subsequently become employed in that establishment or part [Section 18 (3)].

It should be noted that the main object of the Industrial Dispute Act is the settlement of industrial disputes. It is not merely the enactment bearing on terms and conditions of service. From this point of view, an award or settlement continues to regulate the relationship between the parties until it is replaced by new one. Hence distinction between award and settlement from the view point of their legal force need not be made [Life Insurance Corporation of India V. D. J. Bahadur and Others (AIR-1980-Supreme Court - 2181]. It must also be remembered that every settlement is always an agreement or arrangement. However every agreement or arrangement cannot be a settlement in the eyes of law [India Tobacco Company V. Deputy Labour Commissioner (1971-75-C.W.N. 217].

Period of Operation of a Settlement and an Award

(1) Period of operation of settlement: Provisions of Section 19 (1) and (2) throw light on the period of operation of a settlement. Section 19 (1) makes it clear that if any settlement arrived at in the course of conciliation proceedings before a Conciliation Officer or a Board of Conciliation, as the case may be, it shall come into operation (i) on such date as is agreed upon by the parties to the dispute, and (ii) if no such date is agreed upon, on the date on which the memorandum of the settlement is signed by the parties to the dispute.

Section 19 (2) provides that such settlement, thus arrived at, shall be binding for such period as is agreed upon by the parties. However, if no such period is agreed upon, it shall be binding for a period of six months from the date on which the memorandum of settlement is signed by the parties to the dispute. Section 19 (2) further states that it shall continue to be binding on the parties after the expiry of the period aforesaid, until the expiry of two months from the date on which a notice in writing of an intention to terminate the settlement is given by one of the parties to the other party or parties to the settlement." Thus, a settlement continues to be binding until any one of the parties gives in writing a notice of termination of the settlement and the settlement ceases to be binding on the expiry of two months from such notice of termination given.

Any notice thus given under Section 19 (2) shall not be operative unless it is given by a party representing the majority of persons bound by the settlement [Section 19 (7)].

(2) Period of operation of an award: So far as the period of operation of an award is concerned, the following provisions have been made in Section 19 of the Industrial Disputes Act of 1947.

(a) Subject to other provisions of Section 19, an award shall remain in operation for a period of one year from the date on which the award becomes enforceable under Section 17-A. [Section 19 (3)].

(b) The appropriate Government has been authorised to reduce this period of one year and to fix such period as it thinks fit [Proviso 1 to Section 19].

(c) The appropriate Government has also been authorised, before the expiry of the said period of one year, to extend the period of operation by any period not exceeding one year at a time as it thinks proper. But the total period of operation of any award shall not exceed three years from the date on which it came into operation [Proviso 2 to Section 19 (3)].

(d) Section 19 (5) lays down that, "Nothing contained in Section 19 (3) shall apply to any award which by its nature, terms or other circumstances does not impose, after it has been given effect to, any continuing obligations on the parties bound by the award."

(e) Provisions have been made in Section 19 (4) relating to shortening of period of operation of award on a material change in the circumstances.
These provisions are as follows:
Where the appropriate Government considers that since award was made, there has been a material change in the circumstances on which it was based, the appropriate Government, either on its own motion or on the application of any party bound by the award, may refer the award or a part

of it (i) to a Labour Court, if the award was that of a Labour Court, or (ii) to a Tribunal, if the award was that of a Tribunal or of a National Tribunal, for a decision whether the period of operation of the award should not, by reason of such change, be shortened. The decision given by Labour Court or the Tribunal in that respect, one such reference, shall be final.

(f) Section 19 (6) states that, "Notwithstanding the expiry of the period of operation under Section 19 (3), the award shall continue to be binding on the parties until a period of two months has elapsed from the date on which notice is given by any party bound by the award to the other party or parties intimating its intention to terminate the award". Thus, the award continues to be binding on the parties until the expiry of the period of two months from the date of notice of its termination by a party and then such award ceases to be binding on the expiry of two months from such notice.

(g) The notice thus given by any party under Section 19 (6) shall not have any effect unless such notice is given by a party representing the majority of persons bound by the award [Section 19 (7)].

2.2 Provisions under Chapter V - Strikes and Lockouts

1. Strikes

Lock-outs and strikes are the weapons in the hands of employers and workmen, respectively, to compel one other to agree to their demand(s).

Strike has been defined in Section 2(g) of this Act to mean cessation of work by a body of persons employed in any industry acting in combination or a concerted refusal or a refusal under a common understanding of any number who are or have been so employed to continue to work or to accept employment. Strike is a powerful weapon in the hands of employees for collective bargaining. The employees through this mechanism can in a way compel the employers to sit across with them for settling their disputes in the form of collective bargaining. When all other methods to resolve the industrial disputes fail, this weapon of strike is used as a last resort. The right to go on strike has been given to the workmen, but this Act imposes certain restrictions on the rights of workmen. This Act prohibits strikes under certain circumstances. It also makes separate provisions for public utility service and private enterprises.

Characteristics of Strikes

(1) A strike is a weapon which is used by employees or workmen acting together to force their employer to agree to the demands made by them.

(2) A strike implies a stoppage of work by a number of employees acting together. But mere absence from work on personal grounds does not amount to cessation or stoppage or refusal of work. There should be premeditation or plan to cease or to refuse to work in a body of workmen.

(3) The duration or stoppage or cessation of work is immaterial. If the workmen acting together cease their work even for an hour or a part thereof, it can be called a strike.

(4) When workmen go on strike against the provisions of this Act, such strike is considered illegal.

(5) Even a partial refusal of work by a body of workmen may constitute a strike.

(6) A strike can be a 'stay-in strike' or 'go-slow strike.'

(7) In certain industries, overtime work is considered essential and it is a legal obligation. While in certain industries, overtime work is done habitually and is customary. Refusal of overtime work in such cases is considered as against the conditions of service. If overtime work is refused, then, it may be considered as a strike.

From the definition and the important points mentioned above, we come to know that the following two factors must exist to constitute a strike.

(a) The workmen must be absent from work either in a body or in a group. They must refuse to work when they are expected to do under legal or contractual obligation for their employer.

(b) The cessation or refusal to do the work is voiced either in concerted form of all workmen or in a group of workmen. Mere absence from duty or work on any personal ground does not amount to cessation or refusal of work. There must exist some form of predetermination or some plan to cease or refuse to do the work in a body of workmen.

Important Provisions Relating to Strikes

Provisions relating to Prohibition of Strike [Section 22]

(1) No person employed in a public utility service shall go on strike, in breach of contract –

   (a) Without giving a notice of strike to the employer, as hereinafter provided, within six weeks before striking; or

   (b) Within fourteen days on giving such notice; or

   (c) Before the expiry of the date of strike specified in such notice as aforesaid; or

   (d) During the pendency of any conciliation proceeding before a conciliation officer and seven days after the conclusion of such proceedings [Section 22(1)].

(2) The notice of strike under the provisions mentioned above in Section 22(1) shall not be necessary where there is already in existence a strike in public utility services. But, it is very essential for the employer to send an intimation of such

strike to such authority as may be specified by the Appropriate Government, on the day on which the strike is declared, either generally or for a particular area or for a particular class of public utility services [Section 22(3)].

The notice of strike referred to in Section 22(1) must be given by such number of persons to such person or persons and in such manner as may be prescribed [Section 22(4)].

(3) If on any day an employer receives from any person employed by him any such notices as are referred to in Section 22(1), he must within five days thereof, report to the Appropriate Government or to such authority as that Appropriate Government may prescribe the number of such notices receive on that date [Section 22(6)].

General Prohibition of Strike [Section 23]

No workman who is employed in any industrial establishment will go on strike in breach of contract under the following circumstances:

(1) During the pendency of conciliation proceedings before a Board and seven days after the conclusion of such proceeding.

(2) During the pendency of proceedings before a Labour Court, an Industrial Tribunal or National Tribunal and two months after the conclusion of such proceedings.

(3) During the pendency of arbitration proceedings before an arbitrator and two months after the conclusion of such proceedings, where a notification has been issued under Section 10-A(3-A), or

(4) During any period in which a settlement or award is in operation, in respect of any of the matters covered by the settlement or award.

Illegal Strikes [Section 24]

(1) A strike shall be illegal if it is commenced or declared in contravention of Sections 22 or 23 or if it is continued in contravention of an order made under Section 10(3) or under Section 10-A(4-A) [Section 24(1)].

(2) Where a strike in pursuance of an industrial dispute has already commenced and is in existence at the time of the reference of the dispute to a Board, an arbitrator, a Labour Court, Tribunal or National Tribunal, the continuance of such strike shall not be deemed to be illegal, provided that such strike was not at its commencement in contravention of the provisions of this Act or the continuance thereof was not prohibited under Section 10(3) or under Section 10-A(4-A) [Section 24(2)].

(3) Any strike declared in consequence of an illegal lock-out shall not be deemed to be illegal [Section 24(3)].

2. Lock-outs

A 'lock-out' has been defined in Section 2(1) of this Act. A Lock-out means the temporary closing of a place of employment, or the suspension of work, or the refusal by an employer to continue to employ any number of workmen employed by him. Thus, a lock-out is resorted to by the given employer to compel the employees to accept his/her terms of working.

A lock-out is a coercive weapon available to the employer to impose his terms and conditions. In short, it is an antithesis of a strike. But it must be remembered that lock-out should not be misunderstood as closure. Closure and lock-out are two different terms.

Characteristics of Lock-outs

From the above mentioned definition of lock-out and the discussion we had so far, we can gather its following important characteristics. They are -

(1) Lock-out is an act of management and it is generally intended to put some pressure on the workers in order to make them agree to the terms and conditions of work of their employer.

(2) Mere suspension of work on account of shortage of raw materials, coal, supply of energy, water etc., does not amount to a lock-out.

(3) Lock-out indicates the temporary closure of the place of business and not the closure of the business itself.

(4) Lock-out is generally caused by strike, fear of disorder, fear of destruction of the properties of the firm, company etc. Most of these causes are the results of industrial disputes.

(5) Lock-out indicates the temporary closing of a place of employment, or the suspension of work, or the refusal of an employer to continue to employ any number of persons employed by him.

(6) Lock-out and discharge do not mean one and the same thing. In a lock-out, the relationship between an employer and his employees continues. But, in the case of discharge, this relationship is cut off.

(7) Lock-out does not indicate closure. Closure implies discontinuation of the business.

Important Provisions Relating to Lock-outs

The important provisions relating to lock-out made in this Act are as follows:

Provisions relating to Prohibition of Lock-out [Section 22]

(1) It is mentioned in Section 22(2) that, "No employer carrying on any public utility service shall lock-out any of his workmen –

   (a) Without giving them notice of lock-out as hereinafter provided, within six weeks before locking-out; or

(b) Within fourteen days of giving such notice; or

(c) Before the expiry of the date of lock-out specified in an such notice as aforesaid; or

(d) During the pendency of any conciliation proceedings before a Conciliation Officer, and seven days' after the conclusion of such proceedings."

(2) The notice of lock-out under this Section 22 shall not be necessary where there is already in existence a lock-out of any public utility service. However, the employer shall send the intimation of such lock-out on the day on which it is declared, to such authority, as may be specified by the Appropriate Government either generally or for a particular area or for a particular class of public utility services [Section 22(3)].

(3) The notice of lock-out referred to in Section 22(2) is required to be given in such manner as may be prescribed [Section 22(5)].

(4) If an any day an employer gives to any persons employed by him any such notices as are referred to in Section 22(2), he shall within five days thereof report to the Appropriate Government or to such other authority as that Government may prescribe, the number of such notices given on that date [Section 22(6)].

Provisions relating to General Prohibition of lock-out [Section 23]

According to the provisions of Section 23, No employer shall declare a lock-out –

(1) During the pendency of conciliation proceedings before a Board and seven days after the conclusion of such proceedings;

(2) During the pendency of proceedings before a Labour Court, Tribunal or National Tribunal and two months after the conclusion of such proceedings;

(3) During the pendency of arbitration proceedings before an arbitrator and two months after the conclusion of such proceedings, where a notification has been issued under Section 10-A(3-A); or

(4) "During any period in which a settlement or award is in operation, in respect of any of the matters covered by the settlement or award."

Provisions relating to Illegal Lock-out [Section 24]

(1) A lock-out shall be illegal, if (a) it is commenced or declared in contravention of Sections 22 or 23 which are mentioned above, or (b) it is continued in contravention of an order made under Section 10(3) or Section 10-A(4-A) [Section 24(1)].

(2) Where a lock-out in pursuance of an industrial dispute has already commenced and is in existence at the time of reference of the dispute to a Board, an arbitrator, a Labour Court, Tribunal or National Tribunal, the continuance of such lock-out shall not be deemed to be illegal, provided that such lock-out was not at its

commencement in contravention of the provisions of this Act, or the continuance thereof was not prohibited under Section 10(3) or under Section 10-A(4-A) [Section 24(2)].

(3) Any lock-out declared in consequence of an illegal strike shall not be deemed to be illegal [Section 24(3)].

3. Distinction between 'Strike' and 'Lock-out'

Strike	Lock-out
(1) 'Strike' means a cessation of work by a body of persons employed in any industry acting in combination, or a concerted refusal, or a refusal under a common understanding of any number of persons who are or have been so employed to continue to work or to accept employment [Section 2(q)].	(1) 'Lock-out' means the temporary closing of a place of employment, or the suspension of work, or the refusal by an employer to continue to employ any number of persons employed by him [Section 2(1)].
(2) A strike is a weapon used by the employees or workmen acting together to force their employer to agree to the demands made by them.	(2) Lock-out is an act resorted to by the management. It is the employer's weapon which is used by him to put pressure on the workers to make them agree to his terms and conditions as regards work. Lock-out can be described as an antithesis of a strike.
(3) A strike implies a stoppage or cessation of work by the employees acting together. A strike can be 'stay-in strike' or 'Go-slow' strike.	(3) Lock-out indicates the temporary closure of the place of business by an employer; but not the closure of the business itself.
(4) In the case of a strike, an employer is not liable to pay wages for the period of strike.	(4) In the case of a lawful lock-out, no compensation is payable by an employer. But, if it is illegal, an employer is liable to pay compensation for the period of lock-out to his employees.
(5) A strike declared in consequence of an illegal lock-out, such strike is not deemed to be illegal [Section 24 (3)].	(5) A lock-out declared in consequence of an illegal strike, such lock-out is not deemed to be illegal [Section 24(3)].

Strike	Lock-out
(6) Any workman who commences, continues or otherwise acts in furtherance of a strike which is illegal, is punishable with imprisonment for a term which may extend upto one month, or with a fine which may extend upto ₹ Fifty, or, with both [Section 26(1)].	(6) Any employer who commences, continues or otherwise acts in furtherance of a lock-out which is illegal, is punishable with imprisonment for a term which may extend upto one month or with a fine which may extend upto ₹ One Thousand or, with both [Section 26(2)].

2.3 Provisions under Chapter VA - Lay-off and Retrenchment

The provisions relating to 'lay-off' and 'retrenchment' have been included in Chapter V-A of this Act. However, both the definitions of the aforesaid terms are given in Section 2 of this Act.

1. **Lay-off**

Section 2(kkk) of this Act defines lay-off and, accordingly, 'lay-off' means the refusal, failure or inability of an employer to provide or to give employment to a workman whose name is borne on the muster rolls of his industrial establishment and who has not been retrenched. Such failure, refusal or inability to provide employment to a workman may be due to one of the following causes, such as –

   (1) The accumulation of stocks.
   (2) Shortages of coal, power, fuel or raw materials.
   (3) The breakdown of machinery.
   (4) Natural calamity.
   (5) Any other connected reason –

A workman is deemed to have been laid off for any day if he presents himself for work at the establishment at the appointed time for the purpose and during the normal working hours on that day and is not given employment by the employer within two hours of his so presenting himself, but if the workman, instead of being given an employment at the commencement of any shift for any day is asked to present himself for the purpose during the second half of the shift for the day and is given employment, then, he shall be deemed to have been laid off only for one-half of that day. It is further provided in this section that if he is not given any such employment even after so remaining present he shall not be deemed to have been laid-off for the second half of the shift for the day and shall be entitled to full basic wages and dearness allowance for that part of the day.

2. **Retrenchment**

The term 'retrenchment' is defined in Section 2(oo) of the Industrial Disputes Act as follows:

'Retrenchment' means the termination by the employer of the services of a workman for any reason whatsoever, otherwise than as punishment inflicted by way of disciplinary act.

To retrench means to end, cease or to conclude. However, retrenchment does not include (i) voluntary retirement of a workman, or (ii) retirement of a workman on reaching the age of superannuation if the contract of the employment between the employer and the workman concerned contains a stipulation in that behalf, or (iii) termination of service of a workman on the ground of continued ill health or (iv) termination of service of the workmen as a result of the non-renewal of the contract of employment between the employer and the workmen concerned on its expiry or of such contract being terminated under a stipulation in that behalf contained therein.

Thus, it seems that it is only when the services of a workman are dispensed with on the ground of surplus labour, then, the termination of services of such workman may be called retrenchment.

Right of Workman Laid-off for Compensation [Section 25-C]

Section 25-C of this Act provides the workman concerned with the right to receive lay-off compensation. It is given to a workman to relieve the hardship on the grounds of human public policy. The principle of social justice is followed in awarding lay-off compensation. The provisions regarding the payment of compensation to a workman who is laid off are contained in Section 25-C, is reproduced as follows:

The important provisions of Section 25-C can be summarised as follows:

(1) For entitlement of compensation, the workman should not be a *badli* or casual workman and his name must appear on the muster-rolls of the industrial establishment.

(2) The workman must have completed not less than one full year of continuous service.

(3) When the above mentioned conditions are fulfilled, the workman, whether laid-off continuously or intermittently, shall be paid compensation by his employer for all days during which he is laid-off, of course, except for such weekly holidays as may intervene.

(4) The rate at which the compensation is to be paid shall be equal to fifty per cent of the total basic wages as well as dearness allowance that would have been payable to the workman had he not been laid-off.

(5) Compensation shall not be payable to a workman during any period of twelve months after the expiry of the first forty-five days if there is an agreement to that effect between the employer and the workmen.

(6) Where a workman is laid-off for a period of forty-five days during the period of twelve months, the employer can retrench the workman, according to the provisions contained in Section 25-F at any time after the expiry of the first forty-five days of lay-off.

(7) When the employer retrenches the workman, any compensation paid to the workman for having been laid-off during the preceding twelve months may be set-off against the compensation payable for retrenchment of the workman.

Conditions Precedent to Retrenchment of Workmen [Section 25-F]

We have already studied the meaning of the term 'retrenchment'. Now, let us consider the conditions precedent to retrenchment of workmen under this Act.

No workman employed in an industry who has been in continuous service for not less than one year under an employer shall be retrenched by the employer until –

(1) The workman has been served one month's notice in writing indicating the reasons for retrenchment and the period of notice has expired or the workman has been paid in lieu of such notice, wages for the period of such notice.

(2) The workman has been paid at the time of retrenchment, compensation which shall be equivalent to fifteen days average pay for every completed year of continuous service or any part thereof of six months; and

(3) Notice in the prescribed manner is served on the Appropriate Government or such authority as may be specified by the Appropriate Government by notification in the Official Gazette [Section 25-F].

Procedure for Retrenchment

Section 25-G of this Act makes clear the procedure for retrenchment. This section applies the rule of 'Last come First go' to retrenchment. Section 25-G states that where any workman in an industrial establishment, who is a citizen of India, is to be retrenched and he belongs to a particular category of workmen in that establishment, in the absence of any agreement between the employer and the workman in this behalf, the employer shall ordinarily retrench the workman who was the last person to be employed in that category, unless for reasons to be recorded, the employer retrenches any other workman.

Re-employment of Retrenched Workman [Section 25-H]

The provisions relating to re-employment of retrenched workman is made in Section 25-H of this Act as under:

Where any workmen are retrenched and the employer proposes to take into his employment any persons, he shall, in such manner as may be prescribed, give an opportunity to the retrenched workmen who are citizens of India, to present themselves for re-employment and, such retrenched workmen, who offer themselves for re-employment shall have preference over other persons.

3. Distinction between 'Retrenchment' and 'Lay-off'

Retrenchment	Lay-off
(1) By retrenchment is meant the termination of service of a workman by an employer for any reason, whatsoever, otherwise than as punishment inflicted by way of disciplinary action. Retrenchment does not include voluntary retirement, because of reaching the age of superannuation, termination of services either because of continued ill health of a workman or because of non-renewal of employment contract.	(1) Lay-off means the failure, refusal or inability of an employer to provide employment to the workmen employed by him on account of the following reasons: (a) Storage of coal, power, fuel, raw materials. (b) Accumulation of stock. (c) Breakdown of machinery. (d) Natural calamity. (e) Any other connective reason. The names of workmen who are laid off must appear on the muster-rolls and they must not be retrenched.

Retrenchment	Lay-off
(2) Workmen are retrenched to remove surplus labour.	(2) Workmen are laid off because of the reasons mentioned above which are beyond the control of the given employer.
(3) Retrenchment is permanent.	(3) Lay-off is temporary.
(4) In retrenchment, the relationship between the employer and his workmen comes to an end.	(4) In lay-off, the relationship between the employer and his workmen is suspended temporarily.

2.4 Provisions under Chapter VC - Unfair Labour Practices

Unfair Labour Practices

1. **On the part of employers and trade unions of employees**
    (1) To interfere with, restrain from or coerce, workmen in the exercise of their right to organise, form, join or assist a trade union or to engage in concerted activities for the purposes of collective bargaining or other mutual aid or protection, that is to say –
    (a) Threatening workmen with discharge or dismissal, if they join a trade union;
    (b) Threatening a lock-out or closure, if a trade union is organised;
    (c) Granting wage increase to workmen at crucial periods of trade union organisation, with a view to undermining the efforts of the trade union at organisation.
    (2) To dominate, interfere with or contribute support, financial or otherwise, to any trade union, that is to say –
    (a) An employer taking an active interest in organising a trade union of his workmen; and
    (b) An employer showing partiality or granting favour to one of several trade unions attempting to organise his workmen or to its members, where such a trade union is not a recognised union.
    (3) To establish employer sponsored trade unions of workmen.
    (4) To encourage or discourage membership in any trade union by discriminating against any workman, that is to say.
    (a) Discharging or punishing a workman, because he urged other workmen to join or organise a trade union;
    (b) Discharging or punishing a workman for taking part in any strike (not being a strike which is deemed to be an illegal strike under this Act).
    (c) Changing seniority rating of workmen because of trade union activities.
    (d) Refusing to promote workmen to higher posts on account of their union activities.
    (e) Giving unmerited promotions to certain workmen with a view to creating discord amongst other workmen, or to undermine the strength of their trade union;

(f) Discharging officer-bearers or active members of the trade union on account of their trade union activities.

(5) To discharge or dismiss workmen –
   (a) By way of victimisation;
   (b) Not in good faith, but in the colourable exercise of the employer's rights;
   (c) By falsely implicating a workman in a criminal case on false evidence or on concocted evidence;
   (d) For patently false reasons;
   (e) On untrue or trumped up allegations of absence without leave;
   (f) In utter disregard of the principles of natural justice in the conduct of domestic enquiry or with undue haste;
   (g) For misconduct of a minor or technical character, without having any regard to the nature of the particular misconduct or the past record or service of the workman, thereby leading to a disproportionate punishment.

(6) To abolish the work of a regular nature being done by workmen and to give such work to contractors as a measure of breaking a strike.

(7) To transfer a workman *mala fide* from one place to another place, under the guise of following management policy.

(8) To insist upon individual workmen, who are on a legal strike to sign a good conduct bond, as a pre-condition to allowing them to resume work.

(9) To show favouritism or partiality to one set of workers regardless of merit.

(10) To employ workmen as 'badlis', casuals or temporaries and to continue them as such for years, with the object of depriving them of the status and privileges of permanent workmen.

(11) To discharge or discriminate against any workman for filing charges or testifying against an employer in any enquiry or proceeding relating to any industrial dispute.

(12) To recruit workmen during a strike which is not an illegal strike.

(13) Failure to implement award, settlement or agreement.

(14) To indulge in acts of force or violence.

(15) To refuse to bargain collectively, in good faith with the recognised trade unions.

(16) Proposing or continuing a lock-out deemed to be illegal under this Act.

2. On the part of workmen and trade unions of workmen

(1) To advise or actively support or instigate any strike deemed to be illegal under this Act.

(2) To coerce workmen in the exercise of the right to self organisation or to join a trade union or refrain from joining any trade union, that is to say –
   (a) For a trade union or its members to picketing in such a manner that non-striking workmen are physically debarred from entering the work places;
   (b) To indulge in acts of force or violence or to hold out threats of intimidation in connection with a strike against non-striking workmen or against managerial staff.

(3) For a recognised union to refuse to bargain collectively in good faith with the employer.
(4) To indulge in coercive activities against certification of a bargaining representative.
(5) To stage, encourage or instigate such forms of coercive actions as willful 'go slow', squatting on the work premises after working hours or 'gherao' of any of the members of the managerial or other staff.
(6) To stage demonstrations at the residence of the employers or the managerial staff members.
(7) To incite or indulge in willful damage to employer's property connected with the industry.
(8) To indulge in acts of force or violence or to hold out threats of intimidation against any workman with a view to prevent him from attending work.

2.5 Provisions under Chapter VI - Penalties

Penalties

The provisions of penalties for various offences are made in this section of this as follows:

(1) Penalty for Closure [Section 25-R]

Any employer who closes down an undertaking without complying with the provisions of sub-section (1) of Section 25-O shall be punishable with imprisonment for a term which may extend upto six months or with fine which may extend upto five thousand rupees or, with both [Section 25(1)].

Any employer, who contravenes an order refusing to grant permission to close down an undertaking under sub-section (2) or Section 25-O or a direction given under Section 25-P shall be punishable with imprisonment for a term which may extend upto one year, or with fine which may extend upto five thousand rupees, or with both, and where the contravention is a continuing one, with a further fine which may extend upto two thousand rupees for every day during which such contravention continues after the conviction [Section 25-R(2)].

(2) Penalty for Committing Unfair Labour Practices [Section 25-U]

No employer or workman or a trade union, whether registered under the Trade Union Act, 1926, or not shall commit any unfair labour practice [Section 25-T]. Unfair labour practice relates to those practices as specified in the Fifth Schedule [Section 2(ra)]. Any person who commits any unfair labour practice is punishable with imprisonment for a term which may extend upto six months or with fine which may extend upto Rupees one thousand or with both [Section 25-U].

(3) Penalty for Illegal Strikes and Lock-outs [Section 26]

Any workman who commences, continues or otherwise acts in furtherance of a strike which is not legal under this Act is punishable with imprisonment for a period which may be extended upto one month or with a fine which may be extended upto fifty rupees or with both [Section 26(1)].

Any employer who commences, continues or otherwise acts in furtherance of a lock-out which is not legal under this Act, is punishable with imprisonment for a term which may extend to one month or with a fine which may be imposed upto rupees one thousand or with both [Section 26(2)].

The remedy which is indicated in this Section 26 is the statutory remedy. No other relief outside this Act can be available on general principles of jurisprudence. The relief, therefore, of compensation by proceedings in arbitration is contrary to law.

(4) Penalty for Instigation [Section 27]

The terms 'Instigation' or 'Incitation' have some deeper meaning than a mere asking a person to do any particular act. These words or terms seem to convey the meaning "to good or urge forward or to encourage the doing of an act. Any person who instigates or incites others to take part in, or otherwise acts in furtherance of a strike or lock-out which is not legal under this Act, is punishable with imprisonment for a term which may extend to six months or with a fine which may also be imposed up to Rupee one thousand or, with both.

(5) Penalty for giving Financial Aid to Illegal Strikes and Lock-outs [Section 28]

Any person who knowingly applies or expends any money in direct furtherance or supports any illegal strikes or lock-out is punishable with imprisonment for a term which may be extended upto six months or with fine which may be extended upto one thousand rupees or, with both.

(6) Penalty for Breach of Settlement or Award [Section 29]

Any person who commits a breach of term of any settlement or award, which is binding on such person under this Act, is punishable with imprisonment for a period which may extend upto six months or with a fine of ₹ …….. or, with both; and where the breach is a continuing one, with a further fine which may extend upto Rupees two hundred for every day during which the breach continues after the conviction for the first breach and the Court trying the offence, if it imposes a fine on the offender, may direct that the whole or any part of the fine realised from him shall be paid, by way of compensation, to any person who, in the opinion of the Court, has been injured by such breach.

This Section 29 of this Act covers strikes in violation of settlement.

(7) Penalty for Disclosing Confidential Information [Section 30]

Any person who purposely or wilfully discloses any such information as is referred to in Section 21 of this Act in contravention of its provisions, on complaint made by or on behalf of the trade union or individual whose business is affected, is punishable with imprisonment for a term which may extend upto six months, or with a fine which may extend upto Rupees one thousand or, with both [Section 30].

(8) Penalty for Closure without Notice [Section 30-A]

Any employer who closes down any undertaking without complying with the provisions of Section 25-FFA of this Act is punishable with imprisonment for a period which may be extended upto six months, or with a fine which may extend upto Rupees five thousand or, with both [Section 30-A].

(9) Penalty for other Offences [Section 31]

Any employer who contravenes the provisions of Section 33 of this Act is punishable with the imprisonment for a period which may extend upto six months or with fine which may extend upto Rupees one thousand or, with both [Section 31(1)].

Any person who contravenes any provisions of this Act or any rule made thereunder is punishable, if not other penalty elsewhere is provided by or under this Act for such contravention, with fine which may extend upto Rupees one hundred [Section 31(2)].

(10) Offences Committed by Companies, Association of Persons, etc.

According to Section 32 of this Act, "Where a person committing an offence under this Act is a company, or other body corporate, or an association of persons (whether incorporated or not), every director, manager, secretary, agent or other officer or person concerned with the management thereof shall, unless he proves that the offence was committed without his knowledge or consent, be deemed to be guilty of such offence."

(11) Cognisance of Offences [Section 34]

(a) No Court shall take cognisance of any offence punishable under this Act or of the abetment of any such offence, save on complaint made by or under the authority of the Appropriate Government [Section 34(1)].

(b) No Court inferior to that of [a Metropolitan Magistrate or a Judicial Magistrate of the First Class] shall try any offence punishable under this Act [Section on 34(2)].

2.6 Provisions under Chapter VII - Miscellaneous

1. Offence by Companies, Associations of Persons [Section 32]

According to Section 32 of this Act, "Where a person committing an offence under this Act is a company, or other body corporate, or an association of persons (whether incorporated or not), every director, manager, secretary, agent or other officer or person concerned with the management thereof shall, unless he proves that the offence was committed without his knowledge or consent, be deemed to be guilty of such offence."

2. Recovery of Money Due from an Employer [Section 33]

(1) Where any money is due to a workman from an employer under a settlement or an award or under the provisions of Chapter V-A or Chapter V-B, the workman himself or any other person authorised by him in writing in this behalf, or, in the case of the death of the workman, his assignee or heirs may, without prejudice to any other mode of recovery, make an application to the appropriate Government for the recovery of the money due to him, and if the appropriate Government is satisfied that any money is so due, it shall issue a certificate for that amount to the Collector who shall proceed to recover the same in the same manner as an arrear of land revenue [Section 33 (1)].

It is provided that every such application shall be made within one year from the date on which the money became due to the workman from the employer [Proviso 1 to Section 33-C (1)].

It is provided further that any such application may be entertained after the expiry of the said period of one year, if the appropriate Government is satisfied that the applicant had sufficient cause for not making the application within the said period [Proviso 2 to Section 33-C (1)].

(2) Where any workman is entitled to receive from the employer any money or any benefit which is capable of being computed in terms of money and if any question arises as to the amount of money due or as to the amount at which such benefit should be computed, then the question may, subject to any rules that may be made under this Act, be decided by such Labour Court as may be specified in this behalf by the appropriate Government within a period not exceeding three months [Section 33-C (2)].

It is also provided that where the presiding officer of a Labour Court considers it necessary or expedient so to do, he may, for reasons to be recorded in writing, extend such period by such further period as he may think fit [Proviso to Section 33-C (2)].

(3) For the purposes of computing the money value of a benefit, the Labour Court may, if it is so thinks fit, appoint a Commissioner who shall, after taking such evidence as may be necessary, submit a report to the Labour Court and the Labour Court shall determine the amount after considering the report of the Commission and other circumstances of the case [Section 33-C (3)].

(4) The decision of the Labour Court shall be forwarded by it to the appropriate Government and any amount found due by the Labour Court may be recovered in the manner provided for in sub-section (1) of Section 33-C [Section 33-C (4)].

(5) Where workmen employed under the same employer are entitled to receive from him any money or any benefit capable of being computed in terms of money, then, subject to such as may be made in this behalf, a single application for the recovery of the amount due may be made on behalf of or in respect of any member of such workmen [Section 33-C (5)]

In this section "Labour Court" includes any Court constituted under any law relating to investigation and settlement of industrial disputes in force in any State [Explanation to Section 33-C].

3. **Cognizance of Offences [Section 34]**
   (1) No Court shall take cognizance of any offence punishable under this Act or of the abetment of any such offence, save on complaint made by or under the authority of the appropriate Government [Section 34 (1)].
   (2) No Court inferior to that of [a Metropolitan Magistrate or a Judicial Magistrate of the first class] shall try any offence punishable under this Act [Section 34 (2)].

4. **Representation of Parties [Section 36]**

Provisions relating to the representation of parties to a dispute have been made in Section 36 of this Act which are as follows:
   (1) A workman who is a party to a dispute shall be entitled to be represented in any proceeding under this Act by –
      (a) Any member of the executive or other office bearer of a registered trade union of which he is a member;

(b) Any member of the executive or other office bearer of a federation of trade unions to which the trade union referred to in clause (a) is affiliated;

(c) Where the worker is not a member of any trade union, by any member of the executive or other office bearer of any trade union connected with, or by any other workman employed in the industry in which the worker is employed and authorised in such manner as may be prescribed [Section 36 (1)].

(2) An employer who is a party to a dispute shall be entitled to be represented in any proceeding under this Act by,

(a) An officer of an association of employers of which he is a member;

(b) An officer of a federation of association of employers to which the association referred to in clause (a) is affiliated;

(c) Where the employer is not a member of any association of employers, by an officer of any association of employers connected with, or by any other employer engaged in, the industry in which the employer is engaged and authorised in such a manner as may be prescribed [Section 36 (2)].

(3) No party to a dispute shall be entitled to be represented by a legal practitioner in any conciliation proceedings under this Act or in any proceedings before a Court [Section 36 (3)].

(4) In any proceeding before a Labour Court, Tribunal or National Tribunal, a party to a dispute may be represented by a legal practitioner with the consent of the other parties to the proceeding and with the leave of the Labour Court, Tribunal or National Tribunal, as the case may be [Section 36 (4)].

5. Protection of Action taken under the Act [Section 37]

No suit, prosecution or other legal proceeding shall lie against any person for anything which is in good faith done or intended to be done pursuance of this Act or any rules made thereunder [Section 37].

6. Power to Make Rules [Section 38]

(1) The appropriate Government may, subject to the condition of previous publication, make rules for the purpose of giving effect to the provisions of this Act [Section 38 (1)]

(2) In particular and without prejudice to the generality of the foregoing power, such rules may provide for all or any of the following matters, namely –

(a) The powers and procedure of conciliation officers, Boards Courts, Labour Courts, Tribunals and National Tribunals including rules as to the summoning of witnesses, the production of documents relevant to the subject-matter of an inquiry or investigation, the number of members necessary to form a quorum and the manner of submission of reports and awards;

(aa) The form of arbitration agreement, the manner in which it may be signed by the parties, the manner in which a notification may be issued under sub-section (3-A) of Section 10-A, the powers of the arbitrator named in the arbitration agreement and the procedure to be followed by him;

(aaa) The appointment of assessors in proceedings under this Act;

(b) The constitution and functions of and the filling of vacancies in Works Committees, and the procedure to be followed by such Committees in the discharge of their duties;

(c) The allowances admissible to members of Courts and Boards and presiding officers of Labour Courts, Tribunals and National Tribunal and to assessors and witnesses;

(d) The ministerial establishment which may be allotted a Court, Board Labour Court, Tribunal or National Tribunal and the salaries and allowances payable to members of such establishment;

(e) The manner in which and the persons by and to whom notice of strike or lockout may be given and the manner in which such notice shall be communicated;

(f) The conditions subject to which parties may be represented by legal practitioners in proceedings under this Act before a Court, Labour Court, Tribunal or National Tribunal;

(g) Any other matter which is to be or may be prescribed [Section 38 (2)].

(3) Rules made under this section may provide that a contravention thereof shall be punishable with fine not exceeding fifty rupees [Section 38 (3)].

(4) All rules made under this section shall, as soon as possible after they are made, be laid before the State Legislature or, where the appropriate Government is the Central Government, before both Houses of Parliament [Section 38 (4)].

(5) Every rule made by the Central Government under this section shall be laid, as soon as may be after it is made, before each House of Parliament while it is in session for a total period of thirty days which may be comprised in one session or in two or more successive sessions, and if before the expiry of the session immediately following the sessions or the successive sessions aforesaid both Houses agree in making any modification in the rule, or both Houses agree that the rule should not be made, the rule shall thereafter have effect only in such modified form or be of no effect, as the case may be; so, however, that any such modification or annulment shall be without prejudice to the validity of anything previously done under that rule [Section 38 (5)].

7. **Provisions Relating to Delegation of Powers [Section 39]**

The appropriate Government may, by notification in the Official Gazette, direct that any power exercisable by it under this Act or rules made thereunder shall, in relation to such matters and subject to such conditions, if any, as may be specified in the direction, be exercisable also –

(a) Where the appropriate Government is the Central Government, by such officer or authority subordinate to the Central Government or by the State Government, or by such officer or authority subordinate to the State Government, as may be specified in the notification; and

(b) Where the appropriate Government is a State Government, by such officer or authority subordinate to the State Government as may be specified in the notification [Section on 39].

[H] Powers of the Appropriate Government to Amend Schedules [Section 40]

(1) The appropriate Government may, if it is of opinion that it is expedient or necessary in the public interest so to do, by notification in the Official Gazette, add to the First Schedule any industry, and on any such notification being issued, the First Schedule shall be deemed to be amended accordingly [Section 40 (1)].

(2) The Central Government may, by notification in the Official Gazette, add to or alter or amend the Second Schedule or the Third Schedule and on any such notification being issued, the Second Schedule or the Third Schedule, as the case may be, shall be deemed to be amended accordingly [Section 40 (2)].

(3) Every such notification shall, as soon as possible after it is issued, be laid before the Legislature of the State, if the notification has been issued by a State Government, or before Parliament, if the notification has been issued by the Central Government [Section 40 (3)].

Exercise

1. Describe the machinery for settlement of Industrial Disputes.
2. Describe the various provisions under Chapter V of Industrial Disputes.
3. Explain the various provisions for Lay-off and Retrenchment under Industrial Disputes Act, 1947.
4. State the various provisions for Penaltie s under Industrial Disputes Act, 1947.
5. Write short notes on:
   (a) Notice of change
   (b) Procedure and Powers of Authorities
   (c) Strikes
   (d) Lock-outs
   (e) Unfair Labour Practices
   (f) Cognizance of Offences
   (g) Power to make Rules

Chapter 3...

Trade Union Act, 1926

Contents ...

Trade Union Act, 1926

- 3.1 Introduction
- 3.2 Objects of the Trade Unions Act, 1926
- 3.3 Section 2: Definitions
- 3.4 Chapter II: Registration of Trade Unions
- 3.5 Chapter III: Rights and Liabilities of a Registered Trade Union
- 3.6 Chapter V: Penalties and Procedures

The Maharashtra Recognition of Trade Unions and Prevention of Unfair Labour Practices Act, 1971

- 3.7 Introduction
- 3.8 Objects of M.R.T.U. and P.U.L.P. Act of 1971
- 3.9 Section 3: Defintions
- 3.10 Chapter II: Authorities Under the Act
- 3.11 Chapter III: Recognition of Unions - Section 14
- 3.12 Chapter IV: Obligation and Rights of Recognised Unions and Other Unions
- 3.13 Chapter V: Illegal Strikes and Lock-outs
- 3.14 Chapter VI: Unfair Labour Practices
- 3.15 Chapter VII: Power of Courts
- 3.16 Chapter VIII: Power of Labour and Industrial Courts to Try Offences under this Act
- 3.17 Chapter X: Miscellaneous
- Exercise

Trade Union Act, 1926

3.1 Introduction

The term 'Trade Union' is commonly used to refer to that body or organisation of workers, which is formed not only to protect their rights but also to enhance their welfare.

According to India's former President, Late Shri V. V. Giri, "Trade Unions are voluntary organisations of workers formed to promote and protect their interests by collective action." A trade union must have definite aims, its members must be welded together as a unified front for the good of the whole class of workers. Trade Unions have a definite role to play in countries like India where workers are not yet properly organised. But up to the end of the First World War, there was no beginning of trade union movement in the real sense; though the first important step towards organising labour was taken by Mr. Lokhande, who was a factory worker in Bombay. He laid the foundation in 1890, the first organisation of workers, viz., the Bombay Mill Hands' Association.

The First World War was responsible for a mass awakening in the sense that, situations like discrimination against Indian Workers, the growth of Indian National Movement, the revolution in Russia were some of the concurrent and yet colluding factors happening across the global landscape being responsible for giving a fillip to Indian Labour Movement.

The Indian Trade Union Act, which was passed in 1926, is a landmark in the history of trade union movement in India. This Act gave the Trade Unions legal status and immunity to its officers and members from civil and criminal liability for concerted actions. Subsequently, by Amendment 38 of Act, 1964, the word 'Indian' was deleted. The said Act has been amended many times to suit the circumstances since its enforcement.

In 1937, under provincial autonomy, the registered Trade Unions were given special representation in the provincial legislatures which further encouraged the registration of Trade Unions. Then, immediately after the Independence, the Trade Union Amendment Act, l947, was passed which provided for the compulsory recognition of the Trade Unions by employers under the orders of a Labour Court. A new Trade Union Bill was introduced in May 1982 which aimed at reducing the multiplicity of unions. The Government introduced the Trade Union Bill on 13th May, 1988, to replace the earlier legislation. The Bill suggested comprehensive amendments in the Trade Union Act. Presently, the said Act requires a trade union to be registered within sixty days of the receipt of the application. Thus, the registration of the Trade Unions has become time-bound. Besides this, it is also provided for a statutorily recognised collective bargaining agent for a unit or for an industry and the term of such an agent is fixed for three years. Thus, by amending the Act from time to time, the efforts have been made to safeguard the interests of the workers.

3.2 Objects of the Trade Unions Act, 1926

The object of this Act is made clear in the preamble which states that it is to provide for the registration of trade unions and, in certain respects, to define the law relating to registered trade unions.

Thus, this Act besides aiming to make provisions for the registration of trade unions; goes further to mention the various objects on which general funds of a trade union can be spent. It also provides for the constitution of a separate fund for political purposes. Further, this Act confers certain rights on registered trade unions and makes clear their liabilities.

That apart, it also provides for the protection of the members and officers of registered trade unions from various civil and criminal liabilities which may be incurred while promoting and safeguarding their legitimate interests.

This Act is intended to promote cordial relations between employers and their employees or workmen to facilitate the peaceful settlement of disputes between them by means of adjudication or arbitration [New Gujarat Cotton Mills vs. L.A.T. - AIR - 195 Bombay - 111].

In a sentence, it can be said that this Act has been passed to make provisions for the registration and regulation of trade unions for furthering the interests of the common workmen.

3.3 Section 2: Definitions

In the Trade Union Act which came into force from 1st June, 1927, and extends to the whole of India, the definitions of certain words, concepts and expressions are given in Section 2 which is as follows:

1. **Appropriate Government [Section 2]**

   In this Act, the Appropriate Government means in relation to trade unions whose objects are not confined to one state, the Central Government and, in relation to other Trade Unions, the State Government.

   Thus, if the jurisdiction of a Trade Union is any particular state, then, in that case, the State Government concerned is the Appropriate Government and if the objects of a trade union are not confined to any one State, then, the Central Government, in that case is the Appropriate Government.

2. **Executive [2(a)]**

   'Executive' means the body by whatever name called to which the management of affairs of a trade union is entrusted.

3. **Office Bearer [2(b)]**

   'Office bearer' in the case of a Trade Union includes any member of the executive thereof but does not include an auditor.

4. **Prescribed [2(c)]**

   "Prescribed' means prescribed by regulations made under this Act.

5. **Registered Office [2(d)]**

   'Registered Office' means office of a Trade Union, which is registered under this Act as the Head Office thereof:

6. **Registered Trade Union [2(e)]**

   Registered Trade Union means a Trade Union registered under this Act.

7. **Registrar [2(f)]**

   'Registrar' means:

   1. A Registrar of Trade Union is appointed by the Appropriate Government under Section 3 and includes an additional or Deputy Registrar of Trade Unions and

2. In relation to any Trade Union, the Registrar appointed for the State in which the head or registered office, as the case may be, of the situated Trade Union.

8. Trade Dispute and Workmen [2(g)]

'Trade dispute' means any dispute between employers and workmen, or between workmen and workmen or between employers and employers which is connected with the employment or non-employment or the terms of employment or the conditions of labour of any persons, and 'workmen' means all persons employed in trade or industry whether or not in the employment of the employer with whom the trade dispute arises.

For any trade dispute, there must be demand made by one of the parties and refusal to accept the same by the other party and so far as this Act is concerned, such trade disputes include any dispute between:

(a) Employers and employers; or
(b) Employers and workmen; or
(c) Workmen and workmen; and such disputes may be connected with
   (i) The employment or non-employment; or
   (ii) The terms of employment; or
   (iii) Conditions of labour of any person.

Section 2(g) of this Act also defines the word 'workmen' and, accordingly, the definition of workmen includes any employee:

(i) Employed in any trade or industry, or
(ii) Dismissed, discharged removed or retrenched.

This Act does not make any distinction between skilled and unskilled workmen; or clerical employees or officers; the only requirement being that the person concerned must be employed in some industry or trade.

Here, it must be remembered that the Trade Union Act is not in *Pari Materia* with the Industrial Disputes Act, 1948, and so the definition of an 'industry' as given in it has no application to the former Act. [Rangaswami vs. Registrar of Trade Unions - AR 1962 - Madras - 321]

9. Trade Union [2(h)]

'Trade Union' means any combination, whether temporary or permanent, formed primarily for the purpose of regulating the relations between workmen and employers or between workmen and workmen; or between employers and employers; or for imposing restrictive conditions on the conduct of any trade or business, and includes any federation of two or more trade unions.

Provided that this Act shall not affect -

(i) Any agreement between partners as to their own business.

(ii) Any agreement between any employer and those employed by him as to such employment; or

(iii) Any agreement in consideration of the sale of goodwill of a business or of instruction in any profession trade or handicraft.

From this definition of a 'trade union', we come to know that:

(a) A Trade Union is any combination.
(b) Such combination can be formed by -
   (i) Employers and employers; or
   (ii) workmen and workmen; or
   (iii) Employers and workmen.
(c) The purposes of forming such combination are to regulate the relations between such persons who form the combination.
(d) Such combination can either be temporary or permanent.
(e) A Trade Union is formed for imposing certain restrictive conditions on the conduct of any trade or business.
(f) A Trade Union may include any federation of two or more trade unions.
(g) The Trade Union Act does not affect any agreement :
   (i) Between partners as to their own business,
   (ii) Between employer and employees regarding their employment, and
   (iii) Which is in consideration of sale of goodwill of a business or of instruction in any profession Trade or handicraft.

In ordinary parlance, trade union means an association of workmen formed to protect their own interest. But the expression 'trade union' includes both workers' and employers' organisations. The intention in covering organisations of employers under this Act is to put both the workers and employers' organisations on par in matters of rights and responsibilities.

3.4 Chapter II: Registration of Trade Unions

It has not been made compulsory under this Act that every trade union must be registered. Unregistered trade unions are not illegal. There are many unions which are not registered under this Act and have remained outside the purview of the provisions of this Act. But the registered Trade Unions get certain benefits because of their registration, which are as follows:

1. Upon registration, a trade union becomes a corporate body by the name under which it is registered. It gets the legal entity which is distinct from its members. It can acquire and hold all types of properties, enter into contracts with the third party, can sue and be sued.

2. The Office bearers and members of a registered trade union are given protection against criminal proceedings for conspiracy in respect of any agreement entered into between the members for furthering such objects of the trade union on which it funds can be spent.

3. No suit is maintainable in any civil court against a registered trade union or its office bearers or members in respect of any act done in contemplation or furtherance of any trade dispute to which a member of trade union is a party on the ground that such act induces some person to break any contract of employment or causes interference with the business or trade of any employer. Such protection is given to trade unions because many times, the activities of trade unions cause interference with the business or trade of the employers and if no such protection is given to the trade unions, the trade unions would be liable for damages under the general law.

4. It is expressly provided for in this Act that any agreement between the members of a registered trade union shall be valid and not void and voidable.

Thus, from the above discussion, it becomes clear that the registered trade unions enjoy certain advantages. Though the unregistered trade unions are not illegal but they run the risk of being held illegal. They do not possess corporate existence neither legal entity nor are they quasi corporations.

In this Act, the procedure has been laid down for registering a trade union. Now, let us study the various provisions related to the registration of a trade union.

(1) Appointment of Registrars [Section 3]

Various provisions have been made in Section 3 of this Act to appoint Registrar, Deputy Registrar and Additional Registrar. It is as follows:

Section 3(1): The Appropriate Government shall appoint a person to be the registrar of the trade unions for each state.

Section 3(2): The Appropriate Government may appoint as many Additional and Deputy Registrars of Trade Unions as it thinks fit for the purpose of the exercising and discharging, under the superintendence and direction of the Registrar, such powers and functions of the Registrar under this Act as it may by order specify and define the local limits within which any such Additional or Deputy Registrar shall exercise and discharge the powers and functions so specified.

Section 3(3): Subject to the provisions of any order under sub-section 3(2), where an Additional or Deputy Registrar exercises and discharges the powers and functions of a Registrar in an area within which the registered office of a trade union is situated, the Additional or Deputy Registrar shall be deemed to be the Registrar in relation to the trade union for the purposes of this Act.

Here, Registrar means a Registrar of Trade Unions appointed by the Appropriate Government under Section 3 and includes Deputy or Additional Registrar of Trade Union and in relation to any trade union, the Registrar appointed for the State in which the head or registered office of the trade union is situated [Section 2(f)].

Certain powers are given to the registrar, for example, he may call for necessary particulars in respect to the registration of the given trade union. If he is satisfied that the requirements in this Act have been complied with, the Registrar has to register such trade union. He may refuse to register the trade union until he gets necessary information. He has also the powers to ask to change the name of the trade union or he may cancel the registration of trade unions, if there are sufficient reasons to do so.

When there are any disputes between two rival factions, i.e., self-interested parties which claim to be the office bearers of a trade union, the Registrar has the powers to hold an enquiry for giving proper decision for the matters mentioned in Section 8. However, his decision in this respect, shall be to either confer any right on one person, or, a group of persons, as the case may be, nor deprive any person or a group of persons of any legal rights.

The Registrar has no powers to issue any directive or to give any direction to the Labour Department of the Government or the employer to recognise and treat any person or a group of persons as the duly elected office-bearers of the union in dealing with the union. The Registrar of Trade unions cannot direct, or has no power to direct the holding of election of the office bearers of a trade union under his own supervision or under any person nominated by him. In the absence of any provision made in the Trade Union Act, 1926, if any dispute of this kind arises, it can only be resolved by filing a suit before a Civil Court. [Bokaro Steel Workers Union vs. State of Bihar [1995 – II C.L.R. 723 (Pat – D.B.)] In Ratan Kumar Dey and Ors vs. Union of India and Ors case [1991 – II – C.L.R. 159 (Gan H.C)], it was held that the Registrar of Trade Unions has no power to decide a dispute between rival bearers of trade union under Section 28.

(2) Mode of Registration [Section 4]

Any seven or more members of a Trade Union may, subscribing their names to the rules of Trade Union and by otherwise complying with the provisions of this Act with respect to registration, apply for registration of the Trade Union under this Act [Section 4(1)] And where an application has been made under this sub-section (1) of Section 4 for the registration of a Trade Union, such application shall not be deemed to have become invalid merely by reason of the fact that, at any time after the date of application, but before the registration of the trade union, some of the applicants, but not exceeding half of the total number of persons who made the application, have ceased to be members of the Trade Union or have given notice in writing to the Registrar disassociating themselves from the application [Section 4(2)].

(3) Application for Registration of a Trade Union [Section 5]

An application for registering a Trade Union is made to the Registrar of Trade Unions and it must be accompanied by (1) a copy of its rules, and (2) a statement of the following particulars, namely - (a) the names, occupations and addresses of members making such application for the registration of the Trade Union, (b) the name of the Trade Union and the address of its head office, and (c) the titles, names, ages, addresses, occupations of the officers of the Trade Union [Section 5(1)].

And where a Trade Union has been in existence for more than one year before the making of an application for its registration, a general statement of assets and liabilities of such trade union prepared in the prescribed form and with other necessary information as required, must be submitted to the Registrar, together with the application of registration [Section 5(2)].

(4) Rules of Trade Union [Section 6]

Section 6 of this Act states the provisions to be continued in the rules of a Trade Union. A trade union cannot be registered under this Act unless the executive thereof is constituted in accordance with the provisions of this Act and the rules thereof provide for the following matters namely:

(a) The name of a Trade Union.

(b) The whole of the objects of the Trade Union for which it is established.

(c) The whole of the purposes for which the general funds of a Trade Union are lawfully applicable under this Act.

(d) The maintenance of a list of the members of the Trade Union and adequate facilities for the inspection thereof by the office bearers and members of the Trade Union.

(e) The admission of ordinary members who shall be persons actually engaged or employed in an industry with which the Trade Union is connected, and also the admission of the honorary or temporary members as office bearers required under Section 22 to form the executive of the Trade Union.

(f) The payment of a subscription by members of the Trade Union which shall not be less than Twenty-Five Naye Paise per month per member.

(g) The conditions under which any member shall be entitled to any benefit assured by the rules and under which any fine or forefeiture may be imposed on the members.

(h) The manner in which the rules shall be amended, varied or rescinded (repealed or cancelled).

(i) The manner in which the members of the executive and other office-bearers of the Trade Union shall be appointed, reappointed and removed.

(j) The safety custody of the funds of the Trade Union, and annual audit in the prescribed manner, of the accounts thereof, and adequate facilities for the inspection of the account books by the office-bearer and members of the Trade Union.

(k) The manner in which the Trade Union may be dissolved.

(5) Registration [Section 8]

Section 8 of this Act states that the Registrar, on being satisfied that the Trade Union concerned has complied with all the requirements of this Act regarding the registration of the Trade Union, shall register the Trade Union by making a proper entry in the register maintained for this purpose in such form as may be prescribed, particulars relating to the Trade Union contained in the statement accompanying the application for registration.

The register of Trade Union, referred to in Section 8 above is maintained in 'Form B', is as follows :

FORM B

Name of Trade Union Registration Number	Date of Registration Number of application form		Remarks :	
Subsequent change of the address of the Head Office.			Names of Members making application	
1. 2. 3. 4. 5. 6. 7. 8.			1. 2. 3. 4. 5. 6. 7. 8.	
Officers (Transfers from one post to another count as relinquishment of appointment held.)				
Year of entering in office — Name — Office held in Union — Age on entry — Address — Occupation — Year of relinquishing Office — Other Offices held in addition to membership of executive with dates				

Thus, if all the conditions of this Act are fulfilled and all necessary provisions are complied with, it is obligatory upon the Registrar of the Trade Union to register a Trade Union. He has no discretionary powers in this regard.

(6) Issue of the Certificate of Registration [Section 9]

The Registrar, after registering a Trade Union under Section 8 has to issue a certificate of registration in the prescribed form to serve as the conclusive evidence that a Trade Union is duly registered under this Act [Section 9].

Once a Trade Union is registered, it acquires the following characteristics:

(a) It becomes a body corporate by that name under which it is registered.

(b) It becomes a legal entity distinct from its members.

(c) It has a common seal.

(d) It has a perpetual succession.

(e) It enjoys the powers to acquire and hold the property, movable as well as immovable.

(f) It gets the powers to enter into contracts.

(g) It can sue and can be sued in its own name.

The procedure of registering any Trade Union can be summarised in the following ways:

(a) Any seven or more members of a Trade Union can apply for the registration of the Trade Union.

(b) Such application is required to be made to the Registrar of the Trade Unions.

(c) Necessary information according to Section 5 of this Act is required to be given in the application.

(d) Every application of the registration is required to be accompanied with a copy of the rules of Trade Union as such rules must provide for various matters as specified in Section 6 of the Act.

(e) If the Trade Union is in existence for more than a year before the application for the registration is made, the application must be submitted to the Registrar of Trade Unions along with a general statement of its assets and liabilities in the prescribed form and other necessary particulars.

(f) After receiving an application with necessary information, if the Registrar is satisfied, he registers the name of the given Trade Union in the register maintained for that purpose and issues a Certificate of Registration.

(g) If all the terms of the Act are complied with, the Registrar has to register a Trade Union and issue the certificate of Registration which is the conclusive evidence of the Trade Union's registration.

The certificate of registration issued by the Registrar under Section 9 is in 'Form C', is as follows:

FORM C

Trade Unions Act, 1926

Certificate of Registration of Trade Unions

Name of Trade Union –

Registration Number

        Office of the Registrar of Trade Unions :

        Bombay.

It is hereby certified that the

        Union has been registered under the Trade Unions Act, 1926, this day of 19..

        Registrar of Trade Unions,

        Maharashtra State, Bombay

Seal

(7) Cancellation of Registration [Section 10]

Section 10 of this Act provides for the cancellation of Registration. It states that a certificate of registration can be withdrawn or cancelled by the Registrar of Trade Unions.

(a) On the application of the Trade Union to be verified in such a manner as may be prescribed or

(b) If the Registrar is satisfied that –
   (i) The Certificate has been obtained by fraud; or
   (ii) It is issued by mistake; or
   (iii) The Trade Union has ceased to exist; or
   (iv) The Trade Union has wilfully and after notice from the Registrar contravened any provision of the Act, or
   (v) It has allowed any rule to continue in force which is inconsistent with any such provision; or
   (vi) The Trade Union has rescinded any rule providing for any matter; provision for which is required by Section 6.

It is also provided in this section that if the cancellation is to be effected on account of clause (b) above, not less than two months prior notice in writing specifying the ground on which it is proposed to withdraw or cancel the certificate must be given by the Registrar to the Trade Union concerned before the certificate of registration is withdrawn or cancelled. [Proviso to Section 10].

Every application by a Trade Union for withdrawal or cancellation of its certificate of registration is required to be sent to the Registrar in Form 'D' which is as follows:

FORM 'D'
Trade Unions Act, 1926
Request to withdraw or cancel Certificate of Registration.

Name, of Trade Union –
Registration Number
(Address) :
Dated this .... day of 20

To
   The Registrar of Trade Unions,
   Mumbai, Maharashtra State.

The above mentioned Trade Union desires that its certificate of registration under the Trade Unions Act, 1926, may be withdrawn (or cancelled) and at a general meeting* duly held on the day of 19 it was resolved as follows :

(Here give exact copy of Resolution)

(Signed)

---

* If not at a general meeting, state in what manner the request has been determined upon.

The Registrar, on receiving an application for withdrawal or cancellation of registration and before granting such application, has to verify whether the application was properly approved in the general meeting of the Trade Union or, if it was not thus approved, that it has the approval of a majority of members of the trade union. For this purpose, the Registrar may call for such further particulars as he may deem necessary and he may examine any office at the trade union. The Registrar of Trade Unions has jurisdiction to cancel registration on being satisfied from legal points of view. It should be noted that a person who ceased to be a member at a Registered Trade Union has no *locus standi* to seek cancellation of registration of the trade union. [D. Munirathnam vs. Additional Registrar of Trade Union – I. – Madras – 6 – 1997 I L.L.J. 509 (Madras H. C.]

3.5 Chapter III: Rights and Liabilities of a Registered Trade Union

The following are the rights and privileges of a registered Trade Union and its members.

1. Incorporation [Section 13].
2. Separate fund for political purposes [Section 16].
3. Immunity from punishment for criminal conspiracy [Section 17].
4. Certain acts not to apply [Section 14].
5. Immunity from civil suits in certain cases [Section 18].
6. No Liability in respect of tortuous Act [Section 18(2)].
7. Enforceability of agreements [Section 19].
8. Right to inspect books of trade union [Section 20].
9. Right of minors to be members [Section 21].
10. Right to change its name [Sections 23, 25 and 26].
11. Right of amalgamation of unions [Sections 24].

Now, let us discuss each of the above mentioned rights and privileges of a Trade Union.

1. Incorporation

Once a Trade Union is registered, it becomes a body corporate by that name under which it is registered. Thereafter, it enjoys perpetual succession and common seal with power to acquire and hold property. As a logical corollary, it becomes empowered to enter into contract in its own name. A Registered Trade Union thus can sue and be sued in its registered name [Section 13]. Thus, thanks to registration, the registered Trade Unions enjoy certain rights and privileges.

2. Separate fund for political purposes

A registered Trade Union has a right to constitute a separate fund, from the contributions separately levied for or made to that fund. The payments can be made from such fund for the promotion of the civic and political interests of its members. The fund can be utilised for achieving the objectives specified in sub-section 2 of Section 16 [Section 16(1)].

However, no member is compelled to contribute to the fund constituted under Section 16(1). A member who does not contribute to the said fund is not excluded from any of the benefits of Trade Union. Contribution to the said fund is not a pre-condition for admission to the Trade Union [Section 16(3)].

3. Immunity from punishment for criminal conspiracy

Section 17 of the Trade Unions Act, 1926, clearly states that no office bearer or any registered Trade Union is liable to punishment under sub-section (2) of Section 120-B of the Indian Penal Code, in respect of any agreement made between the members for the purpose of furthering any such object of the Trade Union as is specified in Section 15 of this Act unless the agreement is an agreement to commit an offence or crime.

Thus, any agreement entered into for committing an offence or crime makes the members of the Trade Union liable for criminal conspiracy. In one case, where a strike was accompanied by violence, intimidation, threat, assault etc., this exemption was not available to the members of the Trade Union concerned. A union leader is not entitled to claim immunity from punishment for any breach of discipline.

4. Certain Acts not to apply

It is already mentioned elsewhere in this chapter that certain Acts, namely, The Societies Registration Act, 1860; the Co-operative Societies Act, 1912; and the Companies Act, 1956, are not applicable to any registered trade unions. If the registration is done under any of these Acts, then, it would be void [Section 14].

5. Immunity from civil suits in certain cases

According to sub-section (1) Section 18 of this Act, no suit or any other legal proceeding shall be maintainable in any Civil Court against any registered Trade Union or its office-bearers or members of any Registered Trade Union in respect of any act done in contemplation or furtherance of a trade dispute to which a member of a Trade Union is a party on the ground only that such act induces some other person or persons to break a contract of employment, or that it is in interference with the trade, business or employment of some other person to dispose off his capital or of his labour, as he wills.

6. No liability in respect of act of torts

Section 18(2) says that a registered Trade Union shall not be liable in any suit or other legal proceeding in any Civil Court in respect of any act of torts done in contemplation or furtherance of a trade dispute by an agent of the Trade Union if it is proved that such person acted without the knowledge of, or contrary to express instructions given by the executive of the Trade Union.

This Section 18 grants certain protection to the members office-bearers of a Trade Union in respect of Civil suits in certain cases and of tortious act, but does not afford immunity to any trade union or its members or office-bearers for any act of deliberate trespass. The Trade Unions have rights to pursue their obligation by means of a strike, so long as it does not indulge in acts unlawful and tortious acts. Even the court concerned cannot prevent or interfere with the legitimate rights of the workers.

The conduct of workers in blocking the passage of men and materials of the plaintiff company was not justified in one case only because of the right of the trade union or a fundamental right under the Article 19 of the Constitution of India. [Simpson and Group Companies Workers and Staff Union vs. Amco Batteries Ltd. 1990 II CLR 832 (Kam H.C.)] Protection under Section 18 of the Trade Union Act, 1926, to the workers does not get enlarged or constricted depending upon the situation of strike or lockout. The consideration and principles are obviously ought to be one and the same for both the situations.

7. Enforceability of agreements

The provision in respect of enforceability of agreements has been made in Section 19 of this Act as follows:

"Notwithstanding anything contained in any other law for time being in force, an agreement between the members of a registered trade union shall not be void or voidable merely by reason of the fact that any of the objects of the agreement are in restraint of trade."

It is further provided that nothing in Section 19 shall enable any of the Civil Courts to entertain any legal proceeding instituted for the express purpose of enforcing or recovering damages for the breach of any agreement concerning the conditions on which any members of a Trade Union shall or shall not sell their goods, transact business, work, employ or be employed.

8. Right to inspect books of trade union

Section 20 of this Act provides for the inspection of books of Trade Union by the office-bearers or members of such Trade Union. Section 20 says that the account books of a registered trade union and the list of its members shall be open for inspection by any office-bearer or member of the Trade Union at such time as may be provided for in the rules of the Trade Union. The object of conferring this right is that the office-bearers and members of Trade Union should be satisfied as to the genuineness of members and of the accounts of the Trade Union.

9. Right of minors to become members

Subject to any rule of the Trade Union to contrary, any one who has completed his fifteen years of age may become a member of a registered trade union and such person may enjoy all the rights and privileges of such membership [Section 21].

10. Right to change the name

Any registered Trade Union has the right to change its name, if:

(a) Two-thirds of the total number of its member give consent to such change of name; [Section 23] and (b) the proposed new name is not identical with that of any other registered Trade Union in existence and in the opinion of the Registrar of Trade Unions, it does not resemble any such name so nearly as to be likely to deceive the public in general and members and office-bearers of either union. Such change in name of the Trade Union must be informed to the Registrar by sending him the notice in writing, signed by the secretary and any seven members of the Trade Union. The Registrar records the change in name of the Trade Union in the registrar if he is satisfied that the provisions of the Act have been complied with properly and such change in name takes effect from the date of registration [Section 25(2) and (3)].

However, the change in the name does not affect any right or obligation of the Trade Union or render defective any legal proceeding by or against such Trade Union. The change in the name does not even affect any legal proceeding which might have been continued or commenced by or against it by its former name may be continued or commenced by or against it by its new name [Section 26(1)].

11. Right of amalgamation of Trade Unions

The registered Trade Unions have got the right under this Act to become amalgamated together as one Trade Union. Section 24 of the Act states that any two or more registered Trade Unions may become amalgamated together as one Trade Union with or without dissolution or division of funds of such Trade Unions or either or any of them, provided that the votes of at least one-half of the members of each or every such Trade Union entitled to vote are recorded and that at least sixty percent of the votes recorded are in favour of the proposal.

Duties and Liabilities of a Registered Trade Union

The Trade Union Act, 1926, imposes certain duties and liabilities on registered trade unions, which are as follows:

1. Change in the address of registered office of a Trade Union: It is the duty of a registered trade union to inform any change in the address of its head office by giving the notice of such change to the Registrar of Trade Unions in writing within fourteen days of such change [Section 12]. Thereafter, such change in the address of the registered office is recorded by the Registrar.

2. Duties relating to the spending of general funds of a registered Trade Union: Section 15 provides that the general funds of a registered trade union shall not spend on any other objects than the following:

(a) The payment of salaries, allowances and expenses to office bearers of the Trade Union;

(b) The payments of expenses for the administration of the Trade Union, including audit of the accounts of the general funds of the Trade Union;

(c) The prosecution or defence of any legal proceeding to which the Trade Union or any member thereof if a party, when such prosecution or defence is undertaken for the purpose of securing or protecting any rights of the Trade Union as such or any rights arising out of the relations of any member with his employer or with a person whom the member employs;

(d) The conduct of trade dispute on behalf of the Trade Union or any member thereof;

(e) The compensation of members for loss arising out of trade disputes;

(f) Allowances to members or their dependents on account of death, old age, sickness, accidents or unemployment of such members;

(g) The issue of, or the undertaking of liability under, policies of assurance on the lives of members, or under policies insuring members against sickness, accident or unemployment;
(h) The provision of educational, social or religious benefit for members (including the payment of the expenses of funeral or religious ceremonies for deceased members) or for the dependants of members;
(i) The upkeep of a periodical published mainly for the purpose of discussing questions affecting employer's workmen as such;
(j) The payment in furtherance of any of the objects on which the general funds of the Trade Union may be spent, of contributions to any cause intended to benefit workmen in general, provided that the expenditure in respect of such contributions in any financial year shall not at any time during that year be in excess of one-fourth of the combined total of the gross income which has up to that time accrued to the general funds of the Trade Union during that year and of the balance at the credit of those funds at the commencement of that year; and
(k) Subject to any conditions contained in the notification any other object notified by the Appropriate Government in the Official Gazette.

Thus, it is the duty and responsibility of a registered trade union to spend its general funds strictly according to the provisions made in Section 15. If such funds are spent on any other objects other than enumerated in Section 15 of the Act, the expenditure incurred is considered unlawful and *ultra vires* the Act. If any trade union does so, it can be restrained by injunction from applying its general funds for any such object.

3. The duty and responsibility of spending of the fund constituted for political purposes: Under Section 16(1), a registered trade union may constitute a separate fund, from contribution separately levied for or made, to that fund, from which payments may be made for the promotion of the civic and political interest of its members in furtherance of any of the objects specified in Section 16(2). The objects of using political funds mentioned in Section 16(2) are as follows:

(a) The payment of any expenses incurred either directly or indirectly, by a candidate or prospective candidate for election to a legislative body under the Constitution or to a local body. Such expenses might have been incurred before, after or during the election. or
(b) The holding of any meeting or the distribution of any literature or documents in support of such a candidate or prospective or a candidate.
(c) The maintenance of a person who is a member of a legislative body under the Constitution or of any local authority. or
(d) The registration of electors or the selection of a candidate for election to a legislative body under the Constitution or any local authority, or
(e) The holding of political meeting of any kind or the distribution of political literature or political documents of any kind.

Thus, it is the duty and the responsibility of a registered trade union to use the political fund for the above objects. In no case, expenditure for political purposes is allowed out of

the general funds and even interest on investments of general funds must be credited to the general fund only. Moreover, while creating political fund, a registered trade union has to follow conditions, according to the provisions of Section 16 as mentioned below:
  (a) Such fund can be created only from contributions separately levied or made to that fund [Section 16(1)].
  (b) Members must be compelled to contribute to the fund.
  (c) A member who does not contribute to the fund must not be excluded from any benefits of the Trade Union or even placed under any kind of disadvantage, disability etc., indirectly or directly.
  (d) Contribution to the political fund must not be made a condition for admission to the Trade Union [Section 16(3)].

4. Proportion of officers to be connected with the industry: Not less than one-half of the total number of the office bearers of every registered Trade Union shall be persons actually engaged or employed in an industry with which the Trade Union is connected [Section 22].

It is also provided that "the Appropriate Government may by special or general order, declare that the provisions of this section shall not apply to any Trade Union or class of Trade Unions as specified in the order" [Provision to Section 22].

The provisions of Section 22 imply that fifty per cent of the office bearers of a registered trade union may be social or political workers. It is also provided in the section that the Appropriate Government can exempt any trade union from the application of these provisions by special or general order. But it is the responsibility of every registered trade union to consider the provisions of this Section 22 while carrying out its functions.

5. Duty and responsibility of a registered trade union relating to returns: The provisions relating to returns have been made in Section 28 as follows:

There shall be sent annually to the Registrar, on or before such date as may be prescribed, a general statement audited in the prescribed manner, of all receipts and expenditure of every registered Trade Union during the year ending on the 31st day of December next preceding such prescribed date, and of the assets and liabilities of the Trade Union existing on such 31st day of December. The statement shall be prepared in such form and shall comprise such particulars as may be prescribed [Section 28(1)].

Together with the general statement there shall be sent to the Registrar a statement showing all changes of office bearers made by the Trade Union during the year to which the general statement refers, together also with copy of the rules of the Trade Union corrected up to the date of the despatch thereof to the Registrar [Section 28(2)].

A copy of every alteration made in the rules of a registered Trade Union shall be sent to the Registrar within fifteen days of the making of the alternation [Section 28(3)].

For the purpose of examining the documents referred to in sub-sections (1), (2) and (3), the Registrar, or any officer authorised by him, by general or special order, may at all reasonable times inspect the certificate of registration, account books, registers and other documents, relating to Trade Union, at its registered office or may require their production at such place as he may specify in this behalf, but such place shall be at a distance of more than ten miles from the registered office of a Trade Union [Section 28(4)].

Every registered trade union has to comply with the provisions of Section 28.

6. Responsibility of a registered trade union not to appoint office-bearers who are disqualified: Provision relating to disqualification of office bearers of a trade union has been made in Section 21-A. By taking into consideration these provisions, persons who are disqualified should not be appointed as office bearers of trade union.

A person shall be disqualified for being, chosen as and for being a member of the executive or any other office bearer of a registered Trade Union, if –
(a) he has not attained the age of eighteen years;
(b) he has been convicted by a Court in India of any offence involving moral turpitude and sentenced to imprisonment, unless a period of five years has elapsed since his Release [Section 21-A(1)].

Any member of the executive or other office bearer of a registered Trade Union who, before the commencement of the Trade Unions (Amendment) Act, 1964, has been convicted of any offence involving moral turpitude and sentenced to imprisonment, shall on the date of such commencement cease to be such member or office bearer unless a period of five years has elapsed since his release before that date [Section 21-A(2)].

7. Duty and responsibility relating to audit of accounts: The accounts of a registered trade union must be audited annually by an auditor authorised under the Companies Act, 1956. Thus, it is necessary for every trade union to get its accounts duly audited as per rules.

3.6 Chapter V: Penalties and Procedure

Provisions have been made in Sections 31 and 32 for imposing penalties for failure of submitting returns and for supplying false information regarding trade unions. These sections are reproduced below:

1. Failure to submit returns

(a) If default is made on the part of any registered Trade Union in giving any notice or sending any statement or other document as required by or under any provision of this Act, every office bearer or other person bound by the rules of the Trade Union to give or send the same, or, if there is no such office bearer or person, every member of the executive of the Trade Union, shall be punishable with fine which may extend to five rupees and, in the case of a continuing default, with an additional fine which may extend to five rupees for each week after the first during which the default continues [Section 31 (1)].

Provided that the aggregate fine shall not exceed fifty rupees [Proviso to Section 31 (1)].

(b) Any person who wilfully makes, or causes to be made, any false entry in, or any omission from, the general statement required by Section 28, or in or from any copy of rules or alternations of rules sent to the Registrar under that section, shall be punishable with fine which may extend to five hundred rupees [Section 31 (2)].

2. **Supplying false information regarding Trade Union:** Any person who, with intent to deceive, gives to any member of a registered Trade Union or to any person intending or applying to become a member of such Trade Union, any document purporting to be a copy of the rules of the Trade Union or of any alterations to the same which he knows, or has reason to believe, is not a correct copy of such rules or alterations as are for the time being, in force, or any person who, with the like intent, gives a copy of any rules of an unregistered Trade Union to any person on the pretense that such rules are the rules of a registered Trade Union, shall be punishable with fine which may extend to two hundred rupees [Section 32].

The Maharashtra Recognition of Trade Unions and Prevention of Unfair Labour Practices Act, 1971

3.7 Introduction

One of the major and important pre-requisites for industrial progress is the prevalence of industrial peace i.e. a suitable climate in which the industries can thrive. Industrial peace broadly implies the absence of industrial unrest, labour problems or the existence of a harmonious cordial relationship or co-operation between workers and their employers. But the problem of industrial peace is common to almost all the industrially developed and developing countries of the world and ever since industrialisation began, every country is making various efforts to find out solutions for establishing industrial peace. However, the methods and ways used in solving the problem of industrial peace or industrial unrest differ from country to country depending upon its economic, social and political environment in existence. Still the problem has not been solved completely. On the contrary, with the advent of the industrial development, labour problems are becoming more and more complicated.

In India, the magnitude of labour problems has increased with the tempo of industrial activities and with industrial development. Problems of wages, strikes and lock-outs, industrial housing, unemployment, trade unions etc. confront the Government as well as social reformers. These labour problems apart from their economic impact, also have social and other repercussions. The welfare of the working class in industrial sector is important both to the industries as well as to the community at large. The Government concern for the welfare of the industrial workers in our country is evident from the fact that a large number of legislative enactments in this field have been passed or improved upon after 1947. Several labour enactments have been promulagated by the central as well as State Governments to safeguard the interests of the industrial workers. Payment of Wages Act, Minimum Wages Act, Industrial Disputes Act, Factories Act, Trade Unions Act, Workmen's Compensation Act, Payment of Bonus Act are some of such Acts.

So far as the Maharashtra State is concerned, previously, the Bombay Industrial Disputes Act, 1938 was passed. The provisions of this Act were availed extensively by the employers as well as the employees in the textile industry. But, with the passage of time and on the strength of the experience gained after passing the Bombay Industrial Disputes Act of 1938, the Government felt it necessary to build further on the same foundations and hence 'The Bombay Industrial Relations Act of 1946' was passed. That Act also was found to be ineffective to deal fully with the growing problems of the industrial workers and hence 'The Maharashtra Recognition of Trade Unions and Prevention of Unfair Labour Practices Act of 1971 was passed to deal with the problems of trade unions and also to provide for the recognition of trade unions for facilitating collective bargaining for certain undertakings, to make clear their rights and obligations, to confer certain powers on unrecognised unions, to provide for declaring certain strikes and lock-outs as illegal strikes and lock-outs, to define properly certain unfair labour practices and to provide for their prevention, to constitute certain courts as independent machinery for carrying out the purposes of the Act etc. The importance of this M.R.T.U. and P.U.L.P. Act is eminent from its title. Efforts have been made to cover many labour litigations under this Act.

Now let us study important provisions of the M.R.T.U. and P.U.L.P. Act of 1971. But before that let us first consider the important objects of passing the Act, its extent commencement and the definitions as given in Sections 1, 2 and 3 of the Act.

3.8 Objects of the M.R.T.U. and P.U.L.P. Act of 1971

In the preamble of the Act, various objects of the Act are clearly mentioned. In the preamble, it is stated that –

"Act to provide for the recognition of trade unions for facilitating collective bargaining for certain undertakings, to state their rights and obligations; to confer certain powers on unrecognised unions; to provide for declaring certain strikes and lock-outs as illegal strikes and lock-outs; to define and provide for the prevention of certain unfair labour practices; to constitute courts (as independent machinery) for carrying out the purposes of according recognition to trade unions for enforcing the provisions relating to unfair practices; and to provide for matters connected with the purposes aforesaid.

Thus, from the preamble, we come to know the following objectives behind passing the Act.

1. To provide for the recognition of trade unions for facilitating collective bargaining for certain undertakings covered by the Act;
2. To state the rights and obligations of trade unions;
3. To provide for declaring certain strikes and lock-outs as illegal strikes and lock-outs;
4. To define certain unfair labour practices and to provide for their prevention;
5. To constitute courts as independent machinery for carrying out the purposes of according recognition to trade unions for enforcing the provisions relating to unfair practices.

3.9 Section 3: Definitions

In this Act, unless the context requires otherwise, the definitions of eighteen words or terms are given in Section three which are as follows.

1. Bombay Act: "Bombay Act" means the Bombay Industrial Relations Act, 1946, Bombay XI of 1947 [Section 3 (1)].

2. Central Act: Central Act" means the Industrial Disputes Act, 1947, XIV of 1947 [Section 3 (2)].

3. Concern: "Concern" means any premises including the precincts thereof where any industry to which the Central Act applies is carried on [Section 3 (3)].

In the definition of 'concern', the words 'any premises' are used. But, they imply any one premise and not more than one. The word 'concern' as defined in this sub-section implies any premises including the precencts thereof where any industry to which the Central Act i.e. the Industrial Disputes Act of 1947 applies is carried on and the expression 'any' in this context should mean only one premise and not more than one premises.

4. Court: "Court" for the purposes of Chapter VI and VII means the Industrial Court, or as the case may be, the Labour Court [Section 3 (4)].

5. Employee: "Employee" in relation to an industry to which the Bombay Act for the time being applies, means an employee as defined in clause (13) of Section 3 of the Bombay Act; and in any other case, means a workman as defined in clause (s) of Section 2 of the Central Act [Section 3 (5)].

The Section 4 (5) is explanatory. It merely states that the term 'employee', in relation to an industry to which the Bombay Industrial Relations Act applies, means an employee as defined in Section 3 (13) of the Bombay Industrial Relations Act and in other cases, an employee means a workman as defined under Section 2 (s) of the Industrial Disputes Act of 1947. Therefore, let us consider the definitions of an employee and a workman as given in both Acts.

According to Section 3 (13) of the Bombay Industrial Relations Act of 1946, "employee means any person employed to do any skilled or unskilled work for hire or reward in any industry, an includes:

(a) A person employed by a contractor to do any work for him in the execution of a contract with an employer within the meaning of sub-clause (e) of clause (14);

(b) A person who has been dismissed, discharged or retrenched or whose services have been terminated from employment on account of any dispute relating to change in respect of which notice is given or an application made under Section 42 whether before or after his dismissal, discharge, retrenchment or, as the case may be, termination from employment.

but does not include –

(i) A person primarily employed in a managerial, administrative, supervisory, or technical capacity drawing basic pay (excluding allowances) exceeding one thousand rupees per month;

(ii) Any other person or class of persons employed in the same capacity as those specified in clause (i) above irrespective of the amount of pay drawn by such persons which the State Government may, by notification in the Official Gazette, specify in this behalf.

6. Employer: "Employer" in relation to an industry to which the Bombay Act applies, means an employer as defined in clause (14) of Section 3 of the Bombay Act; and in any other case, means an employer as defined in clause (g) of Section 2 of the Central Act [Section 3 (6)].

Section 3 (14) of the Bombay Industrial Relations Act of 1946 defines the term 'Employer' as follows:

"Employer" includes –

(a) An association or a group of employer;

(b) Any agent of employers;

(c) Where an industry is conducted or carried on by a department of the State Government, the authority prescribed in that behalf, and where no such authority is prescribed, the head of the department;

(d) Where an industry is conducted or carried on by or on behalf of a local authority, the Chief Executive Officer of the authority;

(e) Where the owner of any undertaking in the course of or for the purpose of conducting the undertaking contracts with any person for the execution by or under the contractor of the whole or any part of any work which is ordinarily part of the undertaking, the owner of the undertaking.

7. Industry: "Industry" in relation to an industry to which the Bombay Act applies means an industry as defined in clause (19) of Section 3 of the Bombay Act, and in any other case, means an industry as defined in clause (j) of Section 2 of the Central Act [Section 3 (7)].

In the M.R.T. and P.U.L.P. Act of 1971, the term 'Industry' has not been defined. But, the Act merely states that in relation to an industry to which the Bombay Industrial Relation Act applies, means an industry as defined in Section 3 (19) of Bombay I. R. Act and in other cases, an industry means an industry as defined in Section 2 (J) of the Industrial Disputes Act of 1947. Thus, an industry covers all the industries included in these two Acts. Therefore, let us consider the definitions of an industry as given in both the Acts.

The definition of 'Industry' as given in Section 3 (19) of the Bombay Industrial Relations Act of 1946 is as follows:

"industry" means –

(a) Any business, trade, manufacture of undertaking or calling of employers;

(b) Any calling, service employment, handicraft, or industrial occupation or avocation of employees;

and includes –

(i) Agriculture and agricultural operations;

(ii) Any branch of an industry or group of industries which the [State] Government may be notification in the Official Gazette declare to be an industry for the purposes of this Act.

8. Industrial Court: "Industrial Court" means on Industrial Court constituted under Section 4 of the M.R.T.U. and P.U.L.P. Act of 1971 [Section 3 (8)].

9. Investigating Officer: "Investigating Officer" means an officer appointed under Section 8 of the M.R.T.U. and P.U.L.P. Act of 1971 [Section 3 (9)].

10. Labour Court: 'Labour Court' means a Labour Court constituted under Section 6 of the M.R.T.U. and P.U.L.P. Act of 1971 [Section 3 (10)].

11. Member: 'Member' means a person who is an ordinary member of a union, and has paid a subscription to the union of not less than 50 *paise* per calendar month;

It is also provided that, no person shall at any time be deemed to be a member, if his subscription is in arrears for a period of more than three calendar months during the period of six months immediately preceding such time, and the expression "membership" shall be construed, accordingly [Proviso to the clause 11 of Section 3].

Explanation: A subscription for a particular calendar month shall, for the purpose of this clause, be deemed to be in arrears, if such subscription is not paid within three months after the end of the calendar month in respect of which it is due.

12. Orders: "order" means an order of the Industrial or Labour Court" [Section 3 (12)].

13. Recognised Union: "Recognised union" means a union which has been issued a certificate of recognition under Chapter III [Section 3 (13)].

14. Schedule: "Schedule" means a Schedule to this Act [Section 3 (14)]

15. Undertaking: "Undertaking" for the purposes of Chapter III, means any concern in industry to be one undertaking for the purpose of that Chapter [Section 3 (15)].

16. Unfair Labour Practices: "Unfair labour practices" means unfair labour practices as defined in Section 26 [Section 3 (16)].

17. Union: "Union" means a trade union of employee, which is registered under the Trade Unions Act, 1926 [Section 3 (17)].

It is made clear in clause 18 of Section 3 that "words and expressions used in this Act and not defined therein, but defined in the Bombay Act, shall, in relation to an industry to which the provisions of the Bombay Act apply, have the meanings assigned to them by the Bombay Act; and in any other case, shall have the meanings assigned to them by the Central Act.

3.10 Chapter II: Authorities under the Act

1. Constitution of the Industrial Court and Qualifications of the Members of the Industrial Court

The State Government is empowered under this Act to constitute the Industrial Court, Provisions relating to the constitution and qualifications of the members of the Industrial Court have been made in Section 4 of the Act which are as follows.

(1) The State Government shall by notification in the *Official Gazette*, constitute an Industrial Court.

(2) The Industrial Court shall consists of not less than three members, one of whom shall be the President [Section 4 (2)].

(3) Every member of the Industrial Court shall be a person who is not connected with the complaint referred to that Court, or with any industry directly affected by such complaint [Section 4 (3)].

It is also provided that, every member shall be deemed to be connected with a complaint or with an industry by reason of his having shares in a company which is connected with, or likely to be affected by, such complaint, unless he discloses to the State Government the nature and extent of the shares held by him in such company and in the opinion of the State Government recorded in writing such member is not connected with the complaint, or the industry [Proviso to Section 4 (3)].

(4) Every member of the Industrial Court, shall be a person who is or has been a Judge of a High Court or is eligible for being appointed a Judge of such Court [Section 4 (4)].

It is further provided that one member may be a person who is not so eligible if he possesses in the opinion of the State Government expert knowledge of labour or industrial matters" [Proviso to Section 4 (4)].

Thus, by the notification in the Official Gazette, the State Government has constituted the Industrial Court. The Industrial Court consists of three members and one of them works as the President. Sub-section (3) and (4) of Section 4 throw light on the qualifications of the members of the Industrial Court and also make clear certain restrictions on the State Government to appoint these members. Section 2 (4) provides that every member of the Industrial Court must be person who is or has been a Judge of the High Court or he must be such person who is eligible for being a Judge of the High Court. But it is also provided in clause 4 of Section 4 that there can be one member who is not so qualified. However, such member, in the opinion of the State Government, must have the expert knowledge of labour or industrial matters.

It is also provided in Section 2 (3) that any member of the Industrial Court must not be person who is connected with the complaint referred to that court or with any industry directly affected by such complaint.

Every member is considered to be connected with a complaint or with an industry by reason of his having shares in a company which is connected with or likely to be affected by, such complaint, unless such member discloses to the State Government the nature and the extent of his share holding in such company and in the opinion of the State Government recorded in writing such member is not connected with the complaint, or the industry [Proviso to Section 4 (3)].

Duties of the Industrial Court

There are certain duties entrusted to the Industrial Court under this Act. These duties are enumerated in Section 5 of this Act which are as follows:

Section 5 states that it shall be the duty of the Industrial Court:

(1) To decide an application by a union for grant of recognition to it;

(2) To decide an application by a union for grant of recognition to it in place of a union which has already been recognised under this Act;

(3) To decide an application from another union or an employer for withdrawal or cancellation of the recognition of a union;

(4) To decide complaints relating to unfair labour practices excess unfair labour practice falling in item 1 of Schedule IV;

(5) To assign work and to give directions to the Investigating Officers in matters of verification of membership of unions and investigation of complaints relating to unfair labour practices;

(6) To decide references made to it on any point of law either by any civil or criminal court; and

(7) To decide appeals under Section 42.

2. Labour Court – Its Constitution and Duties

(1) Constitution of Labour Court

The State Government is empowered under this Act to constitute one or more Labour Courts and to appoint persons to preside over such Courts. The provisions relating to the constitution of Labour Courts and to the appointment of persons to preside over such Courts, their qualifications have been made in Section 6 which are as follows:

The State Government shall by notification in the *Official Gazette,* constitute one or more Labour Courts, having jurisdiction in such local areas, as may be specified in such notification, and shall appoint persons having the prescribed qualifications to preside over such Courts".

So far as qualifications of persons to be appointed to preside over Labour Courts under this Act, it is provided that, "no person shall be so appointed, unless he possesses qualifications (other than the qualification of age), prescribed under Article 234 of the Constitution for being eligible to enter the judicial service of the State of Maharashtra; and is not more than sixty years of age" [Proviso to Section 6].

(2) Duties of Labour Court

Following duties have been entrusted to the Labour Court or Labour Courts constituted under this Act.

(a) To decide complaints relating to unfair labour practices which are mentioned or described in item 1 of the Schedule IV; and

(b) To try offences punishable under the Act.

Section 7 lays down that, "It shall be the duty of the Labour Court to decide complaints relating to unfair labour practices described in item 1 of Schedule IV and to try offences punishable under this Act".

Thus, the jurisdiction of the Labour Courts appointed under this Act is limited to give decisions in respect of the complaints relating to unfair labour practices described in item 1 of the Schedule IV appended to this Act and also to try offences punishable under this Act.

In Schedule IV appended to this Act, various general unfair labour practices on the part of employers are given. But the duty of the Labour Courts constituted under this Act is to decide complaints only relating to unfair labour practices described in item 1 of this schedule IV. This item 1 of the said schedule provides that the discharge or dismissal of employees by the employer shall amount to an unfair labour practice if such discharge or dismissal is

(a) By way of victimisation;
(b) Not in good faith, but in the colourable exercise of the employer's rights;
(c) By falsely implicating an employee in a criminal case on the false evidence or on concocted evidence;
(d) For patently false reasons;
(e) On unture or trumped up allegations of absence without leave.
(f) In utter disregard of the principles of natural justice in the conduct of domestic enquiry or with undue haste;
(g) For misconduct of a minor or technical character, without having any regard to the nature of the particular misconduct, so as to amount to a shockingly disproportionate punishment.

3. Investigating Officers – Their Appointment and Duties

(1) Appointment of the Investigation Officers

The Investigating Officers are appointed by the State Government to assist the Industrial Court and Labour Courts in discharge their duties. Such Investigating Officers are appointed for different areas as the State Government considers necessary. The provision relating to the appointment to Investigating Officers are made in Section 8 which is as follows.

"The State Government may, by notification in *Official Gazette*, appoint such number of Investigating Officers for any area as it may consider necessary, to assist the Industrial Courts and Labour Courts in the discharge of their duties".

(2) Duties of Investigating Officers

(a) The Investigating Officer shall be under the control of the Industrial Court, and shall exercise powers and perform duties imposed on him by the Industrial Court [Section 9 (1)].

(b) It shall be the duty of an Investigating Officer to assist the Industrial Court in matters of verification of membership of unions, and assist the Industrial and Labour Courts for investigating into complaints relating to unfair labour practices [Section 9 (2)].

(c) It shall also be the duty of an Investigating Officer to report to the Industrial Court, or as the case may be, the Labour Court the existence of any unfair labour practices in any industry or undertaking, and the names and addresses of the persons said to be engaged in unfair labour practices and any other information which the Investigating Officer may deem fit to report to the Industrial Court, or as the case may be, the Labour Court [Section 9 (3)].

The Investigation Officers work under the control of the Industrial Court and they exercise various powers and perform certain duties as imposed on them by the Industrial Court. Their important duties are as follows:

(a) The Investigation Officers have to assist the Industrial Court in the matters which are mentioned below:
  (i) Verification of membership of unions.
  (ii) Investigation into complaints relating to unfair labour practices in order to assist the Industrial as well as Labour Courts [Section 9 (2)].
(b) The duty of the Investigating Officers is to report to the Industrial Court or the Labour Court, as the case may be, relating to the following matters:
  (i) The existence of any unfair labour practices in any industry or undertaking;
  (ii) Information relating to the names and addresses of persons said to be engaged in unfair labour practices; and
  (iii) Any other information which the Investigation Officers deem fit to report to the Industrial Court or the Labour Court, as the case may be [Section 9 (3)].

3.11 Chapter III: Recognition of Unions [Section 14]

Section 14 provides for granting the status of a recognised union to other union in place of a recognised union which is already registered as such subject to certain essential conditions. These conditions are laid down in Section 14 in clauses (1) to (4). In brief, these conditions are as follows:

1. Applicant union must have largest membership of employees;
2. A period of two years must have elapsed since the date of registration of recognised union, or/and;
3. A period of one year has elapsed since the date of disposal of the provisions application of that union;
4. The applicant union complies with the conditions necessary for recognition, as specified in Sections 11 and 19 of this Act;
5. Its membership during the whole period of six months, (immediately preceding the calendar month in which it made application was larger than the membership of the recognised union.

Section 14 also lays down the procedure to be followed by the Industrial while taking action in respect of recognition of other union. Section 14 is reproduced below in order to understand fully the essential conditions and the procedure to be followed while giving recognition to other union.

3.12 Chapter IV: Obligation and Rights of Recognised Unions and Other Unions

1. Obligations of Recognised Unions [Section 19]

According to the provisions of Section 19 which relates to the obligations of recognised union, "The rules of a union seeking recognition under this Act shall provide for the following matters, and the provisions thereof shall be duly observed by the union, namely:

(1) The membership subscription shall be not less than fifty paise per month;

(2) The Executive committee shall meet at intervals of not more than three months;

(3) All resolutions passed, whether by Executive Committee or the General Body of the union, shall be recorded in a minute book kept for the purpose;

(4) An auditor appointed by the State Government may audit its account at least once in each financial year".

Above mentioned four conditions have been imposed upon a union seeking recognition under this Act. But so far as last condition i.e. an auditor appointed by the State Government may audit its account at least once in each financial year, is concerned this condition is not within the control of the union as it is the State Government to appoint the auditor for the purpose of auditing its accounts. If the State Government appoints any auditor, it is obligatory on the part of a union seeking recognition under this Act to get its account duly audited. Section 13 (1) (iii) empowers the Industrial Court to cancel the recognition or to suspend the rights of a recognised union if it fails to observe the conditions mentioned in Section 19. Thus, a recognised union or any union seeking recognition must comply with the conditions as are laid down in Section 19. Besides these conditions, a union seeking recognition has to fulfil the conditions mentioned in section 12 of this Act. Provisions of Section 12 have been already discussed.

2. Rights of Recognised Unions [Section 20]

Recognised unions enjoy certain rights. The provisions relating to such rights have been made in Section 20 of the Act. Section 20 lays down that –

(1) Such officers, members of the office staff and members of a recognised union as may be authorised by or under rules made in this behalf by the State Government shall, in such manner and subject to such conditions as may be prescribed have a right:

(a) To collect sums payable by members to the union on the premises, where wages are paid to them;

(b) To put up or cause to be put up a notice board on the premises of the undertaking in which its members are employed and affix or cause to be affixed notice thereon;

(c) For the purpose of the prevention or settlement of an industrial dispute:

(i) To hold discussion on the premises of the undertaking with the employees concerned, who are the members of the union but so as not to interfere with the due working of the undertaking;

(ii) To meet and discuss, with an employer or any person appointed by him in that behalf, the grievances of employees employed in this undertaking;

(iii) To inspect, if necessary, in an undertaking any place where any employee of the undertaking is employed;

(d) To appear on behalf of any employee or employees in any domestic or departmental inquiry held by the employer [Section 20 (1)].

(2) Where there is a recognised union for any undertaking:

(a) That union alone shall have the right to appoint its nominees to represent workmen on the Works Committee constituted under Section 3 of the Central Act;

(b) No employee shall be allowed to appear or act or be allowed to be represented in any proceedings under the Central Act (not being a proceedings in which the legality or propriety of an order to dismissal, discharge, removal retrenchment, termination of service, or suspension of an employee is under consideration), except through recognised union and the decision arrived at, or order made, in such proceeding shall be binding on all the employees in such undertaking; and accordingly, the provisions of the Central Act, that is to say, the Industrial Disputes Act, 1947, XIV of 1947, shall stand amended in the manner and to the extent specified in Schedule I [Section 20 (2)].

3. **Rights of Unrecognised Unions [Section 22]**

Unrecognised unions also enjoy certain rights under this Act. Such rights are given in Section 22 where are as follows:

"Such officers, members of the office staff and members of any union (other than a recognised union) as may be authorised by or under the rules made in this behalf by the State Government shall, in such manner and subject to such conditions as may be prescribed, have a right –

(1) To meet and discuss with an employer or any person appointed by him in that behalf, the grievances of any individual member relating to his discharge, removal, retrenchment, termination of service and suspension;

(2) To appear on behalf of any of its members employed in the undertaking in any domestic or departmental inquiry held by the employer" [Section 22].

Thus, the officers, members of the office staff and members of a recognised union have a right to (1) discuss with an employer in the matters related to discharge, removal, retrenchment, termination of service and suspension of any individual member, and (2) to appear an behalf of its members in any domestic or departmental inquiry held by the employer under Section 22.

3.13 Chapter V: Illegal Strikes and Lock-outs

1. **Illegal Strikes**

Section 24 (1) states that, "*In this Act, unless the context requires otherwise "illegal strike" means a strike which is commenced or continued –*

(1) Without giving to the employer notice of strike in the prescribed form, or within fourteen days of the giving of such notice;

(2) Where there is a recognised union, without obtaining the vote of the majority of the members of the union, in favour of the strikes before the notice of the strike is given;

(3) During the pendency of conciliation proceeding under the Bombay Act or the Central Act and seven days after the conclusion of such proceeding in respect of matters covered by the notice of strike;

(4) Where submission in respect of any of the matters covered by the notice of strike is registered under Section 66 of the Bombay Act, before such submission, is lawfully revoked;

(5) Where an industrial dispute in respect of any of the matters covered by the notice of strike has been referred to the arbitration of a Labour Court or the Industrial Court voluntarily under sub-section (6) of Section 58 or Section 71 of the Bombay Act, during the arbitration proceeding or before or the date on which the arbitration proceedings are completed or the date on which the award of the arbitrator comes into operation, whichever is later;

(6) During the pendency of arbitration proceedings before an arbitrator under the Central Act and before the date on which the arbitration proceedings are concluded, if such proceedings are in respect of any of the matters covered by the notice of strike;

(7) In cases where an industrial dispute has been referred to the arbitration of a Labour Court or the Industrial Court under Sections 72, 73 or 73-A of the Bombay Act, during such arbitration proceedings or before the date on which the proceeding is completed or the date on which the award of the Court comes into operation, whichever is later, if such proceedings are in respect of any of the matters covered by the notice of strike;

(8) In case where an industrial dispute has been referred to the adjudication of the Industrial Tribunal or Labour Court under the Central Act, during the pendency of such proceeding before such authority and before the conclusion of such proceeding, if such proceeding is in respect of any of the matters covered by notice of strike.

It is further provided that, nothing in clauses (g) and (h) shall apply to any strike where the union has offered in writing to submit the industrial dispute to arbitration under sub-section (6) of Section 58 of the Bombay Act or Section 10-A of the Central Act, and –

(1) The employer does not accept the offer, or

(2) The employer accepts the offer but disagreeing on the choice of the arbitrator, does not agree to submit the dispute to arbitration without naming an arbitrator as provided in the Bombay Act,

and thereafter, the dispute has been referred for arbitration of the Industrial Court under Section 73-A of the Bombay Act, or where the Central Act applies, while disagreeing on the choice of the arbitrator, the employer does not agree to submit the dispute to arbitration of the arbitrator recommended by the State Government in this behalf, and thereafter, the dispute has been referred to adjudication of the Industrial Tribunal or the Labour Court, as the case may be, under the Central Act; or

(3) During any period in which any settlement or award is in operation, in respect of any of the matters covered by the settlement or award; [Proviso to Section 24 (1)].

Provisions of clauses (a) and (b) of Section 24 (1) imply that if the following conditions for commencement or continuation of a strike are not fulfilled, such strike becomes illegal.

(a) Before giving the notice of a strike, where there is a recognised union, it must obtain the vote of majority of its members in favour of the strike;

(b) The notice of the strike must be given to the employer in the prescribed form. Rule 22 of the M.R.T.U. and P.U.L.P. Rules of 1975 prescribes that the notice of the strike must be in Form I and the same must be sent to the employer by the registered post. The format of Form I is as follows:

FORM – I
(See Rule 22)

Name of the Trade Union:
Names of 5 elected representatives of the workmen, where no Trade Union exists:
Address: ....
Dated the .... day of .... 20 ......
To,
    (Here mention name of the employer and full address of the undertaking)
Dear Sir (s)/Madam,

In accordance with the provisions contained in sub-section (1) of Section 24 of the Maharashtra Recognition of Trade Unions and Prevention of Unfair Labour Practices Act, 1971, I/we.
(Here insert name of the persons (s))
hereby give you Notice that I/we propose to call a strike of the workmen employed in you undertaking propose to go on strike along with the other workmen employed in your undertaking from the .... day of .... 20 .... , for the reason (s) explained in the Annexure attached hereto.

2. This Union being a recognised Union in your undertaking has obtained the vote of majority of the members in your undertaking in favour of the strike, before serving this notice on you, under clause (b) of sub-section (2) of Section 24 of the Act.

        Yours faithfully,
Place ....

        Signature
        General Secretary/Secretary
        ....
        (Here insert name of the Union)
             *Strike off whichever is not applicable.

Annexure
Statement of Reasons

Copy to:
1. The Investigating Officer
   (Here enter office address of the Investigating Officer, for the area concerned)
2. The Registrar, Industrial Court, Maharashtra, Bombay.
3. The Judge, Labour Court ....
   (Here enter address of the Labour Court, of the area concerned).
4. The Commissioner of Labour, Bombay.

(c) The strike should not be commenced or continued within 14 days of giving such notice clauses (c) to (h) of Section 24 (1) imposes various restrictions on the commencement or continuation of strike during the pendency of the proceedings and within certain period from the conclusion of such proceedings.

2. **Illegal Lock-outs**

Provisions of Section 24 (2) lay down the conditions under which a lock-out becomes illegal. Section 24 (2) states that, *"illegal lock-out" means a lock-out which is commenced or continued* –

(1) Without giving to the employees, a notice of lock-out in the prescribed form or within fourteen days of the giving of such notice;

(2) During the pendency of conciliation proceeding under the Bombay Act or the Central Act and seven days after the conclusion of such proceeding in respect of any of the matters covered by the notice of lock-out;

(3) During the period when a submission in respect of any of the matters covered by the notice of lock-out is registered under Section 66 of the Bombay Act, before such submission is lawfully revoked;

(4) Where an industrial dispute in respect of matter covered by the notice of lock-out has been referred to the arbitration of a Labour Court or the Industrial Court voluntarily under sub-section (6) of Section 58 or Section 71 of the Bombay Act, during the arbitration proceeding or before the date on which the arbitration proceeding is completed or the date on which the award of the arbitrator comes into operation, whichever is later;

(5) During the pendency of arbitration proceedings before an arbitrator under the Central Act and before the date on which the arbitration proceedings are concluded, if such proceedings are in respect of any of the matters covered by the notice of lock-out;

(6) In cases where an industrial dispute has been referred to the arbitration of a Labour Court of the Industrial Court compulsory under Sections 72, 73 or 73-A of the Bombay Act, during such arbitration proceeding or before the date on which the proceeding is completed, or the date on which the award of the Court comes into operation whichever is later, if proceedings are in respect of any of the matters covered by the notice of lock-out; or

(7) In cases where an industrial dispute has been referred to the adjudication of the Industrial Tribunal or Labour Court under the Central Act, during the pendency of such proceeding before such authority and before the conclusion of such proceeding, if such proceeding is in respect of any of the matters covered by the notice of lock-out;

Provided that, nothing in clauses (f) and (g) shall apply to any lock-out where the employer has offered in writing to submit the industrial dispute to arbitration under sub-section (6) of Section 58 of the Bombay Act, or Section 10-A of the Central Act; and

(a) The union does not accept the offer;

(b) The union accepts the offer, but disagreeing on the choice of the arbitrator does not agree to submit the dispute to arbitration without naming an arbitrator as provided in the Bombay Act, and thereafter, the dispute has been referred for arbitration of the Industrial Court under Section 73-A of the Bombay Act, or where the Central Act applies, while disagreeing on the choice of the arbitrator, the union does not agree to submit the dispute to arbitration of the arbitrator recommended by the State Government in his behalf, and thereafter, the dispute has been referred to adjudication of the Industrial Tribunal or the Labour Court, as the case may be, under the Central Act;

(8) During any period in which any settlement or award is in operation, in respect of any of the matters covered by the settlement or award".

Clause (a) of Section 24 (2) makes it clear that if the lock-out is commenced or continues without giving the notice to the employees in the prescribed form or within fourteen days of giving such notice, such lock-out is considered illegal. Such notice of lock-out must be given in Form – J which is prescribed under Rule 23 of the M.R.T.U. and P.U.L.P. Rules of 1975. Moreover, the reasons of lock-out are required to be given in the annexure annexed to the notice, and further the date on which the lock-out is to be intended is required to be mentioned in the notice. The format of the Form-J is as follows:

FORM – J
(See Rule 23)
Notice of Lock-out

Name of the employer: ....
Full address of the undertaking: ....
Dated the .... day of .... 20 ....

In accordance with the provisions of sub-section (2) of Section 24 of the Maharashtra Recognition of Trade Unions and Prevention of Unfair Labour Practices Act, 1971, I/We .... hereby give notice to all concerned that it is my/our intention to effect a lock-out in .... departments (s)/sections (s) of my/our undertakings, with effect from .... day of ..... 20 ... for the reasons explained in the Annexure attached thereto.

        Signature ....

Place: ....

        Designation ....
        (Here insert name of the undertakings)

Annexure

Statement of Reasons

Copy to –
1. The Investigating Officer: ....
   (Here enter office address of the Investigating Officer for the area concerned)
2. The Registrar, Industrial Court, Maharashtra, Bombay ....
3. The judge, Labour Court ....
4. The Commissioner of Labour, Bombay ....

Copy forwarded to:
1. Investigating Officer of the area at ....
2. Commissioner of Labour ....
3. Labour Court at ....

Thus, clauses (a) to (h) of Section 24 (2) make clear the circumstances under which the lock-out declared by the employer becomes illegal.

3. **Reference to the Labour Court for Declaration Whether the Strike or Lock-out is Illegal [Section 25]**

The provisions of Section 25 are passed for the purpose of getting a declaration whether the strike and lock-out which are in contravention of the provisions of this Act are illegal. After such declaration is made, an opportunity is given to the concerned erring employer or employees to rectify the error with the promise that thereupon the illegality in the action already taken would be withdrawn [Section 25 (5)]. Now let us consider the provisions of Section 25.

Section 25 (1) lays down that "*Where the employees in any undertaking have proposed to go on strike or have commenced a strike, the State Government or the employer of the undertaking may make a reference of the Labour Court for a declaration that such strike is illegal*".

Where the employer of any undertaking has proposed a lock-out or has commenced a lock-out, the State Government or the recognised union or, where there is no recognised union, any other union of the employees in the undertaking may a reference to the Labour Court for a declaration whether such lock-out will be illegal [Section 25 (2)].

For the purposes of this section recognised union includes a representative union under the Bombay Act [Explanation to Section 25 (2)].

No declaration shall be made under this section, save in the open [Section 25 (3)].

The declaration made under this section, shall be recognised as binding, and shall be followed in all proceeding under this Act [Section 25 (4)].

Where any strike or lock-out declared to be illegal under this section is withdrawn within forty-eight hours of such declaration, such strike or lock-out shall not, for the purposes of this Act, be deemed to be illegal under this Act [Section 25 (5)].

3.14 Chapter VI: Unfair Labour Practices

In this Act, unless the context requires otherwise, unfair labour practices mean any of the practices listed in Schedules II, III and IV [Section 26]. It is laid down in Section 27 that "no employer or union and no employee shall engage in any unfair labour practice".

Various unfair labour practices on the part of the employers are given in Schedule II.

SCHEDULE II

Unfair Labour Practices on the part of the employers

1. To interfere with, restrain or coerce employees in the exercise of their right to organise, form, join or assist a trade union and to engage in concerted activities for the purposes of collective bargaining or other mutual aid or protection, that is to say –

(a) Threatening employees with discharge or dismissal, if they join a union;

(b) Threatening a lock-out or closure, if a union should be organised;

(c) Granting wage increase to employees at crucial periods of union organisation, with a view to undermining the efforts of the union at organisation.

2. To dominate, interfere with, or contribute, support - financial or otherwise - to any union, that is to say –
(a) An employer taking an active interest in organising a union of his employees; and
(b) An employer showing partiality or granting favour to one of several unions attempting to organise his employees or to its members, where such a union is not a recognised union.
3. To establish employer sponsored unions.
4. To encourage or discourage membership in any union by discriminating against any employee, that is to say -
(a) Discharging or punishing an employee because he urged other employees to join or organise a union;
(b) Discharging or dismissing an employee for taking part in any strike (not being a strike which is deemed to be an illegal strike under this Act);
(c) Changing seniority rating of employee because of union activities;
(d) Refusing to promote employees to higher posts on account of their union activities;
(e) Giving unmerited promotions to certain employees, with a view to show discord amongst the other employees, or to undermine the strength of their union;
(f) Discharging office-bearers or active union members, on account of their union activities.
5. To refuse to bargain collectively, in good faith, with the recognised union.
6. Proposing or continuing a lock-out deemed to be illegal under this Act.

Various unfair labour practices on the part of trade unions are given in Schedule III.

SCHEDULE III
Unfair Labour Practices on the part of Trade Unions

1. To advise or actively support or instigate any strike deemed to be illegal under this Act.
2. To coerce employees in the exercise of their right to self-organisation or to join unions or refrain from joining any union, that is to say –
(a) for a union or its members to picketing in such a manner that non-striking employees are physically debarred from entering the workplace;
(b) to indulge in acts of force or violence or to hold out threats of intimidation in connection with a strike against non-striking employees or against managerial staff.
3. For a recognised union to refuse to bargain collectively in good faith with the employer.
4. To indulge in coercive activities against certification of a bargaining representative.
5. To stage, encourage or instigate such forms of coercive actions as willful "go-slow" squatting on the work premises after working hours or of "gherao" of any of the members of the managerial staff.
6. To stage demonstrations at the residence of the employers or the managerial or other staff members.

In schedule IV, the general unfair labour practises on the part of employers are given.

SCHEDULE IV
General Unfair Labour Practices on the Part of employers

1. To discharge or dismiss employees –
  (a) By way of victimisation;
  (b) Not in good faith, but in the colourable exercise of the employer's rights;
  (c) By falsely implicating an employee in a criminal case on false evidence or on concocted evidence;
  (d) For patently false reasons;
  (e) On untrue or trumped up allegations of absence without leave;
  (f) In utter disregard of the principles of natural justice in the conduct of domestic enquiry or with undue haste;
  (g) For misconduct of a minor or technical character, without having any regard to the nature of the particular misconduct or the past record of service of the employee, so as to amount to a shockingly disproportionate punishment.
2. To abolish the work of a regular nature being done by employees, and to give such work to contractors as a measure of breaking a strike.
3. To transfer an employee *mala fide* from one place to another place, under the guise following management policy.
4. To insist upon individual employees, who were on legal strike, to sign a good conduct-bond, as a pre-condition to allowing them to resume work.
5. To show favouritism or partiality to one set of workers, regardless of merits.
6. To employ employees as "badlis", casuals or temporaries and to continue them as such for years, with the object of depriving them of the status and privileges of permanent employees.
7. To discharge or discriminate against any employee for filing charges or testifying against an employer in any enquiry or proceeding relating to any industrial dispute.
8. To recruit employees during a strike which is not an illegal strike.
9. Failure to implement award, settlement or agreement.
10. To indulge in act of force or violence.

3.15 Chapter VII: Power of Courts

1. **Power of Labour Court**

(1) Where a Court decides that any person named in the complaint has engaged in, or is engaging in, any unfair labour practice, it may in its order –

  (a) Declare that an unfair labour practice has been engaged in or is being engaged in by that person, and specify any other person who has engaged in, or is engaging in the unfair labour practice;

(b) Direct all such persons to cease and desist from such unfair labour practice, and take such affirmative action (including payment of reasonable compensation to the employee or employees affected by the unfair labour practice, or reinstatement of the employee or employees with or without back wages, or the payment of reasonable compensation), as may in the opinion of the Court necessary to effectuate the policy of the Act.

(c) Where a recognised union has engaged in or is engaging in, any unfair labour practice, direct that its recognition shall be cancelled or that all or any of its rights under sub-section (1) of Section 20 or its rights under Section 23 shall be suspended [Section 30 (1)].

(2) In any proceeding before it under this Act, the Court may pass such interim order including any temporary relief or restraining order) as it deems just and proper (including directions to the person to withdraw temporarily the practice complained of, which is an issue in such proceeding), pending final decision [Section 30 (2)].

It is further provided that, the Labour Court may, on an application in that behalf, review any interim order passed by it [Proviso to Section 30 (2)].

(3) For the purpose of holding an enquiry or proceeding under this Act, the Court shall have the same powers as are vested in Court in respect of –

(a) proof of facts by affidavit;

(b) summoning and enforcing the attendance of any person, and examining him on oath;

(c) compelling the production of documents; and

(d) issuing commissions for the examination of witnesses [Section 30 (3)].

(4) The Court shall also have powers to call upon any of the parties to proceedings before it to furnish in writing, and, in such forms as it may think proper, any information, which is considered relevant for the purpose of any proceedings before it, and the party so called upon shall thereupon furnish the information to the best of its knowledge and belief, and if so required by the Court to do so, verify the same in such manner as may be prescribed [Section 30 (4)].

2. Powers of Industrial Court

(1) Where a Court decides that any person named in the complaint has engaged in, or is engaging in, any unfair labour practice, it may in its order –

(a) Declare that an unfair labour practice has been engaged in or is being engaged in by that person, and specify any other person who has engaged in, or is engaging in the unfair labour practice;

(b) Direct all such persons to cease and desist from such unfair labour practice, and take such affirmative action (including payment of reasonable compensation to the employee or employees affected by the unfair labour practice, or reinstatement of the employee or employees with or without back wages, or the payment of reasonable compensation), as may in the opinion of the Court be necessary to effectuate the policy of the Act.

(c) Where a recognised union has engaged in or is engaging in, any unfair labour practice, direct that its recognition shall be cancelled or that all or any of its rights under sub-section (1) of Section 20 or its right under Section 23 shall be suspended [Section 30 (1)].

(2) In any proceeding before it under this Act, the Court may pass such interim order (including any temporary relief or restraining order) as it deems just and proper (including directions to the person to withdraw temporarily the practice complained of, which is an issue in such proceeding), pending final decision [Section 30 (2)].

It is further provided that, the Court may, on an application in that behalf, review any interim order passed by it [Proviso to Section 30 (2)].

(3) For the purpose of holding an enquiry or proceeding under this Act, the Court shall have the same powers as are vested in Court in respect of –

(a) Proof of facts by affidavit;
(b) Summoning and enforcing the attendance of any person, and examining him on oath;
(c) Compelling the production of documents; and
(d) Issuing commissions for the examination of witnesses [Section 30 (3)].

(4) The Court shall also have powers to call upon any of the parties to proceedings before it to furnish in writing, and, in such forms as it may think proper, any information, which is considered relevant for the purpose of any proceedings before it, and the party so called upon shall thereupon furnish the information to the best of its knowledge and belief, and if so required by the Court to do so, verify the same in such manner as may be prescribed [Section 30 (4)].

Powers of the Industrial Court when the concerned parties to the suit do not appear before the Court [Section 31]

The Industrial Court is empowered either to adjourn the matter or proceed ex-parte and to pass necessary orders as it thinks fit. Provisions of Section 31 are as follows:

Consequences of Non-appearance of Parties

(1) Where in any proceeding before the Court, if either party, inspite of notice of hearing having been duly served on it, does not appear, when the matter is called on for hearing the Court may either adjourn the hearing of the matter to a subsequent day, or proceed *ex parte*, and made such order as it think fit [Section 31 (1)].

(2) Where any order is made *ex parte* under sub-section (1), the aggrieved party may, within thirty days of the receipt of the copy thereof, make an application to the Court to set aside such order.

If the Court is satisfied that there was sufficient cause for non-appearance of the aggrieved party, it may set aside the order so made, and shall appoint a date for proceeding with the matter [Section 31 (2)].

It is also provided that, no order shall be set aside on any such application as aforesaid, unless notice thereof has been served on the opposite party [Proviso to Section 31 (2)].

The Power of the Industrial Court to decide all Connected Matters [Section 32]

Section 32 confers the power to the Industrial Court which is in addition to the powers given under other provisions of this Act. The Industrial Court can decide all matters which are not covered under the other provisions of the Act and also can deal with various matters arising out of any application or complaint, if any, referred to it.

It must be noted here that the Industrial Court has the power to invoke the provisions only if there is no specific provision or if the Act is silent about the power of the Court and the matter is referred to the Court. This implies that Section 32 does not enlarge the jurisdiction of the Industrial Court beyond what is conferred upon it by the other provisions of this Act.

For example, the Industrial Court has no jurisdiction to deal with the unfair labour practices mentioned in item 1 of schedule IV appended to this Act. Section 32 does not confer any power to the Industrial Court to deal with the unfair labour practices mentioned in item 1 on the Schedule IV of this Act. Section 32 is reproduced below for your information.

Power of the Industrial Court to decide all connected matters: "*Notwithstanding anything contained in this Act, the Court shall have the power to decide all matters arising out of any application or a complaint referred to it for the decision under any of the provisions of this Act*".

3.16 Chapter VIII: Power of Labour and Industrial Courts to Try Offences under this Act

1. Powers of Labour Courts in relation to Offences [Section 38]

Section 38 empowers the Labour Courts constituted under this Act to try offences which are punishable under this Act. The provisions of Section 38 are as follows:

A Labour Court shall have power to try offences punishable under this Act [Section 38 (1)].

Every offence punishable under this Act shall be tried by a Labour Court within the limits of whose jurisdiction it is committed [Section 38 (2)].

Thus, section 38 provides the forum to try various offences punishable under this M.R.T.U. and P.U.L.P. Act of 1971. It is only the Labour Court which has jurisdiction to try all such offences, which have been committed within the limits of its jurisdiction.

2. Powers of the Labour Courts to take Cognizance of Offences [Section 39]

Section 39 states that, "*No Labour Court shall take cognizance of any offence except on a complaint of facts constituting such offence made by the person affected thereby or a recognised union or on report in writing by the Investigating Officer*".

Thus, this Section 39 empowers the Labour Court to take cognizance of offences punishable under this Act. However, Section 39 lays down two important conditions. The Labour Court can take cognizance of offences only on fulfillment to these two conditions. These two conditions are –

(1) There must be a complaint of facts constituting an offence under this Act; and

(2) Such complaint must have been made by –
   (a) the person affected thereby, or
   (b) a recognised union, or
   (c) by the investigating officer on submitting his report in writing.

3. Powers and Procedure of the Labour Courts in Trials [Section 40]

In Section 40, provisions relating to the power and procedure of the Labour Courts in trial have been made clear. It states that, "In respect of offences punishable under this Act, a Labour Court shall have all the powers under the Code of Criminal Procedure, 1898, V of 1898, of a Presidency Magistrate in Greater Bombay and a Magistrate of the First Class elsewhere, and in the trial of every such offence, shall follow the procedure laid down for in Chapter XXII of the said Code of summary trial in which an appeal lies; and the rest of the provisions of the Code shall so far as may be, apply to such trial".

Section 40 confers upon the Labour Courts all powers of a Presidency Magistrate in Greater Bombay and Magistrate of the First Class elsewhere in respect of offences punishable under this Act. These powers are as provided under the Code of Criminal Procedure of 1898.

However, the provisions have been made in Section 42 to make an appeal to the Industrial Court notwithstanding anything contained in Section 40. Section 42 is reproduced below:

(1) Notwithstanding anything contained in Section 40, an appeal shall lie to the Industrial Court –
   (a) Against a conviction by a Labour Court, by the person convicted;
   (b) Against an acquittal by a Labour Court in its special jurisdiction, by the complainant;
   (c) For enhancement of a sentence awarded by a Labour Court in its special jurisdiction, by the State Government [Section 42 (1)].

(2) Every appeal shall be made within thirty days from the date of conviction, acquittal or sentence, as the case may be [Section 42 (2)].

It is provided that, the Industrial Court may, for sufficient reason, allow an appeal after expiry of the said period [Proviso to Section 42 (2)].

4. Powers of Labour Courts to Impose Higher Punishment [Section 41]

Any Labour Court is empowered to pass sentence authorised under this Act even in excess of its powers under Section 32 of the Code of Criminal Procedure of 1898. Section 41 says that, "Notwithstanding anything contained in Section 32 of the Code of Criminal Procedure, 1898, V of 1898, it shall be lawful for any Labour Court to pass sentence authorised under this Act in excess of its powers under Section 32 of the said Code".

5. Power of the Industrial Court to Exercise Superintendence over Labour Courts [Section 44]

Section 44 states that, "the Industrial Court shall have superintendence over all Labour Courts and it may –

(1) Call for returns;
(2) Make and issue general rules and prescribe forms for regulating the practice and procedure of such Courts in matters not expressly provided for by this Act, and in particular, for securing the expeditious disposal of the cases;

(3) Prescribe form in which books, entries and accounts shall be kept by officers of any Courts; and

(4) Settle a table of fees payable for process issued by a Labour Court or the Industrial Court.

Thus, Section 44 confers wide powers of superintendence over the Labour courts. These powers help the Industrial Court to have administrative and judicial control over all Labour Courts and also include the powers to direct the Labour Courts to carry out the orders given.

6. Power of the Industrial Court to Transfer Proceedings [Section 45]

Section 45 empowers the Industrial Court to transfer proceedings from one Labour Court to another. It states that, – *"The Industrial Court may by order in writing, and for reasons to be stated therein, withdraw any proceeding under this Act pending before a Labour Court, and transfer the same to another Labour Court for disposal and the Labour Court to which the proceedings is so transferred may dispose of the proceeding, but subject to any special direction in the order of transfer, proceed either de novo or from the stage at which it was so transferred"*.

It is made clear in Section 46 that *"no order of the Industrial Court in appeal in respect of offences tried by it under this Act shall be called in question in any Criminal Court"*.

3.17 Chapter X: Miscellaneous

1. **Periodical returns to be submitted to industrial and labour courts [Section 52]:** Every recognised union shall submit to the Industrial Court and Labour Court on such dates and in such manner as may be prescribed periodical returns of its membership.

2. **Modifications of Schedules [Section 53]:** The State Government may, after obtaining the opinion of the Industrial Court, by notification in the Official Gazette, at any time make any addition to, or alteration in, any Schedule II, III or IV and may, in the like manner, delete any item therefrom.

   Provided that, before making any such addition, alteration or deletion, a draft of such addition, alteration or deletion shall be published for the information of all persons likely to be affected thereby, and the State Government shall consider any objections or suggestions that may be received by it from any person with respect thereto.

   Every such notification shall as soon as possible after its issue, be laid by the State Government before the Legislature of the State).

3. **Liability of executive of union [Section 54]:** Where anything is required to be done by any union under this Act, the person authorised in this behalf by the executive of the union, where no person is so authorised, every member of the executive of the union shall be bound to do the same, and shall be personally liable, if default is made in the doing of any such thing.

   Explanation: For the purpose of this section; the executive of a union means the body by whatever name called to which the management of the affairs of the union is entrusted.

4. **Offence under Section 48 (1) to be cognizable [Section 55]:** *The* offence under sub-section (1) of section 48, shall be cognizable.
5. **Certain officers to be public servants [Section 56]:** Investigating Officers, a member of the Industrial or Labour Court and a member of the staff of any such Court shall be deemed to be public servants within the meaning of, Section 21 of the Indian Penal Code.
6. **Protection of action taken in good faith [Section 57]:** No suit, prosecution or other legal proceeding shall lie against any person for anything which is in good faith done or purported to be done by or under this Act.
7. **Pending proceedings [Section 58]:** Any proceeding pending before the State Government or before any tribunal or any other authority, or any proceedings relating to the trial of offences punishable under the provisions of the Central Act or Bombay Act before the commencement of this Act shall be continued and completed as if this Act had not been passed and continued in operation, and any penalty imposed in such proceedings shall be recorded under such Central, or as the case may be, Bombay Act,
8. **Bar of proceedings [Section 59]:** If any proceeding in respect of any matter falling within the purview of this Act is instituted under this Act, then no proceeding shall at any time be entertained by any authority in respect of that matter under the Central Act or, as the case may be, the Bombay Act; and if any proceeding in respect of any matter within the purview of this Act is instituted under the Central Act, or as the case may be, the Bombay Act, then, no proceeding shall at any time be entertained by the Industrial or Labour Court under this Act.
9. **Bar of suits [Section 60]:** No civil court shall entertain any suit which forms or which may form the subject-matter of a complaint or application to the Industrial Court or Labour Court under this Act; or which has formed the subject of an interim or final order of the Industrial Court or Labour Court under this Act.

Exercise

1. Explain the various provisions of Registration of Trade Unions.
2. Describe the Rights and Liabilities of Registered Trade Unions.
3. Describe the various authorities under the M.R.T.U. and P.U.L.P. Act, 1971.
4. Explain the various provisions relating to illegal strikes and illegal lock-outs under the M.R.T.U. and P.U.L.P. Act, 1971.
5. State the various provisions of Chapter VIII under the M.R.T.U. and P.U.L.P. Act, 1971.
6. Write short notes on:
   (a) Penalties and Procedures (Trade Union Act, 1926)
   (b) Labour Court (M.R.T.U. and P.U.L.P. Act, 1971)
   (c) Industrial Court (M.R.T.U. and P.U.L.P. Act, 1971)
   (d) Unfair Labour Practices (M.R.T.U. and P.U.L.P. Act, 1971)
   (e) Miscellaneous Provisions (M.R.T.U. and P.U.L.P. Act, 1971) - Chapter X.

Chapter 4...

The Industrial Employment (Standing Orders) Act, 1946

Industrial Employment (Standing Orders) Act, 1946

- 4.1 Introduction
- 4.2 Objects of the Act
- 4.3 Extent, Scope and Application of the Act
    - 4.3.1 Short Title
    - 4.3.2 Extent
    - 4.3.3 Scope and Application or Coverage of the Act
- 4.4 Definitions: [Section 2]
- 4.5 Provisions relating to the Procedure for Submission of Draft Standing Orders [Section 3]
- 4.6 Procedure for the Certification of the Standing Orders [Section 5]
- 4.7 Provisions of the Act relating to Appeals [Section 6]
- 4.8 Date of Operation of Standing Orders or Amendments [Section 7]
- 4.9 Posting of Standing Orders [Section 9]
- 4.10 Provisions of the Act relating to Duration and Modification of Standing Orders [Section 10 (1)]
    - 4.10.1 Duration of Standing Orders [Section 10 (1)]
    - 4.10.2 Procedure for Modification of Standing Orders
- 4.11 Provisions of the Act relating to the Payment of Subsistence Allowance
- 4.12 Powers of the Certifying Officer and Appellate Authority for the Enforcement of the Act [Sections 11 and 12]
- 4.13 Interpretation etc. of Standing Orders [Section 13-A]
- 4.14 Power to Exempt [Section 14]
- 4.15 Delegation of Powers [Section 14-A]
- 4.16 Penalties and Procedure [Section 13]

Contract Labour Act (Regulation and Abolition Act), 1970

4.17 Introduction
4.18 Objects of the Act
4.19 Definitions: [Section 2]
4.20 Chapter III: Registration of Establishments Employing Contract Labour
4.21 Chapter IV: Licensing of Contractors [Sections 11 to 15]
4.22 Chapter V: Welfare and Health of Contract Labour
4.23 Chapter VI: Penalties and Procedure
4.24 Chapter Vii: Miscellaneous
- Exercise

4.1 Introduction

Before passing of this Industrial Employment (Standing Orders) Act of 1946, employers were free to contract different terms and conditions of service with their employees. The conditions of service also were not uniform in industries carrying on the similar type of work. In many cases, the terms and service conditions were not well defined and reduced in writing and they were governed by oral agreements. As a result, there was more ambiguity or doubt regarding the nature and scope of terms and service conditions. Naturally, it lead to conflicts resulting in unnecessary industrial disputes. Hence, it was thought that there should be definiteness and similarity in service conditions in order to have equality, industrial harmony and peace. As a result, this Act was passed. In this Act, necessary provisions have been made for making the standing orders which constitute the statutory terms of employment between the industrial establishments to which this Act applies and their employees.

4.2 Objects of the Act

This Act is a beneficent piece of legislation. In the preamble and title of the Act, the basic object is given and accordingly, its object is to require the employers in industrial employments to define with sufficient precision the conditions of employment of workmen employed under them and to make the said conditions known to such workmen. The conditions of employment include the conditions of recruitment, discharge, disciplinary action etc.

It is obvious that the object of defining various conditions of employment is to avoid the disputes arising from the uncertainty and vagueness or ambiguity in the terms and conditions of the employment. Thus, this Act has been passed to have industrial harmony and industrial peace.

Besides the above mentioned objects, yet another object of passing this Act was to introduce uniformity in terms and conditions of employment in respect of those workmen who belong to the same category of employment and doing the same or similar type of work in various industrial establishments to which the Act is made applicable.

Thus, in short, it can be said that the Industrial Employment (Standing Order) Act of 1946 is designed basically to provide service rules for the workmen working in the industrial establishments to which this Act applies.

4.3 Extent, Scope and Application of the Act

We find the provisions of the Act relating to its extent, scope and application in Section 1 and 13-B of the Act. These provisions are given and discussed below.

4.3.1 Short Title

This Act may be called the **Industrial Employment (Standing Orders) Act, 1946** [Section 1 (1)] making clear the short title of the Act.

4.3.2 Extent

This Act extends to the whole of India [Section 1 (2)].

4.3.3 Scope and Application or Coverage of the Act

This Act applies to every industrial establishment wherein one hundred or more workmen are employed, or were employed on any day of the preceding twelve months [Section 1 (3)].

It is further provided that the appropriate Government may, after giving not less than two months' notice of its intention to do so, by notification in the Official Gazette, apply the provisions of this Act to any industrial establishment employing such number of persons less than one hundred as may be specified in the notification [Proviso to Section 1 (3)].

Thus, the Act is applicable to all industrial establishments employing one hundred or more workmen. The term 'industrial establishment' includes factory, transport service, construction work, building activity, transmission of power etc.

Once the Act becomes applicable to an industrial establishment, it does not cease to apply merely because of the fall in the number of workmen in the concerned establishment below fifty.

Section 1 (4) and Section 13-B make clear that the Act does not apply to certain industrial establishments. The provisions of these sections are given below:

1. **Section 1 (4):** "Nothing in this Act shall apply to –

(1) any industry to which the provisions of Chapter VII of the Bombay Industrial Relations Act, 1946, (Bom. Act II of 1947) apply, or

(2) any industrial establishment to which the provisions of the Madhya Pradesh Industrial Employment (Standing Orders) Act, 1961 (M.P. Act 26 of 1961) apply"

It is also provided that notwithstanding anything contained in the Madhya Pradesh Industrial Employment (Standing Orders) Act, 1961 (M.P. Act 25 of 1961) the provisions of this Act shall apply to all industrial establishments under the control of the Central Government [Proviso to Section 1 (4)].

2. **Section 13-B: Act not to apply to certain industrial establishments:** "Nothing in this Act shall apply to an industrial establishment in so far as the workmen employed therein are persons to whom the Fundamental and Supplementary Rules, Civil Services (Classification, Control and Appeal) Rules, Civil Services (Temporary Service) Rules, Revised Leave Rules, Civil Service Regulations, Civilians in Defense Services (Classification, Control and Appeal) Rules or the Indian Railway Establishment Code or any other rules or regulations that may be notified in this behalf by the appropriate Government in the Official Gazette, apply".

3. **Section 14: Power to exempt:** "The appropriate Government may by notification in the Official Gazette exempt, conditionally or unconditionally, any industrial establishment or class of industrial establishments from all or any of the provisions of this Act".

4.3.4 Application of the Act in the Maharashtra State

As already made clear that this Act applies to every industrial establishment wherein fifty or more workmen are employed on any day of the preceding twelve months subject to the provisions of Section 1 (4) and Section 13-B. But, in exercise of powers conferred by the proviso to Section 1 (3) in its application to the Maharashtra Government by notification Industries, Energy and Labour Department dated 15th June, 1982 applied with effect from 15th August 1982 all the provisions of this act to any industrial establishment wherein one hundred or more workmen are employed or were employed on any day of the preceding twelve months.

4.4 Definitions: Section 2

In this Act, in Section 2, the definitions and meaning of certain words, terms, concepts etc. are given by clearly stating that, "unless there is anything repugnant in the subject or context". Now let us consider the definitions of the words, concept, terms etc. as given in Section 2 of this Act.

1. **Appellate Authority [Section 2 (a)]:**

"Appellate authority" means an authority appointed by the appropriate Government by notification in the Official Gazette to exercise in such area as may be specified in the notification the functions of an appellate authority under this Act [Section 2 (a)].

It is further provided that in relation to an appeal pending before the Industrial Court or other authority immediately before the commencement of the Industrial Employment (Standing Orders) Amendment Act, 1963 (39 of 1963) that Court or authority shall be deemed to be the appellate authority [Proviso to Section 2 (a)].

These provisions of Section 2 (a) imply that an authority appointed by the Appropriate Government by notification in the Official Gazette to exercise and perform the functions relating to appeals is the Appellate authority under this Act. The area of the Appellate authority may also be specified in the notification.

2. **Appropriate Government [Section 2 (b)]:**

"Appropriate Government" means in respect of Industrial Establishments under the control of the Central Government or Railway administration or in a major port, mine or oilfield, the Central Government and in all other cases the State Government [Section 2 (b)].

It is also provided that where any question arises as to whether any industrial establishment is under the control of the Central Government, that Government may, either on a reference made to it by the employer or the workman or a trade union or other representative body of the workmen, or on its own motion and after giving the parties an opportunity of being heard, decide the question and such decision shall be final and binding on the parties [Proviso to Section 2 (b)].

3. Certifying Officer [Section 2 (c)]:

"Certifying Officer" means a Labour Commissioner or a Regional Labour Commissioner, and includes any other officer appointed by the appropriate Government, by notification in the Official Gazette, to perform all or any of the functions of Certifying Officer under this Act; [Section 2 (c)].

The functions, duties etc. of the certifying officer are given in Sections 3rd and 5th. Following points give you an idea about the duties, functions etc. of the Certifying Officer.

(1) The Certifying Officer has to accept the copies of the draft standing orders submitted by the employer of an industrial establishment to which this Act applies according to the provisions of Section 3 (1).

(2) On receipt of the draft standing orders under Section 3 (1), the Certifying Officer has to forward a copy thereof to the trade union of the workmen, if any. If there is no trade union, the Certifying Officer has to send the copy of the draft standing orders to the concerned workmen in the prescribed manner [Section 5 (1)].

(3) The Certifying Officer has to send along with a copy of the draft standing orders a notice in the prescribed form requiring objections, if any, which the concerned workmen may desire to make to the draft standing orders [Section 5 (1)].

(4) It is the duty of the Certifying Officer to give an opportunity to the concerned employer, trade union or other representative of the workmen as may be prescribed of being heard if any modifications or addition to standing orders is to be made [Section 5 (2)].

(5) After completing the formalities mentioned above in points a, b, c, and d, the Certifying Officer has to decide whether or not any modification or addition to the draft standing orders submitted by the employer is necessary to render the draft standing orders certifiable under this Act and then, he has to make an order in writing accordingly.

(6) Thereafter, the Certifying Officer has to certify the draft standing orders with the modifications, if any and then, he has to send within seven days copies of the certified standing orders authenticated in the prescribed manner and also of his order to the employer, to the trade union or to other prescribed representatives of the workmen [Section 5 (3)].

4. Employer [Section 2 (d)]:

"Employer" means the owner of an industrial establishment to which this Act for the time being applies, and includes –

(1) in a factory, any person named under clause (f) of sub-section (1) of Section 7 of the Factories Act, 1948 (63 of 1948) as manager of the factory;

(2) in any industrial establishment under the control of any department of any Government in India, the authority appointed by such Government in this behalf, or where no authority is so appointed, the head of the department;

(3) in any other industrial establishment any person responsible to the owner for the supervision and control of the industrial establishment; [Section 2 (d)].

In Maharashtra State, the following sub-clause (b) is added in the definition of employer.

- where a person who, for the purpose of fulfilling a contract with the owner of the industrial establishment, employs workmen on the premises of the establishment for the execution of the whole or any part of any work which is ordinarily part of such establishment then in relation to such workmen the owner of the industrial establishment".

5. **Industrial Establishment [Section 2 (e)]:**

"Industrial establishment" means –

(1) an industrial establishment as defined in clause (ii) of Section 2 of the Payment of Wages Act, 1936 (4 of 1936), or

(2) a factory as defined in clause (m) of Section 2 of the Factories Act 1948 (63 of 1948), or

(3) a railway as defined in clause (4) of Section 2 of the Indian Railways Act, 1890 (9 of 1890), or

(4) the establishment of a person who, for the purpose of fulfilling a contract with the owner of any industrial establishment, employs workmen;

6. **Standing Orders [Section 2 (g)]:**

The term "Standing Orders" means rules relating to matters set out in the Schedule of the Act.

There is only one schedule appended to this Act in which matters to be provided in the standing orders are clearly mentioned. The schedule is given below.

THE SCHEDULE

Matters to be provided in Standing Orders under this Act:

1. Classification of workmen, e.g. whether permanent, temporary, apprentices, probationers, or badlies.
2. Manner of intimating to workmen periods and hours of work, holidays, pay days and wage rates.
3. Shift working.
4. Attendance and late coming.

> 5. Conditions of procedure in applying for, and the authority which may grant leave and holidays.
> 6. Requirement to enter premises by certain gates, and liability to search.
> 7. Closing and re-opening of sections of the industrial establishment, and temporary stoppages of work and the rights and liabilities of the employer and workmen arising therefrom.
> 8. Termination of employment, and the notice thereof to be given by employer and workmen.
> 9. Suspension or dismissal for misconduct, and acts or omissions which constitute misconduct.
> 10. Means of redress for workmen against unfair treatment or wrongful executions by the employer or his agents or servants.
> 11. Any other matter which may be prescribed.

There are certain 'service conditions' or 'service rules' for employees employed in Government offices or departments, banks, insurance companies etc. The Industrial Employment (Standing Orders) Act of 1946 has been designed to provide service rules to workmen employed in industrial establishments to which this Act applies. 'Standing Orders', in simple words, means rules of conduct for workmen employed in industrial establishments. Normally, these rules relate to matters such as classification of workmen, working hours, shift working, transfers, holidays, attendance rules, leave rules, leave eligibility, leave conditions, rules relating to misconduct and termination of employment, suspension, dismissal etc., retirement age, fines that can be imposed and other certain matters included in the schedule.

7. Trade Union [Section 2 (h)]:

"Trade Union" means a trade union for the time being registered under the Indian Trade Unions Act of 1926.

8. Prescribed [Section 2 (f)]:

Prescribed means prescribed by the rules made by the Appropriate Government under this Act.

9. 'Wages' and 'Workman' [Section 2 (i)]:

'Wages' and 'Workman' have the meanings respectively assigned to them in clauses (rr) and (s) of section 2 of the Industrial Disputes Act, 1947 (14 of 1947)".

The definitions of 'Wages' and 'Workman' as given in Section 2 of the Industrial Disputes Act of 1947 are given below for your quick reference.

Wages means all remuneration capable of being expressed in terms of money, which would, if the terms of employment, express or implied, were fulfilled, be payable to a workman in respect of his employment or of work done in such employment.

What is included in 'wages' ? Wages include:

(1) such allowances (including dearness allowance) as the workman is for the time being entitled to;

(2) the value of any house accommodation, or of supply of light, water, medical attendance or other amenity or of any service or of any concessional supply of foodgrains or other articles;

(3) any travelling concession;

(4) any commission payable on the promotion of sales or business or both. This Clause has been added by the Amendment Act of 1982.

What is not included in Wages ? Wages does not, however, include –

(a) any bonus;

(b) any contribution paid or payable by the employer to any pension fund or provident fund or for the benefit of the workmen under any law for the time being in force;

(c) any gratuity payable on the termination of his service.

Workman [Section 2 (s)]: 'Workman' means any person (including an apprentice) employed in any industry to do any manual, unskilled, skilled, technical, operational, clerical or supervisory work for hire or reward. His terms of employment may be expressed or implied. For the purposes of any proceeding under this Act in relation to an Industrial dispute, workman includes any person who has been dismissed, discharged or retrenched in connection with, or as a consequence of, that dispute, or whose dismissal, discharge or retrenchment has led to that dispute.

Persons who are not workmen. Workman does not include any such person –

(1) who is subject to the Air Force Act, 1950, or the Army, 1950, or the Navy Act, 1957; or

(2) who is employed in the police service or as an officer or other employee of a prison; or

(3) who is employed mainly in a managerial or administrative capacity; or

(4) who being employed in a supervisory capacity, draws wages exceeding ₹ 1,600 per mensem or exercises, either by the nature of the duties attached to the officer or by reason of the powers vested in him, functions mainly of a managerial nature.

4.5 Provisions Relating to the Procedure for Submission of Draft Standing Orders [Section 3]

1. The procedure for the submission of draft standing orders begins with the submission of five copies of the draft standing orders to the Certifying Officer. Section 3 (1) states that, "within six months from the date on which this Act becomes applicable to an industrial establishment, the employer shall submit to the Certifying Officer five copies of the draft standing orders proposed by him for adoption in his industrial establishment".

The Industrial Employment (Standing Orders) Central Rules of 1946 provide for the Form No. 1 to be filled in by the employer for submitting the five copies of the standing orders to the Certifying Officer. The Form No. 1 is given below.

FORMS UNDER STANDING ORDERS
FORM I
[Industrial Employment (Standing Orders) Act, 1946 - Section 3 (1)]

Dated 20

To,
  The Certifying Officer,
    [*Vide* Notification No.L.R.11(98), dated 25th July, 1953]
    (Area)
    (Place)

Sir,
  Under the provisions of Section 3 of the Industrial Employment (Standing Orders) Act, 1946, I enclose five copies of the draft Standing Orders proposed by me for adoption in

....
....
         (Name)

....
         (Place)   (Postal address)

an industrial establishment owned/controlled by me, with the request that these orders may be certified under the term of the Act. I also enclose a statement giving the particulars prescribed in Rule 5 of the Industrial Employment (Standing Orders) Central Rules, 1946.

(Signature)

Employer/Manager

---

2. It is mentioned in Section 3 (2) that, "Provision shall be made in such draft for every matter set out in the Schedule which may be applicable to the industrial establishment, and where model standing orders have been prescribed, shall be, so far as is practicable, in conformity with such model".

Thus, the standing orders require to cover every matter set out in the schedule appended to the Act. Where the model standing orders have been prescribed, such standing orders, so far as practicable, should be in conformity with such model.

3. The draft standing orders are required to be accompanied by the particulars of workmen and they should also give the name of the trade union if any, to which the workmen belong.

According to Section 3 (3), "The draft standing orders submitted under this section shall be accompanied by a statement giving prescribed particulars of the workmen employed in the industrial establishment including the name of the trade union, if any, to which they belong".

4. Section 3 (4) provides that the employers in similar establishments are allowed to submit a joint draft of standing orders. This Section 3 (4) runs as follows:

"Subject to such conditions as may be prescribed, a group of employers in similar industrial establishments may submit a joint draft of standing orders under this section".

Thus, it seems that these provisions have been done for the convenience of employers working in similar industrial establishments. However, they have to submit a joint draft of standing orders, subject to the conditions as may be prescribed.

4.6 Procedure for the Certification of the Standing Orders [Section 5])

Procedure for the certification of the standing orders is laid down in Section 5 of this Act. Every employer covered under this Act is required to prepare the standing orders for his establishment covering the matters specified in the schedule appended to the Act or required in the standing orders. They should be sent to the Certifying Officer for approval. Thereafter, the Certifying Officer has to inform to concerned trade union, if any or the representatives of the workmen or workmen as the case may be and hear the objections raised by them. After that, the Certifying Officer has to certify the standing orders for the industrial establishment in question. This Act has also prescribed the model standing orders which are automatically applicable till the employer prepares the standing orders for his own employees and they are approved by the Certifying Officer.

It should be noted that once the standing orders are certified, they supersede any term and condition of employment contained in the appointment letter. If there is any inconsistency between standing orders and appointment letter the provisions of the standing orders prevail [Eicher Goodearth Limited V. R.K. Soni Case (1930 XXIV LLR 524 (Raj HC)].

Now let us consider the provisions of Section 5 as they are given in the Act.

1. A copy of the draft of standing orders to be sent by the Certifying Officer

On receipt of the draft under Section 3, the Certifying Officer shall forward a copy thereof to the trade union, if any, of the workmen, or where there is no such trade union, to the workmen in such manner as may be prescribed, together with a notice in the prescribed form requiring objections, if any, which the workmen may desire to make to the draft standing orders to be submitted to him within fifteen days from the receipt of the notice [Section 5 (1)].

In Section 5 (1), provision has been made that the Certifying Officer has to forward a copy of the draft standing orders to the trade union of workmen, or to the workmen, as the case may be, in the prescribed manner i.e. in the particular manner. The Certifying Officer has to send the copy of the draft standing orders alongwith the Form II which is given in the Industrial Employment (Standing Orders) Rules of 1946. This form is given below to enable you to know the contents of the Form II.

> **FORM II**
>
> **[Notice under Section 5 of the Industrial Employment (Standing Orders) Act, 1946]**
>
> Office of the Certifying Officer for .... area/place ....
>
> Dated the .... 20 ....
>
> *I .... Certifying Officer .... area, forward herewith a copy of the draft* Standing Orders proposed by the employer for adoption in the .... industrial establishment and submitted to me for certification under the Industrial Employment (Standing Orders) Act, 1946. Any objection which the workmen may desire to make to the draft Standing Orders should be submitted to me within fifteen days from the receipt of this notice.
>
> (Certifying Officer)
>
> To,
>
>   The Secretary
>
> Union

2. **Provision of Opportunity of hearing to a trade union/representatives of workmen and then, the Certifying Officer to make an order in writing accordingly –**

   According to Section 5 (2) which relates to the procedure for certification of standing orders, "After giving the employer and the trade union or such other representatives of the workmen as may be prescribed an opportunity of being heard, the Certifying Officer shall decide whether or not any modification of or addition to the draft submitted by the employer is necessary to render the draft Standing Orders, certifiable under this Act, and shall make an order in writing accordingly".

3. **Issue of Certificate pertaining to the draft Standing Orders by the Certifying Officer**

   "The Certifying Officer shall thereupon certify the draft standing orders, after making any modifications therein which is order under sub-section (2) may require, and shall within seven days thereafter send copies of the certified standing orders authenticated in the prescribed manner of his order under sub-section (2) to the employee and to the trade union or other prescribed representatives of the workmen" [Section 5 (3)].

4.7 Provisions of the Act Relating to Appeals [Section 6]

If any one concerned with the standing order is aggrieved by the order of the Certifying Officer can file an appeal to the Appellate Authority within thirty days from the date on which copies are sent under Section 5 (3).

These provisions relating to the Appeals have been made in Section 6 (1) and 6 (2) of the Act.

Section 6 (1): "Any employer, workmen, trade union or other prescribed representatives of the workmen aggrieved by the order of the Certifying Officer under sub-section (2) of Section 5 may, within thirty days from the date on which copies are sent under sub-section (3) of that section, appeal to the appellate authority, and the appellate authority, whose decision shall be final, shall by order in writing confirm the standing orders in the form certified by the Certifying Officer or after amending the said standing orders by making such modifications thereof as it thinks necessary to render the standing orders certifiable under this Act.

Section 6 (2): "The appellate authority shall, within seven days of its order under sub-section (1), send copies thereof to the Certifying Officer, to the employer and to the trade union or other prescribed representatives of the workmen accompanied unless it has confirmed without amendment the standing orders as certified by the certifying officer, by copies of the standing orders as certified by it and authenticated in the prescribed manner".

4.8 Date of Operation of Standing Orders or Amendments [Section 7]

"Standing Orders shall, unless an appeals is preferred under Section 6, come into operation on the expiry of thirty days from the date on which authenticated copies thereof are sent under sub-section (3) of section 5, or where an appeal as aforesaid is preferred, on the expiry of seven days from the date on which copies of the order of the appellate authority are sent under sub-section (2) of Section 6" [Section 7].

4.9 Posting of Standing Orders [Section 9]

The standing orders are, in fact, the rules of conduct or service conditions or service rules made for the workmen employed in industrial establishments. These standing orders include various matters which have been mentioned in Schedule I appended to the Act. The workmen employed in the industrial establishments should know the service conditions or rules which are in the form of standing orders and hence, they must be displayed properly. Hence, the provisions have been made accordingly in Section 9 of this Act which is reproduced below.

Section 9: Posting of Standing Orders:

"The text of the Standing Orders as finally certified under this Act shall be prominently posted by the employer in English and in the language understood by the majority of his workmen on special boards to be maintained for the purpose at or near the entrance through which the majority of workmen enter the industrial establishment and in all departments thereof where the workmen are employed".

4.10 Provisions of the Act relating to Duration and Modification of Standing Orders [Section 10 (1)]

4.10.1 Duration of Standing Orders [Section 10 (1)]

In Section 10 of this Act, the provisions relating to duration and modification of the standing orders or their amendments have been done. So far as the duration of the standing orders is concerned, it is provided in Section 10 (1) that finally certified standing orders, subject to certain exception mentioned in that Section 10 (1), are not liable to be modified until the expiry of six months from the date on which the standing orders or even the last modifications thereof came into the operation. The text of Section 10 (1) is given below.

Standing orders or amendments finally certified under this Act shall not, except on agreement between the employer and the workmen or a trade union or other representative body of the workmen be liable on modification until the expiry of six months from the date on which the standing orders or the amendments or the last modifications thereof came into operation.

4.10.2 Procedure for Modification of Standing Orders

Procedure for the modification of the standing orders is laid down in sub-sections 2, 3, and 4 of Section 10. The concerned party intending to modify the standing orders has to apply to the Certifying Officer alongwith the five copies of proposed modifications to be made. Thereafter, following the same procedure made clear in the provisions contained in Sections from 3 to 9 of this Act are applied which are applicable to the certification of the first standing orders.

The provisions of Section 10 (2) are not applicable to industrial establishments in respect of which the Appropriate Governments make necessary rules in that behalf. This is so because of the powers to make rules have been conferred on the Appropriate Governments under Section 15 of the Act. The provisions of the Section 10 (2), (3) and (4) relating to the procedure of modifying the standing orders are given below.

1. **Procedure for filing copies of the proposed modifications in the standing orders under Section 10 (2)**

Subject to the provisions of sub-section (1), an employer or workmen or a trade union or other representative body of the workmen may apply to the Certifying Officer to have the standing orders modified, and such application shall be accompanied by five copies of the modifications proposed to be made, and where such modifications are proposed to be made by agreement between the employer and the workman or a trade union or other representative body of the workmen a certified copy of that agreement shall be filed along with the application.

2. **Provisions of Sections 3 to 9 of this Act are applicable in respect of an application made under Section 10 (2) which is reproduced above**

"The foregoing provisions of this Act shall apply in respect of an application under sub-section (2) as they apply to the certification of the first amendments" [Section 10 (3)].

3. **Provisions of Section 10 (2) are not applicable to the industrial establishments in respect of which State of Gujarat and State of Maharashtra are the Appropriate Governments.**

According to Section 10 (4) of this Act, "Nothing contained in sub-section (2) shall apply to an industrial establishment in respect of which the appropriate Government is the Government of the State of Gujarat or the Government of the State of Maharashtra.

4.11 Provisions of the Act relating to the Payment of Subsistence Allowance [Section 10-A]

Following are the three important aspects of Section 10-A which are related to the payment of subsistence allowance.

1. When a workman is suspended by his employer for any investigation or inquiry pertaining to the complaints or misconduct against that workman, a question arise as to the payment of subsistence allowance to the workman. Section 10-A (1) provides for the payment of subsistence allowance.

According to Section 10-A (1), "Where any workman is suspended by the employer pending investigation or inquiry into complaints or charges of misconduct against him, the employer shall pay to such workman subsistence allowance –

(1) at the rate of fifty per cent of the wages which the workman was entitled to immediately preceding the date of such suspension for the first ninety days of suspension and;

(2) at the rate of seventy-five per cent of such wages for the remaining period of suspension if the delay in the completion of disciplinary proceedings against such workman is not directly attributable to the conduct of such workman".

2. If there arises any dispute regarding the subsistence allowance to be paid, then it is provided in Section 10-A (2) that such dispute may be referred to the Labour Court. Section 10-A (2) states that, "if any dispute arises regarding the subsistence allowance payable to a workman under sub-section (1), the workman or the employer concerned may refer the dispute to the Labour Court constituted under the Industrial Disputes Act, 1947 (14 of 1947), within the local limits of whose jurisdiction the industrial establishment wherein such workman is employed is situate and the Labour Court to which the dispute is so referred shall, after giving the parties an opportunity of being heard, decide the dispute and such decision shall be final and binding on the parties".

3. It is also provided in Section 10-A (3) that if subsistence allowance to be paid to any workman under this Section 10-A (1) is less beneficial than it is to be paid to the workman under any other law in existence, the provisions of that law are to be made applicable in that respect. Provisions of Section 10-A (3) are as follows:

"Notwithstanding anything contained in the foregoing provisions of this section, where provisions relating to payment of subsistence allowance under any other law for the time being in force in any State are more beneficial than the provisions of this section, the provisions of such other law shall be applicable to the payment of subsistence allowance in that state".

4.12 Powers of the Certifying Officer and Appellate Authority for the Enforcement of the Act [Sections 11 and 12]

For certain purposes and for the enforcement of this Act, necessary powers have been given to every Certifying Officers and Appellate Authorities [Section 11]. While Section 12 of this act states that oral evidence in contradiction of standing orders is not admissible.

In this context, following provisions as are given in Sections 11 and 12 may be noted.

1. "Every Certifying Officer and Appellate Authority shall have all the powers of a Civil Court for the purposes of (1) receiving evidence, (2) administering oaths, (3) enforcing the attendance of witnesses, and (4) compelling the discovery and production of documents [Section 11 (1)]".
2. "Every Certifying Officer and Appellate Authority shall be deemed to be a Civil Court within the meaning of Sections 345 and 346 of the Code of Criminal Procedure, 1973 (2 of 1974) [Section 11 (1)].
3. "Clerical or arithmetical mistakes in any order passed by a Certifying Officer or appellate authority, or errors arising therein from any accidental slip or omission may, at any time, be corrected by that officer or authority or the successor in office of such officer or authority, as the case may be" [Section 11 (2)].
4. "No oral evidence having the effect of adding to or otherwise varying or contradicting standing orders or model standing orders, or model standing orders with all the amendments as finally certified under this Act, as the case may be shall be admitted in any Court" [Section 12].

4.13 Interpretation etc. of Standing Orders [Section 13-A]

Sometimes, questions arise as to the application or interpretation in respect of standing orders certified under this Act. If any controversy relating to application or interpretation of standing orders arises, the same can be referred to the Labour Court constituted under the Industrial Disputes Act of 1947. But, in deciding the controversy, the Labour Court commits any apparent error, the aggrieved party is empowered to maintain a writ petition in the High Court. However, in view of the provisions of Section 13-A, the controversy is first to be referred to the Labour Court. The provisions of Section 13-A relating to interpretation etc. are given below.

Section 13-A: "If any question arises as to the application or interpretation of a standing order certified under this Act, any employer or workman or a trade union or other representative body of the workmen may refer the question to any one of the Labour Courts constituted under the Industrial Disputes Act, 1947 (XIV of 1947), and specified for the disposal of such proceeding by the appropriate Government by notification in the Official Gazette and the Labour Court to which the question is so referred shall, after giving the parties an opportunity of being heard, decide the question and such decision shall be final and binding on the parties".

4.14 Power to Exempt [Section 14]

"The appropriate Government may by notification in the Official Gazette exempt, conditionally or unconditionally, any industrial establishment or class of industrial establishments from all or any of the provisions of this Act".

4.15 Delegation of Powers [Section 14-A]

The appropriate Government may, by notification in the Official Gazette, direct that any power exercisable by it under this Act or any rules made thereunder shall, in relation to such matters and subject to such conditions, if any, as may be specified in the direction, be exercisable also –

1. Where the appropriate Government is the Central Government, by such officer or authority subordinate to the Central Government or by the State Government or by such officer or authority subordinate to the State Government, as may be specified in the notification; [Section 14-A (a)].

2. Where the appropriate Government is a State Government, by such officer or authority subordinate to the State Government, as may be specified in the notification [Section 14-A (b)].

The matters in respect of which the powers are delegated and the conditions under which such delegation is to be made is specified in the direction given by the Appropriate Government.

4.16 Penalties and Procedure [Section 13]

Provisions have been made in Section 13 of the Act for the imposition of penalties for certain offences committed by any employer. However, it is laid down in Section 13 (3) that prosecution for any offence punishable under Section 13 shall not be instituted except with the previous sanction of the Appropriate Government.

The whole Section 13 is reproduced below.

1. An employer who modifies the standing orders, model standing orders or amendments, otherwise than in accordance with the provisions of this Act shall on conviction, be punished with fine which may extend to five thousand rupees, and in the case of a continuing offence with a further fine which may extend to two hundred rupees for every day after the first during which the offence continues [Section 13 (1)].

2. An employer who does any act in contravention of the standing orders, model standing orders or the amendments, as finally certified under this Act for his industrial establishments, as the case may be, shall, on conviction, be punished with fine which may extend to one hundred rupees, and in the case of a continuing offence with a further fine which may extend to twenty-five rupees for every day after the first during which the offence continues [Section 13 (2)].

3. Whoever contravenes the provisions of this Act or of any rule made thereunder in cases other than those falling under sub-section (1) or sub-section (2), shall, on conviction, be punished with fine which may extend to one hundred rupees and in the event of such person being previuosly convicted of an offence under this Act, with fine which may extend to two hundred rupees and in the case of a continuing

offence with a further fine which may extend to twenty-five rupees for every day after the first during which the offence continues [Section 13 (2-A)].

4. The Court convicting an employer under sub-section (1) or sub-section (2) may direct such employer to pay such compensation as it may determine to any workman directly and adversely affected by the modification or contravention of the Standing Orders, Model Standing Orders, or Amendments, as the case may be [Section 13 (2-B).

5. The compensation awarded under sub-section (2-B) may be recovered as if it were a fine and if it cannot be so recovered, the person by whom it is payable shall be sentenced to imprisonment of either description for a term not exceeding three months as the Court thinks fit [Section 13 (2-C)].

6. No prosecution for an offence punishable under this section shall be instituted except with the previous sanction of the appropriate Government [Section 13 (3)].

7. No Court inferior to that [a Metropolitan Magistrate or Judicial Magistrate of the second class] shall try any offence under this section [Section 13 (4)].

The Contract Labour Act (Regulation and Abolition Act), 1970

4.17 Introduction

'Contract Labour' is distinguished from 'Direct Labour' from the view-point of relationship with the principal employment, methods of payment of wages, working conditions etc. Direct labour is borne on the pay or muster-roll of the establishment. Such labour, is thus, entitled to be paid directly, regularly and according to the provisions of the Acts applicable to the establishments. But there are many establishments which entrust the work to the contractors do not have any direct relationship with the labour employed by the contractors. In many cases, the wage rates paid to the contract labour are stipulated, but whether the payment of wages is done on that basis or not done is hardly the concern of the contractors who employ such labour or of the concerned persons or organisations for whom the contractors work. As a result, contract labourers have been exploited and suppressed. Besides this, the contract labourers have to face various problems such as unhealthy working conditions, uncertainty of jobs, irregularity in the payment of their wages etc. Hence, the efforts were made in the direction of the abolition of contract labour. But because of the inevitability of contract labour under certain conditions contract labour is still in existence.

In order to regulate the conditions of contract labour in establishments where its abolition is not possible, the Contract Labour (Regulation and Abolition) Act of 1970 had been passed which came into force with effect from 10th February, 1971. Subsequently, many modifications have been done in the Act and at present, it is applicable to the whole of India.

4.18 Objects of the Act

From the preamble and various provisions of the Act, we come to know the following important objects of the Contract Labour (Regulation and Abolition) Act of 1970.

The Act is basically passed to (a) regulate the employment of contract labour in certain establishments and (b) to provide for the abolition of contract labour in certain circumstances.

Besides the above mentioned basic object, the Act also aims to provide for –

1. Making available certain basic welfare amenities like drinking water, first aid facilities, rest-rooms, canteens etc. in case of employment where more than one hundred contract workmen are employed in order to create fair and healthy working conditions for the workmen employed on contractual basis.
2. Ensuring economic and social justice to contract labourers and eliminating the exploitation and victimisation practices adopted by the contractors.
3. Registration of establishments, licensing of contractors etc.
4. The setting up of Advisory Boards of tripartite character in order to advice the Central as well as State Governments in regard to the administration of the legislation.
5. Imposition of penalties for contravention of provisions of the Act.

4.19 Definitions - Section 2

In Section 2 of the Act, meaning or connotation of the terms, concepts, words etc. used in the Act are given by defining the same. They are given below:

1. Appropriate Government [Section 2 (1) (a)]:

"Appropriate Government" means,

(1) in relation to an establishment in respect of which the appropriate Government under the Industrial Disputes Act, 1947, (14 of 1947) is the Central Government;

(2) in relation to any other establishment, the Government of the State in which that other establishment is situated.

Section (2) (a) of the Industrial Disputes Act of 1947 states the definition of an Appropriate Government in which the list of industries or establishments is given in respect of which the Central Government is an Appropriate Government. The relevant part of Section 2 (a) of the Industrial Disputes Act of 1947 is given below:

2. Appropriate Government [Section 2 (a)]:

'Appropriate Government' means the Central Government in relation to any Industrial dispute concerning –

(1) any industry carried on (i) by or under the authority of the Central Government, or (ii) by a railway company, or (iii) concerning any such controlled Industry as may be specified in this behalf by the Central Government,

(2) (a) a Dock Labour Board established under Sec. 5-A of the Dock Workers (Regulation of Employment) Act, 1948, or

(b) the Industrial Finance Corporation of India established under Section 3 of the Industrial Finance Corporation Act, 1948, or

(c) the Employees' State Insurance Corporation established under Section 3 of the Employees' State Insurance Act, 1948, or

(d) the Board of Trustees constituted under Section 3-A of the Coal Mines Provident Fund and Miscellaneous Provisions Act, 1948, or

(e) the Central Board of Trustees and State Boards of Trustees constituted under Sec. 5-A and Sec. 5-B, respectively, of the Employees Provident Fund and Miscellaneous Provisions Act, 1952, or

(f) the 'Indian Airlines' and 'Air India' Corporations established under Section 3 of the Air Corporations Act, 1952, or

(g) the Life Insurance Corporation of India established under Section 3 of the Life Insurance Corporation Act, 1956, or

(h) the Oil and Natural Gas Commission established under Section 3 of the Oil and Natural Gas Commission Act. 1959, or

(i) the Deposit Insurance and Credit Guarantee Corporation established under Section 3 of the Deposit Insurance and Credit Guarantee Corporation Act, 1961, or

(j) the Central Warehousing Corporation established under Section 3 of the Warehousing Corporations Act, 1962, or

(k) the Unit Trust of India established under Section 3 of the Unit Trust of India Act, 1963, or

(l) the Food Corporation of India established under Section 3, or a Board of Management established for 2 or more contiguous States under Section 16 of the Food Corporation Act, 1964, or

(m) the International Airports Authority of India constituted under Section 3 of the International Airports Authority of India Act, 1971, or

(n) Regional Rural Bank established under Section 3 of the Regional Rural Banks Act, 1976, or

(o) the Export Credit and Guarantee Corporation Limited, or

(p) the Industrial Reconstruction Bank of India, or

(q) the Banking Service Commission established under Section 3 of the Banking Service Commission Act, 1975, or

(r) a banking or an insurance company, or

(s) a mine, an oil field, a Cantonment Board, or a major port.

The definition of an Appropriate Government has a great significance and relevance under this Act. It should be remembered that the definition of an Appropriate Government denotes that may be a dispute between the parties concerned, the Government having jurisdiction over the area is competent to make a reference.

It should be noted that in respect of the Food Corporation of India, the Appropriate Government is the Central Government. But in Food Corporation Workers Union V. Food Corporation of India [1985 (66) FJR 444] case, where contract labour was employed by regional offices and warehouses of Food Corporation of India. It was held that the Appropriate Government for the purpose of that case pertaining to the regional offices and their warehouses in the respective state is the State Government and not the Central Government.

3. Establishment [Section 2 (1) (e)

"Establishment" means –
(i) any office or department of the Government or a local authority; or
(ii) any place where any industry, trade, business, manufacture or occupation is carried on;

4. Workman [Section 2 (1) (i)]

"Workman" means any persons employed in or in connection with the work of any establishment to do any skilled, semi-skilled or un-skilled manual, supervisory, technical or clerical work for hire or reward, whether the terms of employment by express or implied, but does not include any such person.

(1) Who is employed mainly in a managerial or administrative capacity; or
(2) Who, being employed in a supervisory capacity draws wages exceeding five hundred rupees per mensem or exercises, either by the nature of the duties attached to the office or by reason of the powers vested in him, functions mainly of a managerial nature; or
(3) Who is an out-worker, that is to say, a person to whom any articles and materials are given out by or on behalf of the principal employer to be made up, cleaned, washed, altered, ornamented, finished, repaired, adapted or otherwise processed for sale for the purposes of the trade or business of the principal employer and the process is to be carried out either in the home of the out-worker or in some other premises, not being premises under the control and management of the principal employer".

In short, any person employed to do any skilled, semi-skilled or unskilled, supervising, technical or clerical work is called as 'Workman and the Act applies to such person. However, the following three categories of persons are precluded from the coverage of this Act.

(a) A person employed in managerial or administrative capacity, or
(b) A person employed in a supervisory capacity or drawing a scale of more than ₹ Five hundred per month, or
(c) An out-worker who is given raw material for doing his work.

5. Contract Labour [Section 2 (1) (b)]:

A workman shall be deemed to be employed as "contract labour" in or in connection with the work of an establishment when he is hired in or in connection with such work by or through a contractor, with or without the knowledge of the principal employer;

6. Principal Employer [Section 2 (1) (g)]:

"Principal employer" means –

(1) in relation to any office or department of the Government or a local authority, the head of that office or department or such other officer as the Government or the local authority, as the case may be, may specify in this behalf,

(2) in a factory, the owner or occupier of the factory and where a person has been named as the manager of the factory under the Factories Act, 1948, (63 of 1448) the person so named,

(3) in a mine, the owner or agent of the mine and where a person has been named as the manager of the mine, the person so named,

(4) in any other establishment, any person responsible for the supervision and control of the establishment.

For the purpose of sub-clause (iii) of this clause, the expressions "mine", "owner" and "agent" shall have the meanings respectively as signed to them in clause (j), clause (i) and clause (c) of Sub-section (1) of Section 2 of the Mines Act, 1952 (35 of 1952); [Explanation to Section 2 (1) (g) (iii)].

7. Contractor [Section 2 (1) (c)]:

"Contractor" in relation to an establishment, means a person who undertakes to produce a given result for the establishment, other than a mere supply of goods or articles of manufacture to such establishment, through contract labour or who supplies contract labour for any work of the establishment and includes a sub-contractor.

8. Controlled Industry [Section 2 (1) (d)]:

"Controlled Industry" means any industry the control of which by the Union has been declared by any Central Act to be expedient in the public interest;

The definitions of Workman, Contract Labour, Principal Employer and Contractor are very important. If we consider the definitions of workman, contract labour, principal employer and contractor, we come to know that there is the existence of a middle man viz. a contractor and hence, on the basis of the definitions given, the relationship of master and servant is required to be decided for the purposes of this Act.

9. Wages [Section 2 (1) (h)]:

"Wages" shall have the meaning assigned to it in clause (vi) of Section 2 of the Payment of Wages Act, 1936 (4 of 1936);

Definition of the term 'Wages' are given in Section 2 (vi) of the Payment of Wages Act of 1936 is given below for your information.

'Wages' means all remuneration (whether by way of salary, allowance or otherwise) expressed in terms of money or capable of being so expressed which would, if the terms of employment, express or implied, were fulfilled, be payable to a person employed in respect of his employment or of work done in such employment, and includes:

(1) any remuneration payable under any award or settlement between the parties or order of a Court.

(2) any remuneration to which the person employed is entitled in respect of overtime work or holidays or any leave period.

(3) any additional remuneration payable under the terms of employment whether called a bonus or by any other name.

(4) any sum which by reason of the termination of employment of the person employed is payable under any law, contract of instrument which provides for the payment of such sum, whether with or without deductions, but does not provide for the time within which the payment is to be made.

(5) any sum to which the person employed is entitled under any scheme framed under any law for the time being in force.

The expression 'Wages' does not include the following:

(1) any bonus (whether under a scheme of profit sharing or otherwise) which does not form part of the remuneration payable under the terms of employment or which is not payable under any award or settlement between the parties or order of a Court.

(2) the value of any house-accommodation, or of the supply of light, water, medical attendance or other amenity or of any service excluded from the computation of wages by a general or special order of the State Government.

(3) any contribution paid by the employer to any pension or Provident Fund, and the interest which may have accrued thereon.

(4) any travelling allowance or the value of any travelling concession.

(5) any sum paid to the employed person to defray special expenses entailed on him by the nature of this employment or

(6) any gratuity payable on the termination of employment in cases other than those specified in sub-clause (d).

4.20 Chapter III: Registration of Establishments Employing Contract Labour

It has been made compulsory for the principal employer of an establishment employing contract labour and to which, this Act is applicable to apply the registering officer for the purpose of the registration of his establishment. Provisions relating to the appointment of registering officers registration of establishments to which this Act applies revocation of registration in certain cases and effect of non-registration have been made in Section 6th, 7th, 8th and 9th respectively in the Chapter III of this Act.

1. Appointment of Registering Officers [Section 6]

Section 6 states that, "The appropriate Government may, by an order notified in the Official Gazette –

(1) appoint such persons, being Gazetted Officers of Government, as it thinks fit to be registering officers for the purposes of this Chapter; and

(2) define the limits, within which a registering officer shall exercise the powers conferred on him by or under this Act".

2. Registration of certain Establishments [Section 7]

(1) Every principal employer of an establishment to which this Act applies shall, within such period as the appropriate Government may, by notification in the Official Gazette, fix in this behalf with respect to the establishments generally or with respect to any class of them, make an application to the registering officer in the prescribed manner for registration of the establishments: [Section 7 (1)].

It is further provided that the registering officer may entertain any such application for registration after expiry of the period fixed in this behalf, if the registering officer is satisfied that the applicant was prevented by sufficient cause from making the application in time [Proviso to Section 7 (1)].

(2) If the application for registration is complete in all respects, the registering officer shall register the establishment and issue to the principal employer of the establishment a certificate of registration containing such particulars as may be prescribed [Section 7 (2)].

3. Revocation of Registration in certain cases [Section 8]

"If the registering officer is satisfied, either on a reference made to him in this behalf or otherwise, that the registration of any establishment has been obtained by misrepresentation or suppression of any material fact, or that for any other reason the registration has become useless or ineffective and therefore requires to be revoked, the registering officer may, after giving an opportunity to the principal employer of the establishment to be heard and with the previous approval of the appropriate Government, revoke the registration" [Section 8].

4. Effect of non-registration [Section 9]

"No principal employer of an establishment, to which this Act applies, shall –

(1) in the case of an establishment required to be registered under Section 7, but which has not been registered within the time fixed for the purpose under that section,

(2) in the case of an establishment the registration in respect of which has been revoked under Section 8,

employ contract labour in the establishment after the expiry of the period referred to in clause (a) or after the revocation of registration referred to in clause (b) as the case may be [Section 9].

4.21 Chapter IV: Licensing of Contractors [Sections 11 to 15]

Every contractor employing contract labour is required to apply for licence in the prescribed form by sending the prescribed fee and deposit. For that purposes, the licensing officers are appointed under Section 11 of the Act. The license granted under this Act is valid for one year and is required to be renewed. If any person is aggrieved by the decision of the Registering Officer or the Licensing Officer, such person can make necessary appeal under Section 15 of the Act to the Appellate Officer as per provisions of that section. The Licensing Officer is empowered to revoke, suspend or amend the licenses already issued if they have been obtained by misrepresentation or suppression of any material fact or failing to comply with conditions subject to which the licenses have been issued or contravened the provisions of the Act and rules made thereunder. The provisions in respect of these aspects have been made in Sections 11 to 15 of Chapter IV under the heading "Licensing of Contractors". All these provisions are given below for your information.

1. **Appointment of Licensing Officer [Section 11]**

   "The appropriate Government may, by an order notified in the Official Gazette –

   (1) appoint such persons, being Gazetted Officers of Government, as it thinks fit to be licensing officers for the purposes of this Chapter; and

   (2) define the limits, within which a licensing officer shall exercise the powers conferred on licensing officers by or under this Act" [Section 11].

2. **Licensing of Contractors [Section 12]**

   (1) With effect from such date as the appropriate Government may, by notification in the Official Gazette, appoint, no contractor to whom this Act applies, shall undertake or execute any work through contract labour except under and in accordance with a licence issued in that behalf by the licensing officer [Section 12 (1)].

   (2) Subject to the provisions of this Act, a licence under Sub-section (1) may contain such conditions including, in particular, conditions as to hours of work fixation of wages and other essential amenities in respect of contract labour as the appropriate Government may deem fit to impose in accordance with the rules, if any, made under Section 35 and shall be issued on payment of such fees and on the deposit of such sum, if any, as security for the due performance of the conditions as may be prescribed [Section 12 (2)].

   If we consider the provisions of Section 7 read with Section 12, we find that where workmen are employed by a principal employer through a contractor and if two conditions of obtaining registration under Section 7 of the Act by the principal employer and of holding licence by the contractor under Section 12 of this Act are not complied with, the concerned workmen can claim to be the direct employees of the principal employer. In Food

Corporation of India Workers' Union V. Food Corporation of India [1990 I CLR 829 (Guj. H.C.)] Case, where in relation to period for which the Food Corporation of India did not possess the Certificate of Registration and contractors through whom workmen were employed also had no license and hence, it was held that workmen could claim to be the direct employees of the Food Corporation of India.

3. Grant of Licences [Section 13]

(1) Every application for the grant of a licence under sub-section (1) of Section 12 shall be made in the prescribed form and shall contain the particulars regarding the location of the establishment, the nature of process, operation or work for which contract labour is to be employed and such other particulars as may be prescribed [Section 13 (1)].

(2) The licensing officer may make such investigation in respect of the application received under sub-section (1) and in making any such investigation the licensing officer shall follow such procedure as may be prescribed [Section 13 (2)].

(3) A licence granted under this Chapter shall be valid for the period specified therein and may be renewed from time to time for such period and on payment of such fees and on such conditions as may be prescribed [Section 13 (3)].

4. Revocation, Suspension and Amendment of Licenses [Section 14]

(1) If the licensing officer is satisfied, either on a reference made to him in this behalf or otherwise, that

    (a) a licence granted under Section 12 has been obtained by misrepresentation or suppression of any material fact, or

    (b) the holder of a licence has, without reasonable cause, failed to comply with the conditions subject to which the licence has been granted or has contravened any of the provisions of this Act or the rules made thereunder, then, without prejudice to any other penalty to which the holder of the licence may be liable under this Act, the licensing officer may, after giving the holder to the licence an opportunity of showing cause, revoke or suspend the licence or forfeit the sum, if any, or any portion thereof deposited as security for the due performance of the conditions subject to which the licence has been granted [Section 14 (1)].

(2) Subject to any rules that may be made in this behalf, the licensing officer may vary or amend a licence granted under Section 12 [Section 14 (2)].

5. Appeal [Section 15]

(1) Any person aggrieved by an order made under Section 7, Section 8, Section 12 or Section 14 may, within thirty days from the date on which the order is communicated to him, prefer an appeal to an appellate officer who shall be a person nominated in this behalf by the appropriate Government [Section 15 (1)].

It is further provided that the appellate officer may entertain the appeal after the expiry of the said period of thirty days, if he is satisfied that the appellant was prevented by sufficient cause from filing the appeal in time [Proviso to Section 15 (1)].

(2) On receipt of an appeal under sub-section (1), the appellate officer shall, after giving the appellant an opportunity of being heard, dispose of the appeal as expeditiously as possible [Section 15 (2)].

4.22 Chapter V: Welfare and Health of Contract Labour

Provisions relating to welfare and health of contract labour have been made in sections from sixteen to nineteen of Chapter V of the Act. Following are these provisions.

1. **Canteens [Section 16]**
   (1) The appropriate Government may make rules requiring that in every establishment–
      (a) to which this Act applies,
      (b) wherein work requiring employment of contract labour is likely to continue for such period as may be prescribed, and
      (c) wherein contract labour numbering one hundred or more is ordinarily employed by a contractor, one or more canteens shall be provided and maintained by the contractor for the use of such contract labour [Section 16 (1)].
   (2) Without prejudice to the generality of the foregoing power, such rules may provide for –
      (a) the date by which the canteen shall be provided;
      (b) the number of canteens that shall be provided, and the standards in respect of construction, accommodation, furniture and other equipment of the canteens; and
      (c) the foodstuffs which may be served therein and the charges which may be made therefore [Section 16 (2)].

2. **Rest-Rooms [Section 17]**
   (1) In every place wherein contract labour is required to halt at night in connection with the work of an establishment –
      (a) to which this Act applies, and
      (b) in which work requiring employment of contract labour is likely to continue for such period as may be prescribed, there shall be provided and maintained by the contractor for the use of the contract labour such number of rest-rooms or such other suitable alternative accommodation within such time as may be prescribed [Section 17 (1)].
   (2) The rest-rooms or the alternative accommodation to be provided under sub-section (1) shall be sufficiently lighted and ventilated and shall be maintained in a clean and comfortable condition [Section 17 (2)].

3. **Other Facilities [Section 18]**
   It shall be the duty of every contractor employing contract labour in connection with the work of an establishment to which this Act applies, to provide and maintain –

(1) a sufficient supply of wholesome drinking water for the contract labour at convenient places;
(2) a sufficient number of latrines and urinals of the prescribed types so situated as to be convenient and accessible to the contract labour in the establishment; and
(3) washing facilities [Section 18].

4. First-Aid Facilities [Section 19]

There shall be provided and maintained by the contractor so as to be readily accessible during all working hours a first-aid box equipped with the prescribed contents at every place where contract labour is employed by him [Section 19].

Various welfare and health facilities to be provided under this Act according to the Sections from 16 to 19 are summerized below:

(1) If the work is likely to be continued for the prescribed period or for more than that period when one hundred or more contract labourers are employed, canteen facilities are required to be provided by the concerned contractor.
(2) If the contract work is likely to be continued for the prescribed period or for more than that period, the contractor has to provide rest-room facility to the contract labourers.
(3) Every contractor employing contract labour is required to provide certain other facilities like wholesome drinking water, sufficient number of latrines and urinals, washing facilities to the contract labour.
(4) Every contractor employing contract labour has to provide and maintain well-equipped first aid boxes with the prescribed contents at all places where contract labour is employed by him. Moreover, all such first aid boxes should be readily accessible during working hours.

5. Liability for Principal Employer in Certain Cases [Section 20]

If the contractor does not provide various facilities which have been made compulsory to be provided under this Act e.g. canteen, rest-rooms, latrines and urinals etc., the principal employer has to provide them and then the expenses incurred in that connection by the principal employer can be recovered from the concerned contractor or contractors. The provisions relating to the liability of the principal employer in certain cases are given in Section 20 which is reproduced below:

(1) If any amenity required to be provided under Section 16, Section 17, Section 18 or Section 19 for the benefit of the contract labour employed in an establishment is not provided by the contractor within the time prescribed therefor, such amenity shall be provided by the principal employer within such time as may be prescribed [Section 20 (1)].

(2) All expenses incurred by the principal employer in providing the amenity may be recovered by the principal employer from the contractor either by deduction from any amount payable to the contractor under any contract or as a debt payable by the contractor [Section 20 (2)].

6. Responsibility for Making Payment of Wages [Section 21]

It has been provided in the Act that the wages should be paid by the contractor to the contract labour employed by him and that too in the presence of a representative duly authorised by the principal employer. But if in case the contractor fails to make payment of wages within the prescribed time to his contract labour or if he makes short payment, it is the responsibility of the principal employer to make such wage-payments. However, the principal employer is entitled to recover the wage payments thus made from the contractor. The provisions relating to the responsibility for making payment of wages to the contract labour have been made in exhaustively in Section 21 of the Act which are given below:

(1) A contractor shall be responsible for payment of wages to each worker employed by him as contract labour and such wags shall be paid before the expiry of such period as may be prescribed [Section 21 (1)].

(2) Every principal employer shall nominate a representative duly authorised by him to be present at the time of disbursement of wages by the contract and it shall be the duty of such representative to certify the amounts paid as wages in such manner as may be prescribed [Section 21 (2)].

(3) It shall be the duty of the contractor to ensure the disbursement of wages in the presence of the authorised representative of the principal employer [Section 21 (3)].

(4) In case the contractor fails to make payment of wages within the prescribed period or makes short payment, then the principal employer shall be liable to make payment of wages in full or the unpaid balance due, as the case may be, to the contract labour employed by the contractor and recover the amount so paid from the contractor either by deduction from any amount payable to the contractor under any contract or as a debt payable by the contractor [Section 21 (4)].

4.23 Chapter VI: Penalties and Procedure

Provisions have been made in the Act for imposition of penalties for various offences such as obstructions of the Inspectors, contravention of the provisions regarding employment of contract labour etc. and procedure relating to the imposition of penalties is also laid down.

1. For obstructing the Inspector, the penalty is the imprisonment upto three months or a fine upto ₹ Five hundred or both.

2. For the contravention of the provisions of the employment of the contract labourers, the punishment is the imprisonment upto three months or a fine upto One Thousand Rupees or both. But if the offence of contravention is continued, the fine can be imposed upto ₹ One hundred for every day of contravention.

3. For any other offences, the punishment is the imprisonment upto three months or a fine upto ₹ One thousand or both.

4. For offences by the companies, the company as well as every person incharge of the company are held responsible.

It should be noted that – (1) a complaint is required to be filed within three months from the date on which the commission of the offence comes to the knowledge of the Inspector, and (2) only a Presidency Magistrate or a Magistrate of First Class or any above authority can try the offences punishable under this Act.

In order to know the exact provisions of the Sections from 22 to 27, they are stated below as are given in the Act.

1. Offence of Obstructing the Inspector and Imposition of penalty in that respect [Section 22]

(1) Whoever obstructs an inspector in the discharge of his duties under this Act or refuses or wilfully neglects to afford the inspector any reasonable facility for making any inspection, examination, inquiry or investigation authorised by or under this Act in relation to an establishment to which, or a contractor to whom, this Act applies, shall be punishable with imprisonment for a term which may extend to three months, or with fine which may extend to five hundred rupees, or with both [Section 22 (1)].

(2) Whoever wilfully refuses to produce on the demand of an inspector any register or other document kept in pursuance of this Act or prevents or attempts to prevent or does anything which he has reason to believe is likely to prevent any person from appearing before or being examined by an inspector acting in pursuance of his duties under this Act, shall be punishable with imprisonment for a term which may extend to three months, or with a fine which may extend to five hundred rupees, or with both [Section 22 (2)].

2. Offence of Convention of provisions regarding employment of contract labour

Whoever contravenes any provision of this Act or of any rules made thereunder prohibiting, restricting or regulating the employment of contract labour, or contravenes any condition of a licence granted under this Act, shall be punishable with imprisonment for a term which may extend to three months, or with fine which may extend to one thousand rupees, or with both, and in the case of a continuing contravention with an additional fine which may extend to one hundred rupees for every day during which such contravention continues after conviction for the first such contravention [Section 23].

3. Other offences and imposition of penalty [Section 24]

"If any person contravenes any of the provisions of this Act or of any rules made thereunder for which no other penalty is elsewhere provided, he shall be punishable with imprisonment for a term which may extend to three months, or with fine which may extend to one thousand rupees, or with both [Section 24].

4. Offences by Companies [Section 25]

(1) If the person committing an offence under this Act is a company, the company as well as every person in charge of, and responsible to, the company for the conduct of its business at the time of the commission of the offence shall be deemed to be guilty of the offence and shall be liable to be proceeded against and punished accordingly [Section 25 (1)].

It is also provided that nothing contained in this sub-section shall render any such person liable to any punishment if he proves that the offence was committed without his knowledge or that he exercised all due diligence to prevent the commission of such offence [Proviso to Section 25 (1)].

(2) Notwithstanding anything contained in sub-section (1), where an offence under this Act has been committed by a company and it is proved that the offence has been committed with the consent or connivance of, or that the commission of the offence is attributable to any neglect on the part of any director, manager, managing agent or any other officer of the company, such director, manager, managing agent or such other officer shall also be deemed to be guilty of that offence and shall be liable to be proceeded against and punished accordingly [Section 25 (2)].

Explanation: For the purpose of this section –
(a) "company" means any body corporate and incudes a firm or other association of individuals; and
(b) "director" in relation to a firm, means a partner in the firm.

5. **Cognizance of Offences [Section 26]**

"No Court shall take cognizance of any offence under this Act except on a complaint made by, or with the previous sanction in writing of the inspector and no Court inferior to that of a Presidency Magistrate or a Magistrate of the first class shall try any offence punishable under this Act" [Section 26].

6. **Provisions relating to the limitations of prosecutions [Section 27]**

"No Court shall take cognisance of an offence punishable under this Act unless the complaint thereof is made within three months from the date on which the alleged commission of offence came to the knowledge of an inspector" [Section 27].

But it is provided that where the offence consists of disobeying a written order made by an inspector, complaint thereof may be made within six months of the date on which the offence is alleged to have been committed [Proviso to Section 27].

4.24 Chapter VII: Miscellaneous

Inspecting Staff [Section 28]

1. **Appointment of Inspectors [Section 28 (1)]**

In Section 28 (1) of the Act, provisions have been made to appoint inspectors for the purposes of the Act. It states that, "the appropriate Government may, by notification in the Official Gazette, appoint such persons as it thinks fit to be inspectors for the purposes of this Act, and define the local limits within which they shall exercise their powers under this Act".

2. **Powers, Rights, and Duties of an Inspectors [Section 28 (2)]**

From the provisions of Section 28 (2), we come to know the powers, rights, duties of the Inspectors appointed under Section 28 (1) of the Act. Such duties, powers etc. are as follows:

Subject to any rules made in this behalf, an inspector may, within the local limits for which he is appointed –

(1) enter, at all reasonable hours, with such assistance (if any), being persons in the service of the Government or any local or other public authority as he thinks fit, any premises or place where contract labour is employed, for the purpose of examining any register or record or notices required to be kept or exhibited by or under this Act or Rules made thereunder, and require the production thereof for inspection;

(2) examine any person whom he finds in any such premises or place and who, he has reasonable cause to believe, is a workman employed therein;

(3) require any person giving out work and any workman, to give any information, which is in his power to give with respect to the names and addresses of the persons to, for and from whom the work is given out or received, and with respect to the payments to be made for the work;

(4) seize or take copies of register, record of wages or notices or portions thereof as he may consider relevant in respect of an offence under this Act which he has reason to believe has been committed by the principal employer or contractor; and

(5) exercise such other powers as may be prescribed.

3. Maintenance of Registers and Records [Section 29]

The responsibility of maintaining the registers and records has been placed on the principal employer and contractor under Section 28 of the Act and the Rules made thereunder. Now let us consider the provisions of Section 29 and rules made by the Government of Maharashtra in this behalf.

4. Effects of Laws and Agreements [Section 30]

It is provided in Section 30 of this Act that the Laws and Agreements which are not consistent with the provisions of this Act will not have any over-riding effect. This implies that the provisions of this Act will prevail unless the other laws or/and agreements provide for more favourable terms, than those comtemplated in this Act. The provisions of Section 30 as given in the Act.

Section 30: Effects laws and agreements inconsistent with this Act:

(1) The provisions of this Act shall have effect notwithstanding anything inconsistent therewith contained in any other law or in the terms of any agreement or contract of service, or in any standing order applicable to the establishment whether made before or after the commencement of the Act: [Section 30 (1)].

It is also provided that where under any such agreement, contract of service or standing orders the contract labour employed in the establishment are entitled to benefits in respect of any matter which are more favourable to them than those to which they would be entitled under this Act, the contract labour shall continue to be entitled to the more favourable benefits in respect of that matter, notwithstanding that they receive benefits in respect of other matters under this Act [Proviso to Section 30 (1)].

(2) Nothing contained in this Act shall be construed as precluding any such contract labour from entering into an agreement with the principal employer or the contractor, as the case may be, for granting them rights or privileges in respect of any matter which are more favourable to them than those to which they would be entitled under this Act [Section 30 (2)].

5. Power to Exempt [Section 31]

The Appropriate Government is vested with the power to exempt any establishment from the provisions of this Act. Section 31 states that, "The appropriate Government may, in the case of an emergency, direct, by notification in the Official Gazette, that subject to such conditions and restrictions, if any, and for such period or periods, as may be specified in the notification, all or any of the provisions of this Act or the rules made thereunder shall not apply to any establishment or class of establishments or any class of contractors.

6. Protection of Action Taken in Good Faith [Section 32]

It is provided in Section 32 that no prosecution will lie against any member of the Advisory Board or any Government servant under this Act for the action taken by them under this Act in good faith. According to Section 32 (1), "No suit, prosecution or other legal proceedings shall lie against any registering officer, licensing officer or any other Government servant or against any member of the Central Board or the State Board as the case may be, for anything which is in good faith done or intended to be done in pursuance of this Act or any rule or order made thereunder" [Section 32 (2) further states that, "No suit or other legal proceeding shall lie against the Government for any damage caused or likely to be caused by anything which is in good faith done or intended to be done in pursuance of this Act or any rules or other made thereunder".

7. Power of the Central Government to give directions and to remove difficulties [Sections 33 and 34]

The Central Government is vested with the power to direct the State Government for implementing the provisions of this Act in that State. Section 33 of the Act says that, "The Central Government may give directions to the Government of any State as to the carrying into execution in the State of the provisions contained in this Act".

The Central Government is also empowered to remove the difficulties in giving effect to the provisions of this Act by passing necessary orders and publishing the same in the Official Gazette. According to the provisions of Section 34, "If any difficulty arises in giving effect to the provisions of this Act, the Central Government may, by order published in the Official Gazette, make such provisions not inconsistent with the provisions of this Act, as appears to it to be necessary or expedient for removing the difficulty".

8. Power to make rules [Section 35]

The Appropriate Government is vested with necessary powers to make rules under Section 35 of this Act which is as follows:

(1) The appropriate Government may, subject to the condition of previous publication, make rules for carrying out the purposes of this Act [Section 35 (1)].

(2) In particular, and without prejudice to the generality of the foregoing power, such rules may provide for all company of the following matters, namely:

(a) the number of persons to be appointed members representing various interests on the Central Board and the State Board, the term of their office and other conditions of service, the procedure to be followed in the discharge of their functions and the manner of filling vacancies;

(b) the times and places of the meetings of any committee constituted under this Act, the procedure to be followed at such meetings including the quorum necessary for the transaction of business, and the fees and allowances that may be paid to the members of a committee;

(c) the manner in which establishment may be registered under Section 7, the levy of a fee therefor and the form of certificate of registration;

(d) the form of application for the grant or renewal of a licence under Section 13 and the particulars it may contain;

(e) the manner in which an investigation is to be made in respect of an application for the grant of a licence and the matters to be taken into account in granting or refusing a licence;

(f) the form of a licence which may be granted or renewed under Section 12 and the conditions subject to which the licence may be granted or renewed, the fees to be levied for the grant or renewal of a licence and the deposit of any sum as security for the performance of such conditions;

(g) the circumstances under which licences may be varied or amended under Section 14;

(h) the form and manner in which appeals may be filed under Section 15 and the procedure to be followed by appellate officers in disposing of the appeals;

(i) the time within which facilities required by this Act, to be provided and maintained may be so provided by the contractor and in case of default on the part of the contractor, by the principal employer;

(j) the number and types of canteens, rest-rooms, latrines and urinals that should be provided and maintained;

(k) the type of equipment that should be provided in the first- aid boxes;

(l) the period within which wages payable to contract labour should be paid by the contractor under sub-section (1) of Section 21;

(m) the form of registers and records to be maintained by principal employers and contractors;

(n) the submission of returns, forms in which, and the authorities to which, such returns may be submitted;

(o) the collection of any information or statistics in relation to contract labour and;

(p) any other matter which has to be, or may be, prescribed under this Act [Section 35 (2)].

(3) Every rule made by the Central Government under this Act shall be laid as soon as may be after it is made, before each House of Parliament while it is in session for a total period of thirty days which may be comprised in one session or in two successive sessions, and if before the expiry of the session in which it is so laid or the session immediately following, both Houses agree in making any modification in the rule or both Houses agree that the rule should not be made, the rule shall thereafter have effect only in such modified form or be of no effect, as the case may be, so however, that any such modification or annulment shall be without prejudice to the validity of anything previously done under that rule [Section 35 (3)].

Exercise

1. Explain various provisions relating to procedure for submission of Draft Standing Orders [I.E. (S.O.) Act, 1946].

2. Explain various provisions relating to Duration and Modification of Standing Orders and Procedure [I.E. (S.O.) Act, 1946].

3. Explain the different penalties and procedure [I.E. (S.O.) Act, 1946].

4. Discuss the various provisions regarding registration of establishments employing Contract Labour [C.L. (R & A) Act, 1970].

5. Describe the provisions for Licensing of Contractors [C.L. (R & A) Act, 1970].

6. Describe the various provisions regarding Welfare and Health of Contract Labour [C.L. (R & A) Act, 1970].

7. Explain the powers, rights and duties of an inspector [C.L. (R & A) Act, 1970].

8. Write short notes on:

   (a) Employer [I.E. (S.O.) Act, 1946]

   (b) Certification of Standing Orders [I.E. (S.O.) Act, 1946]

   (c) Payment of Subsistence Allowance [I.E. (S.O.) Act, 1946]

   (d) Wages [C.L. (R and A) Act, 1970].

***

Chapter 5...

IR Initiative

Contents ...
5.1 Workers Participation in Management: Concept, Evolution, Implementation, Challenges
5.2 Collective Bargaining: Concept, Evolution and Implementation
• Questions for Discussion

Learning Objectives ...
- To understand the concept and evolution of Workers Participation in Management
- To discuss the duties and functions of works committee
- To describe the functions of joint and shop council
- To list the challenges of Workers Participation in Management
- To study the concept of collective bargaining
- To elaborate the features of Collective Bargaining
- To explain the importance of collective bargaining
- To know the process of collective bargaining

5.1 Workers Participation in Management: Concept, Evolution, Implementation, Challenges

1. **Meaning of Workers Participation in Management**

The concept of workers' participation in management has been a vague and debatable issue in the field of industrial relations and hence, it has acquired different meanings for different people. It is difficult to define the concept of workers' participation very clearly because it is associated with varying practices in different countries, its content and form being in accordance with the socio-economic objectives of a country. However, it seems that the concept of workers' participation in management has its roots in the human relations movement in the domain of industrial organisations. The humanitarian approach to labour has brought about a new set of values for labour and management.

Definitions of Workers Participation in Management

(1) **Keith Davis:** *"Workers' participation in management is a mental and emotional involvement of a person in a group which encourages him to contribute to the goals and share responsibilities in them".*

(2) **C. B. Mamoria:** *"Workers' participation in management is a system of communication and consultation either in formal or informal way by which employees of organisation are kept informal about the affairs of the undertaking and through which they express their opinion and contribute to management decisions".*

(3) International Labour Organisation [I.L.O.]: *"Workers' participation may, broadly, be taken to cover all terms of association of workers and their representatives with the decision-making process, ranging from exchanging of information, consultations, decisions and negotiations to more institutionalised forms such as the presence of workers' member on management or supervisory boards or even management by workers themselves as practised in Yugoslavia".*

(4) McGregor Douglas: *"The term workers' participation implies a formal method of providing an opportunity for every member of the organisation to contribute his brain and ingenuity as well as his physical efforts to the improvement of organisational effectiveness".*

2. Pre-requisites of Workers Participation in Management

It is needless to say that workers' participation in management, besiders other things, provides a better status to workers and helps to create industrial democracy. It also makes workers more responsible and responsive to the needs of their organisation. Moreover, it creates a feeling of involvement among workers and it acts as a bridge between the management and workers. Hence, it is very essential to create suitable atmosphere for making the workers' participation in management successful. Following are some of the important pre-requisites or conditions for the successful functioning of workers' participation schemes in management.

(1) The attitude of an organisation/management should be constructive and progressive. It must sincerely and whole heartedly accept the concept of workers' participation and must be prepared to give a fair trial to the schemes of workers' participation.

(2) Both parties should have genuine faith, mutual trust in the system and in each other. Moreover, they must be willing to work together.

(3) There should be progressive management and it should recognise its obligations, responsibilities etc. towards their unions.

(4) Trade union must be strong and democratic with a genuine and prudent leadership. The union leaders should have genuine desire to participate in the management. The attitude of union leaders should be positive, co-operative and not aggressive.

(5) There should be closely and mutually formulated objectives for successful participation by management as well as trade unions.

(6) There should be effective two-way communication for making the workers' participation successful. For that purpose, frequent meetings of representatives of workers and their employers /management should be held to discuss various issues relating to workers' participation schemes and to conduct negotiations for the solution of pending problems. Both the parties should do all the efforts to develop a favourable attitude towards the schemes of participative management.

(7) Workers should be given proper education and training as regards the schemes of workers participation. Along with workers, supervisory staff should also be associated with the management.

(8) The follow-up actions on the decisions of the participating forums should be ensured.

(9) There should be full recognition of the rights and claims of both the parties. Workers should be no doubt conscious of their rights, but at the same time, emphasis must also be laid on their responsibilities.

(10) Workers' participation in the management cannot be effective unless the state of labour-management relations in the organisation is healthy. Besides this, workers' participation in management cannot be effective unless there is an adequate machinery for collective bargaining.

3. **Objectives of Workers Participation in Management**

Workers' participation in management is considered as a means of self-realisation in work. Further, it helps to meet the psychological needs of workers at work by eliminating to a large extent the feeling of futility, isolation and consequent frustration that they face in normal industrial setting. The objectives of workers' participation in management may vary from country to country because socio-economic development, political philosophy, industrial relations scene, attitudes of working class and of trade unions are different. However, the objectives of workers' participation in management which are considered as very important are mentioned below.

(1) To develop good industrial relations.

(2) To create and increase better understanding among the workers about their role and place in the process of attainment of organisational goals and objectives.

(3) To stimulate workers for higher productivity for the benefits of themselves for the advantage of their organisations and society at large.

(4) To satisfy the workers' social and esteem needs.

(5) To create among the workers the feeling of dignity and self-respect.

(6) To strengthen labour-management co-operation for maintaining industrial peace and harmony.

(7) To establish industrial democracy.

(8) To avoid external interference.

(9) To build the dynamic human resource systematically.

(10) To share financial and other information about the organisation for the purpose of collective bargaining.

4. **Advantages of Workers Participation in Management**

The basic idea or principle behind the workers' participation in management is to increase the workers' influence in the management of an enterprise or an organisation to which they belong in order to solve their problems relating to their work. Following points make clear the benefits or advantages of workers' participation in management.

(1) It helps to promote good and healthy industrial relations for creating and maintaining industrial peace.

(2) It creates a better understanding in workers about their role, responsibilities and place in the process of attainment of organisational goals. It, in turn, leads to workers' commitment to their work and towards their organisation.

(3) It helps to improve the quality of decision making as workers/ employees can offer useful suggestions and recommendations regarding the working and for solving their problems.
(4) It eliminates the differences of opinion between workers and their management and facilitates team work.
(5) When workers' participation is effective, it increases a sense of confidence and trust in the minds of workers towards the management. As a result, workers give full co-operation and accept the change without much resistance. This also helps to avoid strikes and lockouts.
(6) When workers co-operate fully and whole heartedly, it leads to higher productivity and efficiency.
(7) Workers' participation in management satisfies the social and esteem needs of the workers.

5. Disadvantages of Workers Participation in Management

Workers' participation in management has to overcome a lot of limitations to succeed. Some of these limitations are:
(1) Today technology and organisations are extremely complex and hence specialised work-roles are necessary. Due to this employees can not participate effectively in matters beyond their particular environment.
(2) Everybody need not necessarily want participation.
(3) Trade unions are not pro participative management and hence do not promote it.
(4) Employers are unwilling to share power with the workers' representatives.
(5) Managers consider participative management a fraud.

6. Levels of Workers Participation in Management

Workers' participation in management is important for maintaining the smooth and healthy industrial relations. It helps the workers to protect their interests. Management and workers are benefited thereby. The workers' participation is possible at all levels of management. Much depends upon the nature of functions, the strength of the workers, the attitudes of the trade unions and also that of management. The areas and degrees of the workers' participation can differ considerably at different levels depending upon the circumstances, needs etc.

Broadly speaking, there can be four stages of participation. At the initial stage, participation may be informative and associative participation. In such type of participation, the members are entitled to receive information, to give and discuss suggestions on the general economic condition of their organisation, the state of market, production, sales programmes, organisation, long-term plans of growth and development etc. At the consultative participation level, the workers are consulted on various matters such as welfare facilities, adoption of new technology and the problems emanting from it, safety measures etc. These aspects are directly related to the workers. In administrative participation, there is a greater degree of sharing of authority and responsibility of management functions. In such participation, the members are given a little more autonomy in exercising administrative and supervisory powers in respect of certain matters like welfare and safety measures, operation of training and development programmes, preparation of schedules of working hours, breaks, holidays etc. Decision-making participation is the highest form of participation. However, the management always likes to maintain its decision-making authority intact.

The workers' participation in management involves participation through representative of workers. Hence, its level can be considered in this context also. Generally, there can be following three levels at which workers' participation in management can take place.

- **(1) Shop-floor level:** At shop-floor, shop-floor councils or committees are constituted. In such committees, the representatives of management and workers are included. They consider and discuss various matters, problems relating to a particular shop.
- **(2) Plant level:** There are many plants of an organisation or company which are located in different geographical areas. When this is the situation, plant level participation of workers in management proves to be useful and advantageous for maintaining good industrial relations. Where a company or an enterprise has a single plant, plant level participation is not needed. Various matters, problems are dealt at the plant level which have relevance for all shop-floors and they cannot be solved at shop-floor level.
- **(3) Enterprise level:** At enterprise level, workers' participation for constructive co-operation is much needed. Such participation can be in the forms of management committees, co-partnership representation of workers at the level of Board of Directors.

7. **Types of Workers Participation in Management**

The forms or methods in which workers can participate in management vary, depending upon the pattern of management, levels of management, size of the factory, authority delegated to subordinates, areas in which participation is sought etc. Certain methods are specified by the legal framework while certain methods are evolved in the process. In India some methods have been prescribed by law while many other methods have been suggested through guidelines formulated by the Government.

When workers participate in management either through formal mechanism or through informal procedures, it is considered as an instance of participative management. For this effective functioning, both the parties i.e. labour and management, must be keenly interested. It is obvious that management interest basically lies in reducing cost and in improving the productivity. On the other hand, workers are interested to increase their earnings and to get various facilities. When earnings increase through sharing gains in productivity, a harmony of interests can be promoted. Hence, if participation is to be made effective and successful as a process or device, it should be integrated properly with a scheme of improving productivity as well as gain sharing.

Participation can be ascending participation or descending participation. In ascending participation, workers are given an opportunity to influence managerial decisions at higher levels through their elected representatives. While in descending participation, workers may be given more powers to plan and make decisions about their work.

Following are the important forms or methods of workers' participation in management.

(1) Works Committee

A works committee is a forum provided under the Industrial Disputes Act of 1947 for explaining the difficulties of the parties concerned with the disputes. It endeavours to maintain cordial relationship even though there are disputes or differences between the parties to the disputes. The success of work committees mainly depends on the efforts and co-operation of both the parties to the disputes.

Section 3 (1) of this Act provides for a Works Committee. According to this section, in the case of any industrial establishment in which one hundred or more workmen are employed or have been employed on any day in the preceding twelve months, the appropriate Government may by general or special order require the employer to constitute in the prescribed manner a Works Committee consisting of representatives of employers and workmen engaged in the establishment. However, the number of representatives of workmen on the committee shall not be less than the number of representatives of the employer. The representatives of the workmen shall be chosen in the prescribed manner from among the workmen engaged in the establishment and in consultation with their trade union, if any, registered under the Indian Trade Unions Act, 1926. Section 3 (2) further provides that it shall be the duty of the Works Committee to promote measures for securing and preserving amity and good relations between the employer and workmen and, to that end to comment upon matters of their common interest or concern and endeavour to compose any material difference of opinion in respect of such matters.

Industrial Disputes Act, 1947 promotes the settlement of industrial disputes firstly by voluntary negotiations. The Works Committees are the prominent efforts towards that goal. Works Committees are joint committees having equal number of the representatives of employers and workmen. The constitution of Works Committee is must in an industrial establishment wherein one hundred or more workmen are employed on any day in preceding twelve months. Works Committee is an internal media for settlement of Industrial Disputes Act within the industry.

Duties or Functions of Works Committee

Sub-section 2 of Section 3 of this Act enumerates the duties or functions of a Works Committee which are as follows:

(a) To remove the disparities between employers and workmen;

(b) To promote measures for securing and preserving amity, and friendly and good relations between the employers and workmen;

(c) To that end, to comment upon all matters of their common interest or concern;

(d) To make efforts to compose any material difference of opinion in respect of various matters. These matters include so many aspects such as welfare of workers, provision and supervision of various recreational facilities, training of workmen and their wages, bonus, gratuity, working conditions including discipline, promotions, transfers etc. Thus, it seems that there is no subject concerning the relation between the employers and workmen which the Works Committee is precluded from considering. However, following points must be remembered in this connection.

(i) Findings of the Works Committee are advisory or recommendatory and not mandatory. It cannot decide and pass final judgement. Its duty is only to comment because it is mainly a negotiating organ. It is the function of the Works Committee to promote measures for harmonious, and friendly and good relations between the employers and workmen.

(ii) Works Committees are not intended to supersede or supplement the trade unions for the purpose of collective bargaining. They are not authorised to consider real changes or substantial changes in the service conditions. They are not a substitute of trade unions.

The success of a works committee mainly depends upon (a) the responsible and positive attitude on the part of management and (b) the wholehearted implementation of its recommendations. Being a legal provision, works committees have been constituted in most of the organisations.

(2) Joint Management Councils

A Joint Management Council (JMC) consists of representatives of management and workers. The J. M. Council performs advisory role on various matters specified. The J. M. Council is expected to be consulted on matters relating to the administration of standing orders, welfare measures, rationalisation, retrenchment etc. The important functions performed by a J. M. Council are as follows:

(a) A J.M.C. is to be consulted by the management on the matters like standing orders, rationalisation, retrenchment, closure, reduction of operations.

(b) To receive information, to discuss and offer suggestions on general economic situations, market position, production and marketing programmes, methods of production, long-term capital budgeting decisions, modernisation, development and growth etc.

(c) To shoulder administrative responsibilities like maintaining welfare measures, safety measures, training schemes and progammes, payment of rewards, scheduling of working hours, problems of indiscipline, absenteeism etc. A J. M. Council takes up and suggests the measures in respect of the matters mentioned above.

It should be noted that J. M. Council merely performs the advisory role on the matter specified and its recommendations are not accepted as a mandatory requirement. Further, various matters which are likely to be sorted out through collective bargaining such as wages, bonus etc. are kept out of its purview. Similarly, it does not deal with the personal problems of an individual worker.

In India, a large number of J. M. Councils are established. However, the real contribution of the councils is limited.

Following are the important reasons of the limited success of the J. M. Councils:

(i) Trade unions generally oppose to such councils as the trade unions feel that their importance may be reduced in course of time. Hence, their attitude towards the J. M. Council becomes negative.

(ii) The attitude of employers or managements of the organisations is not progressive and favourable for the effective working of the J. M. Councils.

(3) Workers' Participation on the Board of Directors

Appointments of employees' or workers' representatives on the Board of Directors is an important form or method of workers' participation in management. The basic idea behind this method is that the workers' representation of the Board of Directors' Level may help to establish industrial democracy and to create and maintain better employer- employee relations. As workers' representatives are appointed on the Board of Directors, it is expected that they would do all the efforts to protect the interests of their workers.

Under this method, the representatives are either elected or nominated, may be two or three, by the workers who attend the meeting of the Board and participate in their deliberations. The representatives of workers on the Board of Directors do all the efforts to bring to the notice of other directors the views, problems etc. of the workers and give suggestions. Thus, they participate in the process of problem solving and decision-making at the top level. However, this method is not much effective in bridging the gap between workers and their management because of the following important reasons:

(a) As the workers' representatives are in minority they cannot bring any pressure on the other Directors. As a result, suggestion of the representatives of workers are not given proper or due attention and the gap between the two parties continue.

(b) The Board meetings are held mainly to discuss managerial problems and not the problems of workers. Naturally, the workers' representatives get limited opportunities to discuss views, problems etc. of the.workers.

(c) Decision-making process at the board level is rather complex, complicated which require specific skills than alternative form of participation for which workers' representatives neither possess skills nor they have mental set.

(d) There are rival trade unions. Naturally, workers' representatives appointed on the Board cannot put forward the views, problems, suggestions which are acceptable to all the workers. Moreover, participation at the board level weakens the bargaining power of trade unions as they have to accept the decisions of the Board having their own representatives.

(4) Suggestion Scheme

Under this scheme, workers are associated with the management through their suggestions on various matters relating to their working. A suggestion committee or suggestion screening committee is constituted with equal representation from management and workers. Workers are encouraged to give their suggestions to the management. The committee constituted for that purpose screens and evaluates the suggestions received from workers. The suggestions are accepted if they are found suitable and useful. Rewards are also given to those workers who give constructive suggestions for the benefit of all. Suggestion boxes are kept at convenient places in some organisations. The suggestions also can be given to a joint committee of workers and management or to the departmental heads.

(5) Shop Councils

A shop council is a method or a form of workers' participation in management wherein for each department or a shop in an unit, a shop council is constituted. Each shop council is consisted of an equal number of representatives of employers and workers. The employers' representatives are nominated by the management. All such representatives are nominated from within the unit concerned.

The workers' representatives are obviously from among the workers of their department or shop concerned. The number of members of each shop council is determined by the employers in consultation with the recognised trade union. Generally, the total number of a shop council does not exceed twelve. Various decisions of a shop council are arrived at on the basis of consensus and not by the process of voting. A shop council works for a minimum period of two years. In other words, the tenure of a shop council is for a period of two years. This method of workers' participation was launched in India in 1975.

Functions of Shop Councils

Following are the important functions of the shop councils:

(a) To assist the management in achieving production targets.

(b) To take necessary steps to improve productivity, efficiency and to increase production to the optimum.

(c) To eliminate wastage and to do all efforts to utilise effectively manpower and machine capacity.

(d) To recommend various steps to reduce absenteeism in the shop or department considering the causes of absenteeism.

(e) To make suggestions for providing safety measures.

(f) To assist to maintain general discipline in the shop or department.

(g) To provide various welfare measures for efficient running of the shop or department.

(h) To do all efforts to provide various physical facilities such as lighting, ventilation, dust control, noise control etc.

(i) To ensure proper flow of adequate two-way communication between the management and workers for efficient working of the shop or department.

(6) Joint Councils

There is a participation of management and of workers in the Joint Councils. These councils work for the whole unit and their membership remains confined to those who are actually engaged in the organisation. The tenure of the Joint Councils is for two years.

The Chief Executive of the unit works as the chairman and workers' members of the council nominate the Vice-Chairman. The Secretary is appointed by the Joint Council.

The Joint Councils meet once in four months, but the periodicity of the meeting varies from unit to unit, it may be once in a month, quarter etc.

The decisions are taken in the Joint Council meeting by the process of consensus and the management implements the discussions within one month.

Under the 20-Point Economic Programme, factories employing five hundred or more workers constituted Joint Councils.

A Joint Council performs certain functions.

Functions of Joint Councils

Following are important functions performed by Joint Councils from which their nature becomes clear.

(a) To increase the output by fixation of standards.

(b) To consider various matters which could not be solved by shop councils.

(c) To do all efforts to develop the skills of workers by providing them necessary and adequate training facilities.

(d) To encourage the employees for research and to give awards to workers involving creative work.

(e) To prepare a schedule of working laws.

(f) To ensure full and proper utilisation of finished goods.

(g) To provide general health, welfare and safety measures for the unit of the plant.

(7) Unit Councils

The scheme of workers' participation was launched in 1977 in commercial and service organisations in the public sector. The scheme envisaged setting up of unit councils in those units which employ at least One hundred workers. The organisations where unit councils are set up include hotels, restaurants, hospitals, transport undertakings, (railway air, sea, road transport services), educational institutions, ports and docks, provident fund and pension organisations, banks, insurance companies, municipalities, warehousing corporations etc.

The scheme provides for unit level councils. These councils are basically set up to eliminate factors which hinder progress and hamper operations. Efforts are made to improve methods of operations.

Under this scheme of unit councils, each unit council consists of an equal number of representatives of management and workers. The actual number of the representatives is determined by the management in consultation with the recognised trade union, registered trade unions or the workers as per the needs. However, total number of the representatives does not exceed twelve. The management's representatives are nominated by the management who are from the unit concerned.

The decisions of a unit council are taken on the basis of consensus and not by the process of voting. The unsettled matters are referred to the joint council for consideration. Every decision of a unit council is implemented by the concerned parties within a period of a month, unless otherwise stated in the decision itself. The management makes necessary arrangements for the recording of minutes of the meetings and designate one of its representatives as a secretary for this purpose. The secretary is entrusted the responsibility to report on the action taken on the decisions at the subsequent meetings of the council.

A unit once formed, functions for a period of two years. The council can meet as frequently as is necessary but at least once in a month. The Chairman of the council is a nominee of the management while worker members of the council elect a vice-chairman from amongst themselves. The functions of the unit councils are more or less similar to those of joint councils. However, the main functions of a unit council are to create necessary conditions for attaining higher productivity and efficiency and to provide better customer services.

Functions of Unit Council

Other functions performed by the unit councils are mentioned below.
(a) To create conditions for healthy employer-employee relations.
(b) To create and improve conditions for reducing absenteeism and recommend measure for the purpose.
(c) To identify areas of inadequate or inferior services and to take necessary constructive and corrective steps to eliminate the contributing factors and to evolve improved methods of operations.
(d) To institute a proper and suitable system of rewards for eliminating pilferage and all types of corruption.
(e) To ensure effective flow of adequate two-way communication between the management and workers for making the working of unit councils successful.
(f) To suggest the measures for improving the physical conditions of working such as lighting, ventilation, internal lay-out, setting up of customers' service points etc.
(g) To make recommendations for improving health, safety and welfare measures for an efficient working of the unit.

(8) Co-partnership

Under co-partnership, workers/employees are made equal partners i.e. owners of the organisation in which they work as employees. In co-partnership, workers or employees participate in the equity capital of their organisation. The shares are allotted to them either on cash payment basis or in-lieu of various incentives payable in cash. Thus, they become the shareholders of their organisation and can exercise control over it as other shareholder do. The workers by becoming co-partners, can participate in both i.e. sharing of profits and participating in management as shareholders.

In this way, workers are given a higher status and they are connected with their organisation in a dual capacity. They, thus, can elect their representatives as directors and protect their interests. This helps to create better understanding between the management and employees which is essential for good industrial relations. It also helps in integrating the employees with their organisation and become the part-owner of the organisation to the extent of their shareholding. However, the workers do not get real control over the management and they cannot participate in management because of their negligible shareholding. The scope of workers' participation in management through co-partnership is quite limited.

(9) Auto-management

Under Auto-management scheme, workers are given wider powers in management. The industrial unit is established by the State but the day-to-day management is entrusted in the hands of workers working in the unit. Various targets e.g. production, sales etc. are decided at the government level, but other activities, functions are managed by the workers collectively. It is obvious that this method of workers' participation in management is suitable in socialist or communist countries. It exists in Yugoslavia. But it is not suitable to the Indian Economic System.

(10) Challenges of WPM

(1) **Overall Climate:** The overall climate in the organisation should be favourable to enable workers' participation. For this to be effective, an attitude of mutual co-operation, confidence, and respect for each other, would be needed. In this regard, the management should take genuine interest in the ideas put forth by the workers, as this goes a long way in making the latter feel valued and that, their ideas are productive and useful.

(2) **Time:** There must be sufficient time to participate before action is called for; because participating in decisions which are almost pre-determined or evolving could lead to conflict. This is so, since the process of participation requires time to discuss, debate and, by extension, for arriving at a consensus. Lack of time could thus complicate matters.

(3) **Matter:** The subject matter, on which participation is sought, ought to be relevant to the given enterprise; it should concern something in which both parties would be interested; as otherwise, the parties concerned are likely to become indifferent to the process of participation.

(4) **Ability of Workers' Representatives:** The workers' representatives should have the requisite ability and knowledge, to participate. They should be asked to participate in problems relating to their work, as this type of participation would prove successful. Conversely, asking them to participate in technical aspects of the machinery would not prove very fruitful. The contributions made by the workers should be meaningful and should benefit not only the workers but should also be in the best interests of the management.

(5) **Effective Communication:** There must be effective communication between the two parties. The representatives of both labour and management should be able to understand each other and express themselves without any inhibitions. They should be able to voice their thoughts and listen objectively to others' point of view.

(6) **Status and Authority of Management and Union:** The process of participation should not unfavourably affect the status or authority of the participants. This is so, since if a manager feels his authority would be threatened in case he participates, then, in all likelihood, he would abstain from participating. Similarly, the workers too would hesitate in participating, if they perceive that by doing so, their status would be adversely affected. In fact, for enlisting effective and successful worker's participation, both management and labour should agree to leave aside their egos and come forward to share their ideas.

(7) **Financial Costs:** The financial costs of participation should not exceed its benefits - both in economic and non-economic terms.

(8) **Overall Policy Framework:** Participation should be within the framework of overall policy of the given enterprise. Each and every decision should be viewed in the backdrop of the vision and mission statements of the organisation concerned. Ultimately, participation should be such that the views, ideas and decisions would benefit the organisation in the long run.

(9) **Ongoing Activity:** Participation should be an ongoing activity in the given organisation, and should not therefore be restricted to unfavourable situations alone. Management and labour should meet on a regular basis not only to exchange ideas but also for building a better rapport in order to develop trust and faith in each other. This comes in handy when one has to confront difficult situations.

5.2 Collective Bargaining: Concept, Evolution and Implementation

1. Meaning of Collective Bargaining

The term 'Collective Bargaining' is composed of two words. (1) Collective, and (2) Bargaining. The word 'collective' is opposite to the word 'individual' as it implies 'group'; while 'bargaining' pertains to 'negotiation' or 'haggling'. In other words, by 'collective bargaining' refers to negotiation by a group. It is obvious that collective bargaining or negotiations require joint sessions of the representatives of workers/employers and management/employers.

Thus, collective bargaining is opposite to that of individual bargaining and it takes place between organised groups of employees with either a single employer or multiple employers. It is so-called because employees, as a group, select their representatives to meet and discuss in joint sessions their differences with the management or employer and the collective bargaining helps in ironing out many differences between employees and their management.

The term 'collective bargaining' was coined by Sydney and Beatrice Webb of Great Britain, which is considered the 'home of Collective Bargaining.' This is based on the belief that the bargaining capacity of an individual worker is weak *vis-à-vis* his employer, who is often powerful. To overcome such an inequitable situation, the workers concerned opt for the mechanism of 'collective bargaining' wherein through their collective efforts, they stand a better chance of taking up their cause from a position of strength *vis-à-vis* their employer or employers, as the case may be.

It is this idea (collective bargaining) that gave birth to the establishment of modern day trade unions, which, in turn, helped the workers to stay organised and thereby gain bargaining advantage, which would have otherwise been not possible but for the mechanism of collective bargaining. This plays an important role in the context of wage determination besides many other things.

Many experts in the field of management and economics have defined the term 'Collective Bargaining'. Let us consider some of the important definitions in order to understand their nature and characteristics.

2. Definitions of Collective Bargaining:

(1) In the **Encyclopedia of Social Sciences**, "Collective Bargaining' is defined as, *a process of discussion and negotiation between two parties, one or both of whom is a group of persons acting in concert. The resulting bargain is an understanding as to the terms and conditions under which a continuing service is to be performed. More specifically, collective bargaining is a procedure by which employees and a group of employees agree upon the conditions of work*".

This implies that they both, by understanding each other's problems and viewpoints, develop some framework of good industrial relations by way of collective bargaining and both may carry their daily association by seeking co-operation for their mutual benefits.

(2) **R.F. Hoxie**, *Collective bargaining is the mode of fixing the term of employment by means of bargaining between an organised body of employees and an employer or an association of employers usually acting through organised agents. The essence of collective bargaining is a bargain between interested parties and not a degree from outside parties.*

(3) **Dale Yoder**, "*Collective bargaining is essentially a process in which employees act as a group in seeking to shape conditions and relationships in their employment*".

(4) **Reynolds L.G**, "*Trade unions try to advance the interests of their members mainly by negotiating agreements usually termed, 'Union contracts' or 'Collective Agreements' – with employers. The process by which these agreements are negotiated, administered and enforced are included in the term Collective Bargaining*".

(5) **Archibald Cox**, "*Collective Bargaining is the resolution of industrial problems between the representatives of employers and the freely designated representatives of employees acting collectively with a minimum of government dictation*".

(6) **J. H. Richardson**, "*Collective bargaining takes place when a number of work people enter into a negotiation as a bargaining unit with an employer or group of employers with the object of reaching an agreement on the conditions of the employment of the work people*".

3. Characteristic Features of Collective Bargaining

The following are the important salient features or characteristics of collecting bargaining:

(1) Collective bargaining is opposite to individual bargaining. In collective bargaining, organised group or groups of employees and either a single employer or multiple employers takes part. It is called collective bargaining because the employees through their representatives negotiate with their management about working conditions, terms of employment etc.

(2) It is a two-party process. Obviously, these two parties are the representatives of workers and the employer or employers or people managing the enterprise.

(3) The above mentioned two parties get an opportunity for clear and face-to-face negotiations.

(4) Collective bargaining is a mutual give and take process and not a take it or leave it method of arriving at settlement of any dispute. Collective bargaining can become successful only when the workers through their representatives and management want to make it successful. There must be some bargaining; the attitude of both the parties must be positive. There should not be any animosity or reprisal.

(5) Collective bargaining is a continuous process. When we use the word 'process' it implies time lag. It does not end with merely negotiation. It begins and ends with a contract. Changes, if required, can be made in the contract, according to one's needs. Contracts once entered into cannot be permanent.

(6) Collective bargaining is a dynamic and flexible process. When we say that collective bargaining is a continuous process, it implies that certain or some changes can be brought about. It has fluidity and ample scope for a compromise. If it is not dynamic, flexible, collective bargaining can not became successful.

(7) The ultimate objective of collective bargaining is to solve the problems or disputes and establish regular stable and sound industrial relations between the employees and their employers.

(8) Collective bargaining is the practical way of industrial democracy wherein workers and their employers participate to achieve certain objectives. It is really a process or method of a joint formulation of the policies of the enterprise concerned on various matters which affects the workers directly at the workplace. It is a good form of inter-disciplinary system that helps promote industrial jurisprudence.

(9) Collective bargaining is a process which includes all the efforts from preliminary preparations to the presentation of conflicting viewpoints, collection of related necessary facts of correct decisions in order to solve the problems or disputes of the needs and objectives of employees and employers who work together in the given organisation.

(10) Collective bargaining is not a competitive process but is essentially a complementary process. This implies that each party needs something that the other party has. A worker can do all that he can as far as productive efforts insofar as enhancing efficient production go - one, that is expected of him from the employer concerned; while the employers have the capacity to pay for those efforts in return. Collective bargaining is a special type of transaction involving a complex process. It is not a simple transaction based on 'take–it–or–leave-it' method. In collective bargaining, the workers and management are highly dependent upon each other. Both parties by acting in a spirit of co-operation stand to gain from the agreement reached through its instrumentality.

(11) Collective bargaining is a voluntary process wherein workers and management participate on their own motion in the process of negotiation for discussing the issues concerned thoroughly and, thereafter, arrive at a solution for the well-being and growth of their enterprise, as a whole.

(12) Collective bargaining covers the negotiations of contracts, grievance procedure and settlement of disputes as well as economic sanctions. In the process of collective bargaining, the participation of workers through their trade unions and their management is essential. The end objective of collective bargaining is to help secure labour-management agreement or contract without any assistance from a third party.

4. Importance of Collective Bargaining

We have already studied the various important aspects such as meaning, characteristic features of collective bargaining. The functions and importance of collective bargaining are as follows:

Prof. Arthur D. Butler, the author of the book, *Labour Economics and Institutions,* has classified the important features under the following three heads. They are:

(1) Collective bargaining as a process of social change;

(2) Collective bargaining as a peace treaty between two parties in continual conflicts or disputes;

(3) Collective bargaining as a system of industrial jurisprudence.

    (a) The function of collective bargaining as a process of social change includes various aspects relating to the establishment of adjustment and balance of power between two conflicting groups. It is a technique of bringing about the rearrangements in the power hierarchy of competing groups. It is not merely confined to the economic relations between the employers and their employees.

    It helps the wage-earners to enhance their social as well as economic position.

    (b) It is also an important function of collective bargaining to bring about truce, i.e., stoppage of fighting or disputes by agreement, compromise for establishing peace and cordial relations between the two parties in a state of continual conflict.

    (c) The function of collective bargaining as a system of industrial jurisprudence is also very important. In a real sense, collective bargaining is a method of introducing civil rights into industry. In other words, it is a democratic method of bargaining. It requires the management to follow rules, terms and conditions while managing its organisation. In this sense, it is a rule-making process. It is a judicial process because in every collective bargaining agreement, there are provisions regarding the interpretation of the agreement entered into. In a nutshell, collective bargaining is a system which establishes, revises and administers many of the rules which govern the workplace and its conditions.

Following discussion would make the importance of collective bargaining, clearer.

Collective bargaining is very important for solving the problems of workers arising at the plant or industry level. The solutions to the common problems can be found directly through negotiations between the parties concerned from the standpoint of employees, trade unions and management, and, therefore, is very beneficial. If it works well, it develops a sense of responsibility and self-respect amongst the workers concerned and contributes significantly to workers' morale and productivity.

Moreover, it also helps to restrict management's freedom of action which is beneficial from the view point of workers. Further, the inclusion of provision for seniority and promotions in the collective bargaining agreement promotes a sense of job security among the workers. It helps to reduce the cost of labour turnover to the management.

At the macro level, i.e., from the view of economic and industrial development of the whole economy, successful collective bargaining results in the establishment of peaceful industrial climate which, in turn, increases the pace of the efforts towards economic and social development by eliminating obstacles coming in the way of development which are related to industrial unrest.

It can be said that as vehicle for industrial peace, collective bargaining has no equal. It encompasses the entire spectrum of democratic principles - right from the political field to the industrial field. It facilitates to help build a system of industrial jurisprudence by introducing civil rights in industry. Thanks to collective bargaining, the affairs relating to workers' job, his working conditions, promotions, transfers, wages and overtime payments, and leaves, etc., is conducted by the management through the mechanism of rules rather than arbitrary decisions.

Collective bargaining helps:
(a) to solve the industrial disputes,
(b) to prevent the industrial disputes,
(c) to create industrial peace in a democratic way,
(d) to secure a prompt and fair redressal of grievances,
(e) to avoid interruptions in work which may follow strikes, go-slow tactics, etc.
(f) to achieve efficient operations of the plants,
(g) to improve economic conditions of the employees,
(h) to provide a flexible means for the adjustment of wages and employment terms and conditions to economic changes and technological changes in the industry.
(i) to provide a solution to the problem of sickness in industry, of old age pension benefits and other fringe benefits.
(j) to create healthy and co-operative atmosphere and sound industrial relations in the enterprise concerned.
(k) to promote the stability and prosperity of the given enterprise as well as of the industrial sector.

5. Process of Collective Bargaining

Collective bargaining is a continuous, flexible, dynamic and mobile process which covers the negotiations of contracts, the grievance procedures and the settlement of disputes as well as economic sanctions. In this process, the participation of workers through their trade unions and their management is essential. The end process of collective bargaining is the labour-management agreement or contract without the assistance of any third party. It is both, at the same time, a device and a procedure used by workers to safeguard their interests. It is really a technique by which the needs and objectives of workers and their employers are met, and hence, it is an integral part of the industrial society. The essence of collective bargaining lies in the readiness of the two parties to a dispute to reach an agreed and mutually satisfying settlement. Hence, there are two important stages in collective bargaining. These stages are:

(1) The Negotiation stage, and
(2) The stage of Contract Administration.

(1) The Negotiation Stage

For collective bargaining, there must exist for negotiation purposes, certain issues, problems, and demands. In this regard, certain proposals are put forward for consideration of the parties concerned and, thus, begin the process of collective bargaining. The negotiation stage itself involves four important steps, which are as follows:

(a) Identification of Problem or Issue

If the problem or problems or issues are not identified, how can the collective bargaining process begin? There must be some base to begin collective bargaining. In fact, the nature of problem or issue influences to a great extent the whole process of collective bargaining. If the problem is serious, it is accorded high priority and thereby discussed immediately. The nature of the problems, or issues or demands influences the selection of representatives, their number, periods of negotiation and agreement that is reached ultimately. Hence, it is very important from the point of view of both the parties to be very clear about the problems or issues before entering into negotiations.

(b) Preparation for Negotiations

Negotiations may commence at the instance of workers or of management. When it is decided to solve the problem, to find the solution for the issue through collective bargaining process, both the parties start preparing themselves for negotiations. It is obvious that the preparation starts with the negotiations and the selection of representatives. The selected representatives collect all the necessary information relating to the problem and study various aspects in order to present their views effectively. Their authority and powers during negotiations are also clearly spelt out. Preparation for negotiations also entails fixing up of time for negotiations, period of negotiations etc. The period of negotiation may vary depending upon the circumstances.

(c) Negotiation Procedure or Technique

For the purpose of negotiations, a negotiation committee comprising three to six members is formed, according to one's needs. It is considered that as far as possible, such committee should be small. If such committees are large, they tend to become unwieldy - one, that is, not only difficult to assemble but also prone to be disorderly. The management committee works as a team. A chief spokesman from the management side leads the committee. A chief spokesman is also called as a chief negotiator or principal negotiator.

The committee plans the negotiations and the chief negotiator covers a strategy of action, directs and presides over the process. He presents the nature and contents of problem, its intensity and the views to both the parties. Thereafter, the representatives of both the parties are allowed to present their views. There can be arguments and counter arguments, proposals and counter proposals. For making it successful, the representatives of both the parties must keep a positive attitude and do all that they reasonably can to reach an amicable solution. Finally, when a solution is reached, it is put on the paper after considering all the legal and other aspects. If no amicable solution could be reached, both the parties may opt for arbitration.

(d) Follow-up Action Stage

The contents of the agreement should be circulated among all the employees so that they come to know exactly what has been agreed upon between their representatives and management. This is very important so as to make clear all the factual points to the employees for whom, the collective bargaining is done. For this purpose, meetings of the people concerned should be held so that they can implement the agreement properly and effectively.

(2) Contract Administration Stage

When the process of negotiation is completed, the contract is signed. But the implementation of the contract is as important as making a contract. Prof. Williamson and Prof. Harris remarked in the context that, "If anything is more important to industrial relations than the contract itself, it is the administration of the contract. The progress in collective bargaining is not measured by the mere signing of an agreement. Rather, it is measured by the fundamental human relationships agreement." The trade unions and the management concerned are required to honour the contract in both letter and spirit.

6. Pre-requisites of Collective Bargaining

Insofar as the pre-requisites for collective bargaining are concerned, the apt proverb to quote in this context would be - "where there is a will, there is a way." The same should be remembered and followed. By keeping a positive attitude, both the parties, i.e., the employers and the trade unions must with sufficient determination come together to make the collective bargaining exercise successful for solving the problems at hand.

There are certain essential conditions or pre-requisites which have been suggested by the experts in the field. These conditions must exist so as to make the exercise of collective bargaining meaningful and effective. The basic conditions are stated as below:

(1) The primary condition or pre-requisite for successful collective bargaining is the existence of well-organised and fully recognised trade unions. The trade unions must be unanimously supported by their members. The trade unions too must have well-defined policies in place.

(2) There must be positive attitude all around. The management, the trade unions concerned and their members must understand that collective bargaining does not imply litigation as it does under adjudication. All the parties to the collective bargaining must determine to resolve their differences on their respective claims in a peaceful and co-operative manner.

(3) Collective bargaining can prove to be an effective technique of settling industrial disputes, problems of employees etc., provided there is a spirit of give and take between the parties concerned. The word 'bargaining' implies 'give and take' and not 'take it or leave it' attitude. The former attitude needs to be followed for making collective bargaining successful.

(4) Collective bargaining is best conducted at plant level. If it is done, various problems can be given proper attention, according to the enormity or importance of the problems. As far as possible, there should be one trade union in a plant. If there is more than one trade union, one trade union, that has, more followers should be recognised as the sole bargaining agent of all the workers in the given organisation.

(5) There is no legal sanction behind the terms and conditions voluntarily agreed upon. Hence, all the parties concerned must do all the things and acts in good faith on the basis of mutual agreement. There must be unanimity between the parties on the implementation of collective bargaining contract.

(6) Employees as well as employers through their representatives should negotiate on the points of differences or on demands with a view to reaching an agreement. Trade unions should not put forward unreasonable demands and their management must consider their reasonable demands. There must be proper dialogue between the two parties. In this regard, it must be noted that rigid attitudes prove detrimental to successful collective bargaining and, therefore, must be avoided at all costs.

(7) The success of collective bargaining would depend much upon the moral fibre of trade union leaders as well as the management. Hence, there must be a complete and true understanding and appreciation of each others' viewpoints.

(8) There must be face-to-face meetings between the parties to the collective bargaining and they make all efforts to keep traditional prejudices at bay.

(9) Negotiations must be based on facts and figures.

(10) Unfair labour practices must be avoided for ensuring the collective bargaining functions properly.

(11) There should not be any uncertainty about the fields or areas in which the parties concerned are legally required to bargain collectively.

(12) When negotiations result in an agreement, its terms, conditions etc., should be put down in writing and embodied in a document in order to avoid any ambiguity. If no agreement is reached, the parties in question should be open to the routes of conciliation, mediation or arbitration for resolving the issue at hand.

(13) The agreement once entered into must be honoured and implemented properly.

(14) It is very essential to incorporate a provision of arbitration. There may be disagreement on the interpretation of the terms and conditions of the agreement. If the disputes arise in respect of terms and conditions of the agreement, the same can be referred to a third party for bringing about a amicable solution - one, that is, final and binding - to the problem in question. This is very important pre-requisite for successful collective bargaining.

7. Types of Collective Bargaining

Collective bargaining can be broadly classified under the following three heads. They are, namely:

(1) A single employer or a single plant bargaining.

(2) A multiple plant bargaining.

(3) A multi-employer bargaining.

(1) A Single Employer or a Single Plant Bargaining:

In this form or type, collective bargaining takes place between the management and a single trade union. We find this type of collective bargaining in India. There can also be the bargaining between the management and more than one trade unions in the enterprise.

(2) A Multiple-plant Bargaining:

This type of bargaining usually takes place between a single factory or establishment having many plants and the workers employed in all those plants.

(3) A Multi-employer Bargaining:

It is the type of collective bargaining between all the trade unions in the same industry through their federal organisations and the federations of employers. This type of bargaining is possible both at the local as well as regional level.

It is found that a trade union starts negotiating with a single employer and while still in its course, it so happens that its jurisdiction enlarges to cover the entire region or industry groups. The actual jurisdiction, however, depends upon the strength of the trade unions.

Bargaining on the basis of a single plant is mostly conducted through the local trade unions. But when there are different problems related to an industry or a group of industries, there is national level bargaining.

It is found that there are national federations in India. They have greater control and they exercise their powers in the bargaining process effectively, and hence, there is an increasing tendency toward multi-employers bargaining.

Questions for Discussion

1. What is Workers Participation in Management? State its objectives.
2. State the Advantages and Disadvantages of WPM.
3. Describe the various levels of WPM.
4. Explain the various types of WPM.
5. What is Collective Bargaining? State the features of Collective Bargaining.
6. Describe the process of Collective Bargaining
7. State the types of Collective Bargaining
8. Write short notes on:
    (a) Challenges of WPM
    (b) Importance of Collective Bargaining
    (c) Pre-requisites of Collective Bargaining.

April 2015

1. (a) Explain concept of industrial relations with evaluation of industrial relations. [10]

    OR

    (b) Define industrial relations. Explain approaches to industrial relations.

2. (a) What are the authorities under Industrial Dispute Act 1947? [10]

    OR

    (b) What are the duties of labour courts tribunals and national tribunals?

3. (a) Discuss the rights and liabilities of registered trade unions? [10]

    OR

    (b) Define trade union. Explain the provisions for illegal strikes and lockouts under the Trade Union Act. [10]

4. (a) Explain the procedure for certification and submission of draft under Industrial Employment (Standing Order) Act, 1946. [10]

    OR

    (b) Explain the provisions for welfare and health of Contract Labour Act 1970.

5. (a) Define workers participation in management. What are the challenges to the worker's participation in management. [10]

    OR

    (b) Write short notes (Any Two):
    - (i) Gandhian approach of industrial relations
    - (ii) Unfair labour practices under Trade Union Act
    - (iii) Collective bargaining process
    - (iv) Works committee.

***

www.ingramcontent.com/pod-product-compliance
Lightning Source LLC
Chambersburg PA
CBHW081926170426
43200CB00014B/2852